T0258886

INTEGRATING MARKER-PASSING AND PROBLEM-SOLVING:

A Spreading Activation Approach to Improved Choice in Planning

James A. Hendler
Department of Computer Science
The University of Maryland

Psychology Press
Taylor & Francis Group

New York London

Reprinted 2009 by Psychology Press

Library of Congress Cataloging in Publication Data

Hendler, James A.
  Integrating marker-passing and problem-solving.

  Bibliography: p.
  Includes index.
  1. Artificial intelligence. 2. Parallel processing
(Electronic computers) 3. Cognition. I. Title
Q335.H46 1988   006.3   87-9000
ISBN 0-89859-982-2

10 9 8 7 6 5 4 3 2 1

To my immediate family:
my parents, Marjorie and Samuel,
my siblings, William and Elizabeth,
and my wife, Terry.

Contents

Preface   vii
Acknowledgments   ix

Chapter 0   Foundations   1
1. Motivating Factors   *2*
2. Approach   *4*

Chapter 1   Introduction   7
1. Some Problems with Problem Solving   *10*
2. Integrating Marker-Passing and Problem Solving   *18*
3. SCRAPS and C-SCRAPS: An Implementation   *22*
4. Cognitive Issues   *31*
5. Some Terminological Difficulties   *32*
6. A Reader's Guide to this Book   *35*

Chapter 2   On Problem-Solving and Planning   37
1. Defining Terms   *37*
2. Previous Work   *38*
3. Relationship of our model to past work   *53*

Chapter 3   On Marker-Passing and Spreading Activation   57
1. Defining Terms   *57*
2. Previous Work   *58*
3. How SCRAPS Relates   *71*

Chapter 4   Integrating Marker-Passing and Problem-Solving   **73**
1. Inside SCRAPS   *74*
2. The Integration of Marker-Passing and Problem-Solving   *86*

Chapter 5   Inside the Path Evaluator   **110**
1. Path Evaluation   *111*
2. Path Evaluation in SCRAPS   *112*
3. Digression—A Formal Footing   *118*

Chapter 6   Designing a Marker-Passer   **124**
1. Design Issues   *124*
2. Marker-Passing Issues   *128*
3. How SCRAPS Does It   *145*

Chapter 7   C-SCRAPS—Adding Concurrency   **159**
1. Why Concurrency?   *159*

Chapter 8   Cognitive Aspects   **181**
1. Cognitive Aspects—Spreading Activation   *182*
2. Cognitive Aspects—Planning   *201*
3. Conclusion   *204*

Chapter 9   On Marker-Passing and Connectionism   **205**
1. Themes   *205*

Chapter 10   SCRAPS in Action   **228**
1. NASL vs. SCRAPS   *228*
2. SCRAPS Alone   *238*
3. SCRAPS vs. C-SCRAPS   *250*

Chapter 11   Conclusion   **264**
1. A Brief Summary   *264*
2. Shortcomings   *271*
3. Research Directions   *278*

Bibliography   **285**
Author Index   **297**
Subject Index   **301**

Preface

The whole of science is nothing more than a refinement of everyday thinking.
— Albert Einstein, *Physics and Reality [1936]*

In writing this preface, I find I'm forced to consider what audience to claim that this work is aimed at. If I say it is a heavily computational work, I'll get computer scientists to read it, but they'll be surprised by the amount of time spent digressing into cognitive issues. If instead I claim it as aimed at the psychologist, there will be surprise expressed at the fact that the book is littered with psuedo-code and computer algorithms. If I call the work "connectionism" lots of people will read it, but I'll have been bending the truth. Therefore, I'll describe very quickly a little about the book, and I'll leave it to the reader to decide what field it covers.

The work covered discusses a system which uses an underlying mechanism, a computationally efficient version of spreading activation, to provide heuristic guidance to a traditional Artificial Intelligence (AI) planning program. The motivations behind this particular work are discussed in the introductory Chapter 0, but right here I'll take a moment and talk about the presentation of the work.

This work is one very small baby step in the direction of solving what I believe is the major problem facing AI today — what is sometimes referred to as the problem of "relevance." AI systems function very well, as one can see from reading the Wall Street Journal, as long as they live in extremely small well specified domains. The staggering number of facts that every human being has at his/her finger tips and uses with ease, phone numbers, addresses, routes to places, abilities to function, language use, day to day plans, understanding of goals and motivations, and all the rest, far exceed anything our systems currently even aspire towards. Compared to our rich world, the domains of even the best AI programs are barely analogous to the cliche "fleas on an elephant."

There are many reasons that this is the case, but one that comes up again and again is the difficulty of finding the right information at the right time in a large memory. This issue has been addressed many times in many forms in the cognitive science community. The logicians' cicumscription formalisms, the Schankian memory indexing schemes, the notion of memory models stressing modularity, and many others are all attempts to solve the problem of examining a large memory without having to examine every fact.

One set of algorithms has been interesting in this light — the various forms of activation spreading algorithms discussed in the AI and psychological literature. From Quillian's 1966 semantic memory model to the modern connectionist models, the spread of activation in an associative memory has been seen as a potential contender for the role of a "low level" process that might somehow help in our search for underlying mechanisms that could help us approach the relevance problem.

Most of the work examining this mechanism, however, has centered around language understanding and memory retrieval during linguistic tasks. The work discussed in this book shifts that focus and looks at this process as a component of planning. The presentation centers on the description of an implementation of such an algorithm, the ramifications of applying this process to the planning problem, and the use of the insights gained in creating the planning system to the design of activation spreading algorithms.

As well as examining the design and use of an algorithmic formulation of this problem we have tried to compare this work to other work in the field. This other work appears in several interconnecting bodies of literature, the cognitive literature in the AI field, the parallelism literature in the computer science area, the spreading activation literature gathered as psychological results, and the growing literature in the new field of connectionism. In this book we have tried to do a reasonably thorough comparison of our work to each of these.

I hope this brief note convinces you to read on. Before we get to all of that, however, I must thank the many people who helped me in this effort.

Acknowledgments

Words are but empty thanks.
— Colley Cibber, *Love's Last Shift [1696]*

The work in this book is an expanded form of my doctoral dissertation. The work in this thesis was influenced by many people, but none so much as my advisor, Eugene Charniak. Also involved 'in the thesis were my committee members David Waltz of Thinking Machines Corporation, who also provided help and encouragement during the process of turning the thesis into this book, and my third reader, Peter Wegner, who had many helpful comments.

Between developing the idea, building the program, writing the initial thesis, getting comments while taking the work "on the road," and creating the final version you are now reading, many many people have lent practical aid or intellectual advice. Included in this group are the members of the Brown AI project, the University of Maryland AI community, all of those involved in the Connectionist Models Summer School, and many people I met while interviewing for an academic appointment: Richard Alterman, Trina Avery, Eamon Barrett, Andy Barto, Alan Collins, Garrison Cottrell, Gerald DeJong, Thomas Dean, Joe Dreussi, Matthew Evett, Jerome Feldman, Tim Finin, Michael Gavin, Richard Granger, Mary Harper, Geoff Hinton, Graeme Hirst, David Johnson, Saj-nicole Joni, Laveen Kanal, Wendy Lehnert, Paul Lewis, Robert McCartney, Jay McClelland, David McDonald, David Miller, Jack Minker, Dick Morley, Greg Murphy, Dana Nau, Peter Norvig, Donald Perlis, Brian Phillips, Jordan Pollack, Lisa Rau, James Reggia, Chris Riesbeck, Eric Roberts, David Rumelhart, Terry Sejnowski, David Touretzky, Andy VanDam, Bonnie Webber, Lorin Wilde, Robert Wilensky, Edward Wisniewski, Doug Wong, and Felix Yen. Also instrumental in providing guidance and criticism was David Boynton of Lawrence Erlbaum Associates who helped in the initial shaping of this book, and Julia Hough and Art Lizza of LEA who helped see it through to production.

Chapter 7 discusses the design of this work for three different types of parallel architectures. The machines, manuals, and etc.

needed for this work were provided by the Parallel Computation and the Computer Vision Laboratories of the University of Maryland. Extra information on Connection Machines was provided by Gary Sabot and Dave Waltz of TMC.

My special thanks goes to Lokendra Shastri who gave the preliminary manuscript a thorough review. He suggested some areas that could be formalized but weren't. They still aren't. If the work isn't formal enough for your tastes blame me, not him.

Of course, a special thanks to my wife, Terry Horowit, who married me just before the madness of writing two theses (mine and hers) came upon us, and yet stuck with me nonetheless, even through the intervening year and the crazy final days of getting this book to the publisher.

And finally, an acknowledgement to Dr. Richard Millward, then head of Brown University's Cognitive Science Program, who provided much encouragement during the early work, but didn't live to see it come to fruition.

CHAPTER 0

Foundations

When the writer becomes the center of his attention, he becomes a nudnick. And a nudnick who believes he's profound is even worse than just a plain nudnick.
— Isaac Bashevis Singer, Interview in *The New York Times Magazine*, 1978

This book is an expanded and edited version of a doctoral thesis entitled *Integrating Marker-passing and Problem-Solving: A spreading activation approach to improved choice in planning* (Hendler, 1986). In the year between the completion of the thesis and the delivery of the manuscript, material was added, deleted, and rewritten to turn the work into a more coherent whole, to bring it up to date, and to include material, particularly material on connectionism, that hadn't been published at the time the dissertation was released. Still and all, after all that rewriting it was realized that something was still missing.

Most doctoral dissertations, the aforementioned included, serve as a deliverable in a contract between student and committee. The details of the work, its ramifications, and its importance must be stated clearly. Not needing to be stated, however, is the set of mutual assumptions shared between the candidate and his/her advisor. These are the unwritten rules that provide the initial motivations for the work and guide the research throughout. When, however, an outsider reads this work, he or she is not privy to these assumptions and may be left wondering where the work came from and why it was performed in the way it was. In an effort to prevent the reader of this book from proceeding into the following text without these assumptions, I have included this brief 0th chapter aimed at elucidating some of the motivations and providing background about the approach this work follows.

1

1. Motivating factors

Much of the AI work in the past has focused on knowledge representation issues having to do with the structure and form of knowledge to be used by the system. Devising a "good" representation was key. It was desirable to show, depending on one's paradigm, that a representation was logically complete and sound, or was psychologically viable, or was efficiently realizable on some architecture, or was able to represent some particular piece of information, etc. A plethora of different systems using scripts, frames, plans, schemata, and whatever were designed and built. Other systems concentrated on the different links allowable in a semantic network, or how to classify particular objects once their network attributes were defined.

Secondary to this, however, was a concentration on general purpose mechanisms and control structures for different AI programs. In planning research, for example, most of the modern research focuses on the form of the data, on demonstrating logical properties of various formulations, and on adding capabilities for handling various new domains. The basic control structure that these systems use, that of nonlinear, "complete" planners with a deductive flavor, was proposed in the mid-70's, and has remained basically unchanged.

One of our motivations was to start looking more directly into the control structures, and some corresponding mechanisms, that might be able to shed light on some of the difficult problems arising with our present schemes. Thus, the goal wasn't to examine a particular representation, but rather to look for a mechanism that multiple representations and various models could take advantage of. Marker-passing, which has been gaining popularity in the natural language and cognitive science communities in the past few years, seemed like a possible candidate for such a mechanism. Could we show that this technique could be useful in areas other than natural language processing?

Coupled with the above motivation was a belief that natural language processing and planning had much in common. Given a story understander that could handle a story like

Willa was hungry. She picked up the Michelin guide.[1]

why couldn't the same program plan what to do if informed that it was hungry? Several people[2] have proposed that the knowledge representation these systems use should be the same, but it seemed to us that the relationship should go deeper. If we believe that certain techniques are of use in understanding the above story, shouldn't we also believe that these same techniques will be of use in the planning arena?

The work reported in this book was an attempt, successful we believe, to lend some credence to this claim. We took the marker-passing technique, particularly the approach suggested by Eugene Charniak, and tried to explore whether it could yield fruit in the planning arena. Further, since marker-passer was proving to be helpful primarily in context recognition problems, it seemed that in planning it should help with plan choice — that is, we can view planning and NLP as somewhat inverse operations, and choice corresponds roughly to the inverse of the context recognition task. We therefore focused efforts on examining the role of marker-passing in plan choice, and this research was the result.

Having decided on marker-passing as the underlying mechanism to be explored, the next issue to be decided was what control structure was needed, in general, to promote the use of this approach. We decided on a type of marker-passing that is able to take advantage of parallelism to a large degree, but that dovetails nicely with present-day AI techniques. In essence, a parallel mechanism limits the search space that a more traditional AI mechanism needs to traverse. A massively parallel, but "dumb" algorithm is used to sweep ahead of the symbolic engine (in our case, the planner). When it finds information that might be of use to a planner, a more standard heuristic mechanism checks that information, and if it is truly of use, it causes changes in the behavior of the main symbolic system. Details follow in the rest of this text — the question raised here is "why this approach?"

1- From (Wilensky, 1978).

2- Full citations and more discussion of this issue are offered in Chapters 1 and 2.

This notion of a hybrid between a massively parallel type of connectionist model and a more traditional deductive AI engine is an attempt to avoid, to use a vastly over-used cliche, throwing the baby out with the bath water. We were unwilling to give up the tremendous power of the traditional AI approach, but we wanted desperately to gain from the efficiency available in local computations and massive parallelism.[3] Thus, a key motivation was to prove, by example, that such hybrid systems were not only realizable, as this was clear, but also could be of use in the traditional AI arena.

2. Approach

One difference between this work and much of the present AI work is the approach we took. We started from a belief that AI is still, in its present state of development, at least in part an experimental field. We do not mean to denigrate the ongoing work in logic and mathematical foundations of AI, but we strongly believe that a priori theorizing cannot be the *only* valid approach to performing research. If one examines any mature science, say biology or physics, one finds three major components: theoretical research, applied engineering, and experimentation. Unfortunately, in recent years AI has been losing this third component. Consider the AAAI and IJCAI conferences: we have a "theory" track and an "engineering" track, but some work has trouble fitting into either. It doesn't look like first-order logic, but neither is it an attempt to solve specific problems in a specific domain. It falls into that middle area where one builds a program to *examine* its behavior and to try to build theories from the result. Our work was developed squarely along these lines.

In particular, though many people have used activation spreading algorithms of various types,[4] little work had been done on examining the behavior of these algorithms and trying to formulate a description of what behaviors they must manifest to work in successively larger domains. As an example, several

---

3– And, as will be seen in Chapter 7, from other less extreme forms of parallelism as well.

4– Detailed in Chapter 3.

different attenuation mechanisms had been proposed to limit the spread of activation, but each of these researchers used only one approach. No one had tried to examine a larger range of behaviors and see if one of these approaches generalized better.

Our goal was to explore, via implementation, what behaviors were needed to make these algorithms work. As an example, we tried using several different attenuation mechanisms to see which ones worked best, which might generalize the best, and which might correspond to desired features of the model. We ended up by designing an attenuation model that merged the best features of the other algorithms, could be used in different ways throughout our entire system, and also which corresponded to real-world constraints on a massively parallel architecture.[5]

The primary limitation of taking this experimental approach, and one which this work reflects, is that by building and tinkering one can never prove that the approach is "the best." Nowhere in this book will you find a proof of the necessity and sufficiency of our attenuation mechanism. Instead, we offer examples of it in action and comparisons to other models. The same can be said of many components of this work. Neither the heuristics for the hybrid system, the algorithms described for the implementation of our marker-passer, nor the system design of our system for various parallel processors has been rigorously proven to be the most elegant or the best approach. Instead, we argue for our design decisions and we contrast with other approaches. This done, we are then able to start thinking about demonstrating the rigor. This book stops short of that point. Future work will need to be done to describe more exactly the theoretical necessity of components of our research. Instead, we offer this work as "experimental" verification that we are on what we hope is the right track, and we particularly hope that it will prove evocative to theorists who wish to formalize systems using underlying mechanisms such as our marker-passer, engineers who might be able to apply algorithms like ours to their particular domains, and to other experimentalists who will take up where this work leaves

---

5– Our attenuation scheme is described in detail in Chapter 6.

off and attempt to extend our understanding of underlying mechanisms and hybrid systems.

CHAPTER 1

Introduction

Razors pain you,
Rivers are damp,
Acids stain you,
Drugs cause cramp.

Guns aren't lawful,
Nooses give,
Gas smells awful,
Might as well live.
— Dorothy Parker, *Resume [1927]*

This book describes a system developed to demonstrate some gains achieved in a problem solver via the addition of an efficient, nondeductive, marker-passing component. It will be shown that in many cases this new component enables the problem solver to avoid making certain errors to which it is prone. Further, it will be shown that through concurrency this can be done in a manner that does not impinge upon the efficiency of the planning process.

My research didn't originally start out as a work in problem solving and planning. Originally I was asked to examine the following simple story thought up by Eugene Charniak

Jack wanted to commit suicide. He got a rope.

The question to be answered was: how do we arrive at the inference that poor Jack is planning to hang himself? Of all the possible uses of a rope (jumping rope, hanging up clothes, rescuing people from caverns, and the like) how does the biasing context of "suicide" prescribe which one to use?

Chris Riesbeck, holding to an expectation-based view of understanding, suggested that there were really very few means of committing suicide available. We could just examine "hang," "shoot," and "poison" and look for the rope to be used. Not to be undone, Charniak then proceeded to elucidate more and more elaborate ways of committing suicide such as

>   Jack wanted to commit suicide. He found an abandoned refrigerator.

The explanation Charniak eventually arrived at for the handling of these stories required the use of a "marker-passing" or "spreading activation" mechanism. Such a mechanism works by passing activation markers and information through an associative network. To better understand this idea, consider an associative network as a bunch of hockey pucks connected to one another by springs hanging in midair. If one of these hockey pucks is struck it will start to vibrate. This in turn will start the hockey pucks next to it vibrating, and so on, and so on, and so on. Because of friction, each puck would vibrate a little less than the puck before until we reached some limit where the vibrations were relatively imperceptible. Assume that at this point we struck another hockey puck elsewhere in the entangled web. This puck would also start a set of pucks vibrating.

At some point, a hockey puck already vibrating from the first node might be shaken from the second. The collection of those pucks vibrating from both nodes forms a set with an interesting property: informally, it is the set of all nodes for which some path connects the two first nodes. In a system where the associative network corresponds to the search space for some problem to be solved (as in a planning system), each path found corresponds to some way of traversing the space between the two nodes. (A review of past and present work and more detail about the design of marker-passers can be found in Chapters 3 and 6, respectively.)

Thus, getting back to our suicide examples, a marker-passing mechanism would find a path of the form

>   Jack's suicide → suicide → kill → hang → noose → rope

for the first example, and of the form:

>   Jack's suicide → suicide → kill → asphyxiate → get locked in abandoned refrigerator → abandoned refrigerator

for the second.[1] From these paths we see where the intermediate concepts, "hang" and "asphyxiate," are found — a potential solution to understanding these stories of poor Jack's plight.[2]

The present work is directly derived from some simple problems resulting when, while helping Charniak to implement a marker-passing system for the sake of handling such stories, I started looking at them from another point of view. Suppose that, instead of trying to understand stories about people committing suicide, we wished to get an AI system to plan such an act. That is, suppose we wanted to be able to tell the machine "Commit suicide!" and have it respond by carrying out (or, to spare the department's budget, listing) the appropriate actions to achieve its own demise. How could such a system be written?

Coming up with the notion of examining this problem solving behavior was not much of a novelty in Brown's AI group. Several papers by Charniak and Wong (Charniak, 1975,1985; Wong, 1981) discussed using the same knowledge structures to do both planning and story understanding.[3] Thus, whatever representation is used to understand the stories about Jack's problems should also be usable for the planning of such acts.

One significant departure of the present work derives from pushing these claims of a mutual representation one step further. In addition to assuming that a story comprehender should share the same knowledge base with a problem solver, why not assume that any processes acting on that knowledge base can (and should) be used by both systems? That is, since the marker-passer was being used to understand the suicide stories, could it aid in the planning of such actions? It turned out not only that it could, but that taking a marker-passing approach to planning could shed

---

1– These examples are both simplified and incomplete, and serve here simply to give the basic idea. Elsewhere in this book we describe the exact form of paths and marks in detail. In fact, throughout this introductory Chapter I simplify representations, issues, and various details of the work. All of these are explained in greater depth in later Chapters.

2– I quickly concede that this in no way enables us to truly "understand" the story. We see nothing in these marker-passing paths to explain the pain and anguish Jack must feel: we cannot empathize with his emotional state, nor do we acknowledge the existential angst which has cause this plight. We must, however, start somewhere.

3– See also Wilenksy, 1978; Allen, 1979.

some light on some previously difficult planning problems.

This work contains both a description of what can be gained by the integration of a marker-passing phase in a problem solving system and a discussion of some of the difficulties in implementing such a marker-passing system. It also addresses some concurrency issues of interest in the design of such programs. These are unified by the discussion of two actual systems, SCRAPS and C–SCRAPS, implemented to test the ideas described herein. The remainder of this introductory chapter is a short version of the rest of the book, introducing the basic ideas handled in later chapters and briefly discussing some of the issues involved.

1. Some problems with problem-solving

To show that a marker-passing phase can be beneficial to problem-solving or planning systems,[4] it is important to identify some of the problems arising in present-day AI programs and show how the marker-passer could be used to avoid them. In this section we do that briefly, giving the reader a feeling for the bare bones of the problems and the marker-passing solution. In later sections we describe the process more fully.

1.1. Backtracking and non-optimal solutions

It turns out that the simple domain of planning such suicide stories as the above led me into many of the traditional problems of AI problem-solving systems. How could I plan the correct way to do things? Given several ways of solving a problem (and even my earliest system had knowledge of hanging and abandoned refrigerators), how does one select the appropriate means? Consider the following problem-solving task

You wish to commit suicide. Also, you are holding a rope.

Most problem-solving systems used in AI today solve tasks by a process of stepwise refinement. Each task is broken into subtasks, which break into yet more subtasks, etc., until one finally reaches a level of "primitives" — tasks that can be broken

---

4– We assume here that problem-solving and planning are interchangeable terms. Section 2.9 discusses this issue.

down no further. If multiple ways of achieving a task are known, the problem-solver simply picks one of them, usually guided by some form of planning heuristics. It is here, however, that the problem arises: How can such heuristics be formulated so as to pick the correct path and avoid paths leading to failure?

Figure 1 shows a simplified version of the knowledge base that a suicide planning system would have. At the time at which the system is required to choose which suicide method to use, it has not yet done the search that would find "rope" and "abandoned refrigerator."[5] Thus, most AI systems would make a choice at random, and be prepared to back up if the method fails. Let us assume for now the system pursues the "suffocation" plan. For this plan the abandoned refrigerator is needed. If the agent of the suicide does not own one, the plan fails. A system with only

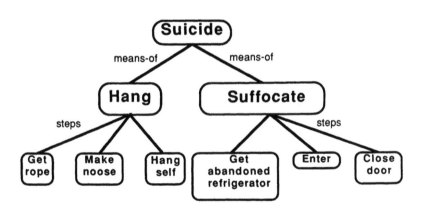

Figure 1: Two ways of commiting suicide.

5– Such a search requires a large amount of work and is quite time consuming. Details about various problem-solving strategies appear in Chapter 2.

the knowledge of Figure 1 would then back up and pursue the "hang" plan. This plan requires the possession of a rope, and therefore succeeds. Avoiding such backing up is highly desirable for efficiency reasons.

Another problem arises when we use more sophisticated knowledge than that shown above. Let us now add to Figure 1 the information about how to obtain things one does not have. Figure 2 is the result. Now, however, instead of failing when a lack is found, the system would proceed to try to "get" an abandoned refrigerator. It would go to a hardware store, buy a refrigerator, take it home, abandon it, and, now having an abandoned refrigerator, enter it and close the door. As an added touch it might even use the rope that it has been carrying all this time to hold the door closed. Thus, present-day systems cannot only fail to find the best approach ("hang" since "rope" is present), but are designed to stop after finding the first "solution" they encounter.

There is no reason why one cannot design a planner that will find all the possible methods of achieving some goal and pick one of these based on some sort of optimality criteria. The problem with such a planner is that it will be arbitrarily slow — the time required to find all possible solutions can be infinite because in principle the problem is undecidable. Even with a parallel planner, we would have no way of knowing when to stop and declare that we had found the best path. The marker-passing approach is to use a heuristic mechanism, designed to run in parallel (see Chapters 6 and 7), which will attempt to check for paths the planner might otherwise ignore. The planner still finds only one plan, but when the mechanism for making decisions is invoked, it will have considered some potential alternatives.

Consider the following examples provided to illustrate the marker-passing solution to both avoiding back-up when a plan would fail and to finding better alternative plans when making a choice. We describe their solutions very briefly here; later we show more examples with more details of the analysis. Let us start by considering the knowledge shown in Figure 1 about suicide planning. Consider a simple system in which (a), that is all the knowledge available and (b), we assert to the system that

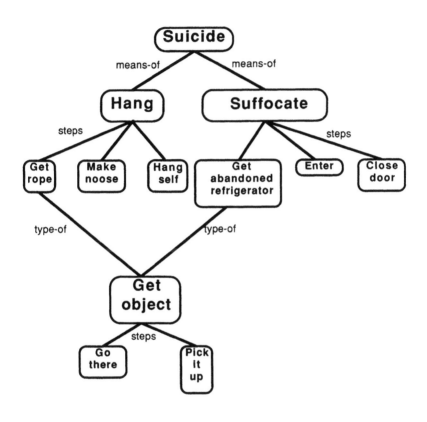

Figure 2: Additional knowledge for a suicide planner.

"ROPE IS UNAVAILABLE." We now start the system going with the goal of "commit suicide." This time, however, instead of picking a plan at random we use the following selection heuristic: pass markers starting at the goal state. If any paths to previously marked items are reported, examine them for more information. If something is found that precludes using this plan, choose a different one. We also add one more piece to our system: if something is "UNAVAILABLE" mark it as such.

Thus, the system would now mark rope, since it is unavailable, and then pass markers starting at suicide. The path

suicide → kill → hang → rope → ROPE IS UNAVAILABLE

would be reported. The problem-solver now examines this path, discovers that the unavailability of rope precludes the hang method, and decides to use a different plan (that of the abandoned refrigerator).

If, instead of asserting that "ROPE IS UNAVAILABLE," we had asserted "YOU HAVE ROPE," the system would mark that. Then, if we pursuing the suicide plan, the path found would be

suicide → kill → hang → rope → YOU HAVE ROPE.

This path would be examined and it would be revealed that we have one of the items necessary to try the "hang" plan, and in the absence of any other plan selection heuristics we would try this plan. Thus, even if we used the knowledge in Figure 2 we would try hanging first, and using a non-optimal solution is avoided.

1.2. Demon invocation

In the course of planning we often wish to notice certain configurations of facts or plans and take approppriate actions when they occur. This is usually done by having production-like rules that recognize a set of conditions and interrupt the usual planning process to add information, when these conditions occur. Thus, for example, if we had an unmanned rover roaming around the moon's surface we might like to have some rule such as

DEMON 1:
IF you are next to a crater
  AND you are carrying a heavy object
  AND the rocks around you are loose
THEN abort present plan and move away.

These rules, usually called "demons," must be applied whenever they are recognized.

The problem with invoking demons during problem-solving is that by the time a demon is ready to fire (that is, to be applied), it is often too late: our lunar robot may already be falling into the crater before it can start to reverse its treads. What is needed is a system that can say, before the actual execution of a plan, "if a demon is going to be fired during this plan, take into account its effects." Thus, instead of going past a crater which was known to contain loose rocks, we would generate a different plan.

We can design a traditional AI planner system to take such rules into account. Such a system must find a plan, simulate its execution, notice any demons being fired during this simulated execution, and change the plan to take the effects of these demons into account. (An example of such a planner, used in Wilensky's, 1983, Unix Consultant System, is described in detail in Chapter 2.) To do this, however, takes a large amount of overhead — not only must planning occur, but a detailed simulation must be run and the original plan amended appropriately.

We contend that marker-passing provides a mechanism that can often predict the invocation of demons without the need for such detailed simulation. Further, as shown in Chapter 7, the marker-passer can run in parallel thus even further reducing the overhead time. Returning to our Lunar rover, if we knew that Tycho was a crater, and had on an earlier mission determined that Tycho has loose rocks, the marker-passer would find paths including the above rule whenever a heavy object was being carried. That is, if we had a plan such as that in Figure 3 the following would occur: First, using the previous analogy, the hockey puck called "proceed to base" would be made to vibrate. This would in turn vibrate those things attached, including the node for Tycho. Since we have links in our knowledge base from Tycho to loose rocks and from loose rocks to DEMON 1, this demon would be vibrating.

Now consider what happens if we have a heavy object (say for example an atomic power plant needed at the base camp). In this case the node associated with that object, atomic plant, would be vibrating. Since the atomic plant is known to be a heavy object, the node for heavy object would now be active. The marker-passer would find a path of the form

atomic plant → heavy object → DEMON 1 → Tycho → proceed to Tycho → path1 → proceed to base

By examining the path, a simpler operation than simulating the plan, we would see that the demon would in fact be invocable, and therefore we would have to abort the present plan prior to

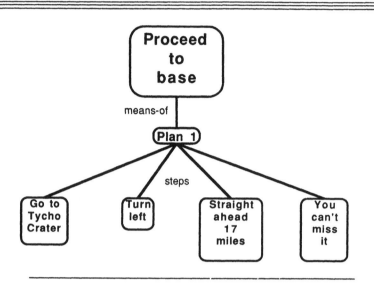

Figure 3: Simple plan for Lunar robot to return to home base.

finishing. Instead, since we would not yet have started the plan we'd find an alternative (path2).

If, on the other hand, we did not have the atomic plant, the path from "proceed to base" would still cause the node for "heavy object" to be activated. This time, however, none of the heavy objects are vibrating, and the marker passer returns no paths. The planner now proceeds as it would if the demon weren't there at all, and takes whatever path it first tries.

1.3. Interactions within plans

Sometimes an often used plan becomes invalid when certain conditions are not met or are violated during the plan's application. Consider the case when John goes to a restaurant -- one of the AI standards for a simple plan.

We would have some such knowledge as is shown in Figure 4. This is easily run in the stepwise refinement paradigm, in which John enters, goes to a table, orders, the waitress tells the cook, the cook cooks the food, the waitress bring it to John, John eats, pays

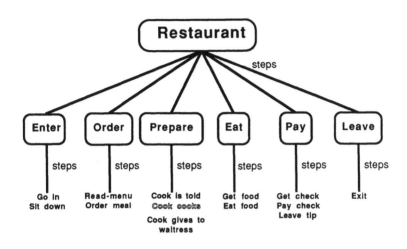

Figure 4: The restaurant plan.
The overall plan "restaurant" is composed of steps (enter, order, etc.) which in turn are composed of the primitive steps shown.

the check, and leaves. No problem. However, suppose that John has had heart trouble and is now wearing a pacemaker. Again, John can execute the restaurant plan with no difficulty — unless, that is, the cook is using a microwave oven. All of a sudden John will be in trouble. Even if it had been asserted that this restaurant used a microwave, we would not see this information until we got to the step in which the cook starts the cooking. At this point, poor John would suffer due to our poor planning abilities.

Once again, we propose invoking marker-passer in this sort of situation. Markers would be passed from John (the agent of this event) and the specific restaurant that he is entering (the object of the plan). These marks would intersect at the node "microwave oven" and would pass over a rule such as "people with pacemakers must not go near a microwave oven." The path might look something like

> John → John has a pacemaker
> → people with pacemakers must
>   not go near a microwave oven
> → this cook uses a microwave oven
> → this restaurant uses this cook
> → this restaurant

The planner could then examine this path and recognize the danger to John. Replanning could then occur and John would eat somewhere else.

2. Integrating marker-passing and problem-solving

The previous Sections have shown some places where a marker-passer could be used in conjunction with a problem-solver. In doing so we have been using terms to do with paths and their analyses very loosely. In this Section we will continue to be vague, but will close in on the issues involved, and on how marker-passing differs from a full search.

2.1. Adding a marker-passer to a problem-solver

Problem-solving is generally formulated as a deductive process. If we wish to plan a "restaurant" event (using knowledge like that shown in Figure 4 above), we must first find out who it is that will play each of the roles (diner, waitress, restaurant, *etc.*) Once this is done we proceed to traverse the knowledge base looking for means to achieve each step, checking features on any steps that are conditionalized, and making sure that we are consistent in our bindings. Thus, for example, if we decide that John is the diner then it is John who must order, eat, pay, *etc.* If we know that the diner must be a human, we must check to make sure that we are talking of a person named John as opposed to, say, a dog with the same name.

This process of searching through the tree and checking all of these bindings and conditions is a complex one. In later Chapters we'll discuss some of the heuristics that have been used in the past and the limitations of present systems. Each system does this seraching and checking somewhat differently: Some use logic and unification, some use pattern-matching and some form of instantiation, some use various semantic network processes and traversal algorithms. In this book we will be using the term **deduction** or **deductive search** to refer to these various activities.

In contrast to this deductive process, marker-passing is a *non-deductive search*. Thus, while the problem-solver needs to check that the agent of the food preparation is human, different from the diner, etc., the marker-passer will simply mark food preparation after marking restaurant. Three important facts follow from this:

(1) *Marker-passing is dependent on being in an associative network, but not on the actual form of the network.* Most network schemes vary in how they keep the knowledge that permits the storage of binding information. The nodes remain relatively constant among different systems, the links vary more greatly. The marker-passing algorithms ignore the format of these links, since they need only traverse them to mark endpoints.

(2) *Marker-passing is different from, and faster than, deductive search.* Since the marker-passer ignores the binding information, it need not consider how the variables are bound and whether they unify[6] together.

(3) *Marker-passing can return incorrect paths.* This, unfortunately, is an inherent problem with marker-passing. Since we are doing non-deductive search, paths may be returned that will not be legal in a deductive sense. Consider the example described earlier in which a suicide planner would choose to hang itself if we assert "YOU HAVE A ROPE." Consider the case where we assert "SOMEONE ELSE HAS A ROPE." The marker-passer would find a path of the form

---

6– The implementation described here is written in a logic-based system (described more fully in Section 3.1). We therefore tend to use logic terminology, though in fact there is no tie between marker-passing systems and logic. In fact, in a system more oriented towards semantic networks, marker-passing is a natural extension, easily implemented (see, for example, Phillips & Hendler, 1982).

suicide → kill → hang → rope → SOMEONE ELSE HAS A ROPE

If the problem-solver decided, therefore, to hang itself, it would be no closer than if it had taken the abandoned-refrigerator route. Thus, if a marker-passing system is to work with our system we must have some sort of *path evaluator* that examines the paths returned and removes those that provide no useful information. The design of such an evaluator is a major part of this work.

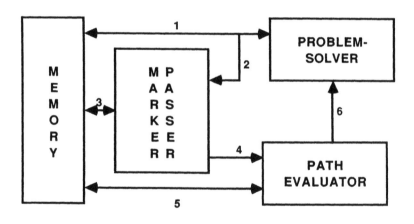

Figure 5: Flow of control in the SCRAPS system.
The problem solver is invoked. As it uses the memory (1) the marker-passer is also invoked (2). The marker-passer runs, using memory information (3), and paths are found. These paths are sent to the path evaluator (4) which uses memory information in determining the relevance of these paths to the present problem solving task (5). When relevant information is found the behavior of the problem solver is influenced (6) as described in the text.

To provide for marker-passing and path evaluation, a system must be designed with a flow of control like that shown in Figure 5. The problem-solver interacts with the memory as it normally would. During these interactions markers are passed through the memory and paths are found. These paths are reported to a path evaluator that uses them to provide feedback to the problem-solver. This feedback includes information about which plans to avoid and which to prefer as described in the previous section.

2.2. The design of marker passing systems

In Chapter 3 we discuss the past work done on the design of marker-passing systems. We talk about systems involving marker-passing and architectures and algorithms for marker-passing. In this section we wish solely to describe some of the issues that must be dealt with in creating such programs.

Let's start by returning, once again, to the hockey pucks and springs analogy given earlier. At that point we mentioned that friction was a damping factor. What happens if friction is removed? Consider: We would strike one puck, it would vibrate, the next set of pucks would vibrate, and so on. Where would it stop? With no frictional damping the system would keep vibrating until every puck was in motion. If we then struck another puck and recorded all the pucks vibrating through both, the intersection set would be the same as the entire network. Further, the set of paths through these nodes of intersection would be incredibly large.[7] In fact, it would be simpler to ignore marker-passing alltogether and just use the memory itself! A marker-passer that marks too much is thus no better (and in fact can be far worse) than a marker-passer that marks nothing at all. To control runaway marking we need only put the friction back into our systems. But how much do we put in? Achieving the correct balance is a major factor in the design of such systems. This is discussed in Chapter 6.

7– Roughly N!B where N is the number of nodes and B is the average outbranching at each. Depending on the exact implementation, this number can be lowered to N! or raised to infinity. In any case it is far too large to consider for computation's sake.

Another factor in the design of marker-passing systems is the use of concurrency. In Chapter 6 we demonstrate that a marker-passing algorithm can be a "local" algorithm: that is, each node can perform a task knowing only its neighboring nodes. As such, marker-passing is formulated to run on a massively parallel machine.[8]

Another issue in the design of marker passing algorithms is how much information to pass. Fahlman (1979) described a system in which markers were binary tags and therefore any node was either marked or unmarked. One problem with such a scheme was the lack of back pointers, which would allow paths, as opposed to intersections, to be found. Another possibility is to pass entire paths: This makes it exceedingly easy to find paths, they are already there, but uses a large amount of extra space. We discuss this issue and some possible solutions in Chapter 6.

Still another issue to be considered is "in what order should the paths be evaluated?" At a quick glance the path evaluator should keep some sort of order in what is examined. It turns out, however, that the same algorithms that provide the "friction" described earlier can provide a path strength that can be used by the path evaluator. In fact, a marker-passer can be designed that will return paths in an order closely corresponding to such strengths. This, too, is described in Chapter 6.

There are other factors to be considered when designing a marker passing system: How long do marks persist? How are they removed? Are all links created equal or are some preferred? Are all nodes treated the same? Computational and cognitive arguments are given in regard to these issues in Chapters 6 and 8, respectively. Chapter 9 also discusses these issues, but from a connectionist standpoint.

3. SCRAPS and C–SCRAPS: An implementation

Many of the ideas described in this book arise from empirical experimentation rather than a priori theorizing. This is particularly true of the details about marker passing described in

---

8– A machine with a large number of interconnected processors (see Chapter 7).

the previous section. I'm tempted to apologize for this or to pretend that they arose from theorizing without mentioning the experimentation that led to them, but in the interest of honesty I won't do so. Instead, those places where empirical evidence helped us to understand the issues involved in designing a marker-passer and developing a problem-solver/marker-passer amalgam are discussed in detail. In this section we will talk about some of the background details of the system and the AI programs for which it was designed.

3.1. AI at Brown: FRAIL and NASL

Rather than starting from scratch to implement a problem-solver, the current system is based on the NASL problem-solver described in McDermott (1977) and implemented at Brown by Doug Wong and Eugene Charniak. NASL is implemented using a frame-based, first-order logic, deductive retrieval system called FRAIL (version 2.1) (Charniak, Gavin & Hendler, 1983). We describe FRAIL and NASL briefly in this section, and talk about some aspects of these later in the book.

FRAIL (FRame-based AI Language) is a system that reads in frames, turns them into first-order predicate logic statements, and stores these in an associative network scheme. Logic statements can be directly asserted and retrieved, and various chaining rules and the like are also implemented.

The basic unit in FRAIL is the "frame," which can be an object or an event. These frames are related by an "isa hierarchy" and information about them is stored in a predicate calculus database. Each frame may contain

1. *Isa:* how this frame fits into the isa hierarchy
2. *Slots:* slots of the frame, and restrictional information
3. *Acts:* the subacts that are performed by an event frame
4. *Facts:* related information about this frame

Some event frames correspond to primitive events; their contents are the same as the above except that no subacts are allowed. Also, a frame that is primitive can add or subtract information in the database. This is done by statements called "TO-ADD" and

"TO-DEL," which cause facts to be asserted into or erased from the database.

The FRAIL input for the HANGING frame (comments in *italics*) is shown in Inset 1. FRAIL takes this input and turns it into predicate calculus statements. Thus, the frame for CARRY would be rendered into the statements

```
(FRAME CARRY)          ;carry is a frame
(ISA CARRY ACTION)     ;this frame is an action
(RESTRICTION (AGENT (CARRY ?X))
             (PERSON ?X)))
       ;the agent is a person
(MOD-MANIP (CARRY ?X))       ;carries are primitive
(TO-DEL (CARRY ?X)
        (LOCATION (PATIENT (CARRY ?X)) ?PL))
       ;the carry will delete any old location
```

These statements are then stored in an associative network by an indexing scheme described in more detail in Chapter 4, Section 1.3, where we discuss how the marker-passer used by the present system is implemented.

NASL is a problem-solver that works via the basic stepwise refinement algorithm. The statements from FRAIL are used as data to guide NASL. NASL is called to SOLVE a problem with some initial conditions. It uses the algorithm shown in Inset 2.

It is the last of these steps that is most interesting to us in this book, since the marker-passer will communicate with the problem-solver via this choice mechanism. This is discussed in the next section.

3.1.1. The choice mechanism for NASL

To understand NASL's choice mechanism, we must look at several different things: how logical implication works in FRAIL, how TO-DO rules work, and what logical predication is used in the choice mechanism. We deal with these issues now, although they are discussed again elsewhere.

The key to using FRAIL as the basis of a problem-solver is its ability to handle logical implication. Specifically, FRAIL allows "if/then" rules via both forward- and backward- chaining rules.

```
(frame: noose
    isa: thing)                             ; a noose is an object

(frame: rope                                ; a rope is an object
    isa: thing
  facts: (material-of noose rope)  ; nooses are made of rope

(plan: hang ?s
    isa: action                     ; hanging is an action with:
  slots: (agent (person))            ; a human agent
         (patient (person))          ; a human patient
         (h-instr (noose))          ; a noose as an instrument
   acts: (h-get-instr-step         ; the agent carries the noose as a step
            (carry (agent(agent ?s))(instr (h-instr ?s))))
         (h-go-victim-step      ; the agent goes to where the patient is
            (get-to (agent(agent ?s))(patient (patient ?s))
               (location (location-of (patient ?s)))))
         (h-use-instr-step       ; the agent does something with the noose
                                  ; we leave out the details for this
                                  ; example
            (DO (agent (agent ?s))(instr (h-instr ?s))))
  facts: (before (h-get-instr-step ?s)    ; getting the noose comes before
            (h-go-victim-step ?s))    ; going to the victim
         (before (h-go-victim-step ?s)    ; going to the victim comes before
            (h-use-instr-step)))      ; doing the hanging

(plan: DO ?u        ;do is a generic primitive for an undescribed action
    isa: action
  slots: (agent (person))  ; a person does something to
         (patient (person))  ; another person using
         (instr (thing))    ; some thing as an instrument
  facts: (mod-manip ?u))  ; This tells FRAIL that DO is a primitive action
                          ; with no specific to-add or to-del

(frame: carry ?p   ; to carry something
    isa: action   ; is an action
  slots: (agent (person))
         (patient (thing))
  facts: (mod-manip ?p)  ; it is primitive
         (to-del ?p (location (patient ?p) ?pl))  ; removes the old location
         (to-add ?p (location (patient ?p) (agent ?p))))
            ; adds the new location
```

Inset 1: FRAIL input for hanging

TO **solve**/*prob, conditions*/

(1)   If the problem is a **primitive action** (a mod-manip statement can be retrieved) then delete all **to-del** statements that match via unification with the initial conditions and add statements for each of the **to-add** assertions (again using unification).

(2)   If the problem matches an **action frame** which contains **subact** statements (generated by FRAIL from the "acts" section of frames) then **solve** each of the sub-acts using the same initial conditions (and any other binding information needed).

(3)   If neither of the above holds, we look for special statements called **to-do** statements that generate a new problem for us to solve. If multiple **to-do** statements are found then we use a **choice mechanism** to determine which one to use.

Inset 1: The basic planning algorithm for NASL

A forward-chaining rule (signalled by the predicate "→") takes two arguments: an antecedent formula and a consequent formula. Whenever a formula is asserted that
unifies with the antecedent, the consequent is also asserted. Thus, a rule to say "If something is a dog then it barks" would look like

$$(\rightarrow \text{(ISA ?X DOG)}$$
$$\text{(BARKS ?X))}.$$

If we now asserted **(ISA SPOT DOG)** the system would add **(BARKS SPOT)**.

A backward-chaining rule is much like a forward-chaining rule except that it is used only at retrieval time. Thus, if we wished to prove **(BARKS SPOT)** after asserting **(ISA SPOT DOG)**, but did not wish to add the "barks" statement to the database, we would assert

(← (BARKS ?X)
　　(ISA ?X DOG)).

In this case "←" is the backward-chaining rule predicate, and this formula would read "We can prove that ?X barks IF we can show that ?X isa dog." Again, unification is the mechanism used for matching the variables.

These implication rules are of particular interest to us when we combine them with the TO-DO rules mentioned previously. To see this, consider how the following TO-DO rule works

(TO-DO (GET-TO (agent ?x)(location ?y))
　　　　(PLANE-FLYING (agent ?x)(destination ?y)))

This rule would say that for some agent to perform the GET-TO frame to some place ?y, the agent could use the PLANE-FLYING frame with the destination bound to that location. Such a rule is usually of more use when it can somehow be conditionalized, since otherwise NASL would consider using planes to go anywhere, no matter how short the distance. This conditionalization is done by using the chaining rules above, usually the backward chaining rules. Thus, the following rule

(← (TO-DO (GET-TO (agent ?x)(location ?y))
　　　　　(PLANE-FLYING (agent ?x)
　　　　　　　　　　　　(destination ?y)))
　　(LARGE-DISTANCE (location-of ?x) ?y))[9]

would say that we should consider PLANE-FLYING only if there is a large distance between where the agent presently is and the destination of travel.

It is often the case, however, that such restrictions are not mutually exclusive. We might have a rule similar to the above that says:

9– FRAIL allows us to call LISP functions during chaining. Thus, the (LARGE-DISTANCE ..) predicate could be rendered as something like
(← (LARGE-DISTANCE ?x ?y)
　　(LISP (> (distance-from ?x ?y) 100)))

$$(\leftarrow (\text{TO-DO (GET-TO (agent ?x)(location ?y))}$$
$$(\text{BUS-TRAVELING (agent ?x)}$$
$$(\text{destination ?y)))}$$
$$(\text{LARGE-DISTANCE (location-of ?x) ?y))}$$

Thus, for a long trip we would discover from such rules that both "plane-flying" and "bus-traveling" are viable. How are such choices made?

The CHOICE mechanism of NASL is performed by gathering a set of TO-DO rules and discarding those alternatives that are ruled-out for some reason or another; then, if more than one alternative still remains, we look for special reasons to rule that method in. The mechanism for discarding bad rules and selecting among the alternatives is to consider logical predicates relating to task choices. Such predicates are called RULE-OUT and RULE-IN. These rules are of the form

(RULE-OUT choose-task method)

and

(RULE-IN choose-task method)

We rule out (or rule in) some specific task if that tasks matches a certain method. Thus

(RULE-OUT ?task (PLANE-FLYING ?action))

would rule out any task that is a plane-flying task.

These rule-in and rule-out rules are almost never used except in conjunction with backward-chaining rules. That is, we only want to rule certain things in or out if certain conditions hold. Thus,

$$(\leftarrow (\text{RULE-OUT ?task (plane-flying ?action}$$
$$(\text{destination ?place)))}$$
$$(\text{LARGE-COST (plane-flying}$$
$$(\text{destination ?place))))}$$

would say to rule out any plane flight that was too expensive. Similarly,

```
(← (RULE-IN ?task (plane-flying ?action
                             (agent ?person)))
   (IN-HURRY ?person))
```

would say to rule in plane flying if the person is in a hurry. Since NASL first rules out the bad options and then uses rule-ins to decide between the remaining options, the net effect of the two rules above would be to say that if plane flying is an option, it is ruled out if too expensive, regardless of whether we are in a hurry. To achieve the reverse effect, that is "rule out plane flying if it is too expensive UNLESS we are in a hurry," we would need to use more complex predication

```
(← (RULE-OUT ?task (plane-flying ?task
                                 (agent ?person)
                                 (destination ?place)))
   (AND (LARGE-COST (plane-flying
                                 (destination ?place)))
        (NOT (IN-HURRY ?person)))))
```

The marker-passer and the problem-solver communicate by having the plan evaluation heuristics assert rule-in and rule-out predicates into the knowledge base used by the planner, thus influencing the planner's choices. In addition, the plan-evaluator can alter the plans used by the problem-solver by adding new subacts to plans, as is shown in more detail elsewhere (Chapters 4 and 5).

3.2. The SCRAPS and C–SCRAPS programs

The programs used to test many of the ideas in this book go by the acronyms of SCRAPS and C–SCRAPS.[10] SCRAPS is the system mentioned previously for demonstrating the integration of

---

10– Later in this work are many examples in which some of FRAIL's frames have multiple agents. Originally, however, FRAIL and NASL assumed that there could only be one agent involved in any frame. This distinction, between single-agent and multiple-agent frames, corresponds to the differentiation between traditional "plans" (*a la* STRIPS, Fikes & Nilson, 1971) and "scripts" (*a la* SAM (Cullingford, 1978). Thus, one of the original "important contributions" of my thesis research was to be the "SCRipt-bAsed Problem-Solver." However, the difference turned out to be minor, and implementing multi-agent plans for NASL turned out to be almost trivial. Thus, the final work makes no mention of this distinction other than this footnote. The acronym, SCRAPS, however, remains.

the marker-passer with the NASL problem-solver, C–SCRAPS is the same but with some concurrent control structure.

In Figure 5 (reiterated here as Figure 6) we showed a block diagram for the setup of SCRAPS. The problem-solver is invoked via the same type of call to SOLVE as in NASL, and proceeds exactly as it would in the algorithm discussed in Section 3.1. However, each time that NASL accesses the FRAIL database the marker-passer is invoked. When marker-passing paths are found they are reported to a path evaluation system, which is implemented as a set of cascaded heuristics (described in detail in Chapter 5). The path evaluation heuristics are able to assert new information that can be used by NASL as it pursues the problem solution.

In SCRAPS the order of operation is that the problem-solver is invoked first. Following this, the marker-passer is invoked.

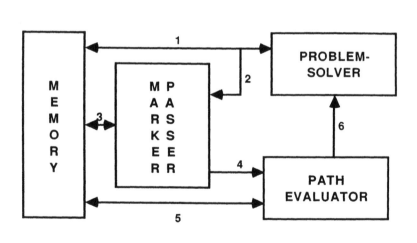

Figure 6: Flow of control in the SCRAPS system (reiterated)
See Figure 5.

When the marker-passer is completed those paths which were found (if any) are examined by the path evaluator. Once all these paths have been processed, the problem-solver continues. It is thus guaranteed that any information added by the marker-passing/path evaluation cycle is there before the problem-solver needs it.

In C–SCRAPS this control structure is changed. The marker-passer, the problem-solver, and the plan evaluator are all running in separate processes, each waiting for messages from the others. It is thus possible for the problem-solver to have already reached, or passed, a decision point before the marker-passing component has finished. Thus, for example, in the "suicide/rope" example described earlier, it would be possible for the CHOICE mechanism to have decided to take the "abandoned refrigerator" path before the marker-passer suggested ruling in "hanging." The issues involved in controlling such concurrency are described in Chapter 7.

4. Cognitive issues

Writing an artificial intelligence book forces an author to decide how much cognitive significance should be attached to the work, and how heavily psychological evidence should be weighted in the design of the systems. In this case, I'd like to consider myself a cognitive scientist and claim great significance for this work. I'd like to, but I can't.

I presently believe that the marker-passer described in this work, and the interaction between this mechanism and the problem-solver, are at best a first order approximation to some actual cognitive mechanism. I thus feel free to use psychological data, but I use it in an almost anecdotal style. There are many differences between my mechanism and the known psychological results. I try to be as honest as possible about these, and try, whenever I can, to show where the boundaries lie. Chapter 8 includes some possible follow-ons that a psychologist might like to pursue.

5. Some terminological difficulties

Many of the terms used by AI researchers, cognitive scientists, and psychologists have no clear meanings. There are other words that have well-defined technical meanings, but are used differently in these different fields. This book is plagued by both. I'll hereby try to define some of the most contrary of the words I use, and at least disclose which things are synonymous, and which not.

5.1. Naming the technique

Primary among the trouble-makers for this book are the terms *Spreading Activation* and *Marker-passing*. Quillian (1966) coined the term "spreading activation" to refer to information passed throughout an associative network to find paths between nodes. (This work, the basis for much of our model, is discussed in detail in Chapter 3). Nowadays, however, psychologists speak of spreading activation as the mechanism accounting for a set of experimental results showing that after the appearance of a target word, words semantically related to that target word are more quickly recognized than random words in memory. (This effect is also called *priming* or *semantic priming*.) These effects are well documented and are discussed in more detail in Chapter 8.

Another body of work models the passing of energy through a network rather than the passing of informational marks as in Quillian's system or ours. This type of energy is usually represented by a set of numerical values that spread throughout a network. The energy at a given node is computed based on the energies of its neighbors. Thus, this process corresponds to a parallel spreading of activation energy, and it too is often referred to as "spreading activation," an alternative usage of the term. (An example of this is the ACT* system of Anderson (1983) discussed in detail in Chapter 8, section 1.2).

The term "marker-passing" is attributed to Scott Fahlman (1979) in the description of his NETL system. This work, described in more detail in Chapter 3, was aimed at designing parallel hardware that would be able to answer certain sorts of semantic queries. NETL worked by passing very simple pieces of information, called *marks*, around a network. Fahlman's work relates to much of the spreading activation work, both of the

Quillian model and the energy passing model, and thus the terms "spreading activation" and "marker-passing" have become blurred.

This blurring of the terms is taken to an extreme here where marker-passing and spreading activation are used interchangeably. The mechanism described here is a computational model that fits Fahlman's original goal (realizability in some form of massively parallel hardware) but relates more directly to the methodology of Quillian and the psychological research. It therefore is somewhere between the two, and rather than creating a new term I will try to distinguish the differences by examples and details throughout this work.

Another terminological confusion arises with the word (and idea of) *connectionism*. Connectionism comes in two flavors: *local connectionism* and *distributed connectionism*. Some people equate the work in marker-passing with local connectionism, while others do not. In this work I will try to separate my work from either form of connectionism and describe the differences. Thus, this work is about *marker-passing* or *spreading activation* and not about *connectionism* or *distributed connectionism*, although they are discussed throughout the work where relevant.[11] Chapter 9 is devoted to a discussion of the relationship between this work and several connectionist models — both local and distributed.

We will also discuss *massively-parallel* computations. This can cause confusion since several different approaches to such computation are presently being examined by the AI community. Some of this work is done on existing machines such as the *connection machine* (Hillis, 1985), other work assumes other architectures and works by running in simulation on serial machines, and yet other work presents "theoretical" machines, which are proposed to describe classes of computation and

---

11- Eugene Charniak (personal communication 8/85) suggested that we refer to ourselves as "von Neumann machine connectionists." I suggested "symbolic connectionists." I won't use these terms in this work, but if they do catch on you heard them here first.

problems, rather than to mean specific hardware.[12] An example of this approach would be the *Boltzmann Machine* (Fahlman, Hinton, and Sejnowski, 1983). In this book we discuss the marker-passing work and it's relations to all of these types of machines. We do attempt to make it clear what type of computation we mean at each point.

5.2. Naming the topic

Another terminological difficulty arises when I try to discuss the topic of this work. To some members of the AI and cognitive communities, *planning* and *problem-solving* are two completely separate entities. To others, they are synonymous. Distinctions have been made with regard to: Whether plans are executable one step at a time or whether a complete plan is generated, whether the domain is formalizable or not, and whether the data structures used refer to a space of plans or a space of states of the world. However, in no case have these distinctions been formal or have the proponents been completely consistent. GPS (for General Problem-Solver) has often been referred to as a planner. Systems built on the planner NOAH are often referred to as problem-solvers.

In this work I adopt the convention of using these terms interchangeably. Problem-solvers generate plans and planners attempt to solve problems. My rational in this is that no matter which of the above distinctions is made, the approach outlined here is germane. All systems that attempt to realize a goal must at some points make choices. In some systems these choices are executed immediately, and thus using marker-passing might prevent the planner from taking improper actions (as discussed previously). In other systems choices are made, but backtracking or replanning can be done if the choice leads to a later contradiction. In these systems a better choice saves later computation. The work in this book is aimed at improving the choices made by a planning (*aka* problem-solving) system while solving a problem (or, shall we say, generating a plan).

12– Thus, these machines are like a "push-down automata" or a "Turing machine" in terms of describing classes of computation, rather than "real" machines.

5.3. Logical terminology

As we've seen earlier, SCRAPS and C–SCRAPS are implemented in a first order predicate world. I try to make it clear throughout this book that most of the ideas herein rest on this logical basis in only the most gentle fashion. At times this may not seem to be the case, since the logical terms for various operations such as *deduction* and *unification* will be used. Again, I try to be clear where this underlying formalism is needed and where it isn't.

5.4. How to describe chunks

One of the true cruxes in writing about AI research is deciding what term to use to define knowledge structures that represent a hierarchical structuring of stereotypic actions and objects. The terms *scripts, frames, schema, chunks,* etc., etc., etc.have been used extensively throughout the AI and cognitive literature, without clear definitions. Trying to differentiate between these terms leads to a morass of complications better left untraversed. I avoid this issue by using the generic term *frame* whenever possible. The reader is invited to replace all occurrences of the word "frame" with his/her favorite neologism.

6. A reader's guide to this book

This book covers two highly interrelated topics: the integration of a marker-passer into a problem-solving system, and the design of a working marker-passing system. I was tempted to try to separate these out into two separate sections, thus sparing the reader interested in only one of these topics from having to do more than skim the other. However, when it came time actually to organize the necessary information it turned out that many of the design issues for the problem-solving component relied on decisions made in regard to the marker-passer, and vice versa. Thus, the book now centers around the SCRAPS system as a unifying concept, and the other issues are discussed as they relate to it.

We follow this introduction with two chapters that define the terms used and discuss previous research. Chapter 2 deals with problem-solving and planning while Chapter 3 concerns marker-passing (primarily from an AI standpoint).

Chapter 4 presents more details about the organization of the program and how the marker-passer and problem-solver interact. Chapter 5 goes into detail about how the paths returned by the marker-passer are evaluated for this interaction. These chapters describe the central ideas of this book and are the "must-read" for those trying simply to extract the main ideas without regard for background or future work.

Chapter 6 contains a detailed discussion of how SCRAPS serves as a working example of a marker-passing system, and discusses some of the issues involved in such a computational implementation. It is aimed at the hard-core computer scientist, and a non-technical reader might wish only to skim this chapter.

Chapter 7 discusses some issues of parallel computation and concurrency. SCRAPS and C–SCRAPS are contrasted and various aspects of both systems concerning concurrency are discussed.

Chapters 8 and 9 describe some research that relates to our work, but not as directly as the research described in Chapters 2 and 3. Chapter 8 concentrates on a cognitive science approach, and presents a review of some of the main psychological theories about spreading activation and semantic priming. We discuss how our research relates to that work, and propose some possible psychological experimentation to explore the role of spreading activation in the planning process. Chapter 9 reviews work in connectionism that is relevant to our approach, compares SCRAPS to this work, and tries to answer the question "Is this work connectionism?"

Chapter 10 shows in extended detail how the SCRAPS program handles several examples. This is designed to pull together the information from all the previous chapters and to show how these issues affected the implementation of SCRAPS.

Chapter 11 discusses some conclusions about this work and some directions for future research. I also face the music and describe some of the more serious limitations of my system, as well as some thoughts on how these can be dealt with in more ambitious future systems.

CHAPTER 2

On Problem-Solving and Planning

The best laid schemes o' mice and men
Gang aft a-gley.
— Robert Burns, *To a Mouse [1785]*

Until now we have been very informal in our use of planning terms and discussion of the problem-solving process. In this section we describe what we mean by these terms in a more precise and technical sense. We also describe past work in the field and relate it to this book.

1. Defining terms

Early AI work used the terms *planning* and *problem-solving* to represent the idea of going from one state of the world to another. A program was presented with information about the present state of the world, called the *initial state*, and a desired future state of the world, the *goal state*. It would attempt to reduce the initial state to the goal state by the sequential application of a set of known procedures called *operators*. A well-ordered list of operators was called the *plan* for solving that particular reduction.

In modern systems the operators may form a very large set and the state of the world may be very complex. This makes the use of the operator/state nomenclature awkward. Instead of moving through a state space, applying operators one to another, one wishes to have a hierarchy of actions to be taken. Problem-solving requires creating a set of *goals* or *tasks* that can be performed by the system. These tasks may involve other tasks, usually simpler ones, for completion. These are called *subgoals* or *subtasks*. Each of these tasks or subtasks may have certain *preconditions* — states that must be achieved before they can work. A task that can be directly applied without any subtasks is

37

called a *primitive task.*[1]

As an example of all these terms we might consider the following. If *John is hungry* we would need to generate a plan by which John would get food. One way to realize this goal would be by the *task* of *John goes to a restaurant.* A *precondition* of this might be *John has some money.* The restaurant task would require *subtasks* such as *order, eat, pay,* etc. These subtasks would in turn be broken down into *primitive tasks* such as *read menu, ingest food, lift money* and the like. The list of the actions taken to achieve this task, or a list of all of the primitive steps, in the order in which they are to be executed, is sometimes referred to as the *plan* for satisfying the original goal.

2. Previous work

AI research in problem-solving is almost as old as the field itself. As such it has had a diverse history encompassing many people and programs. In this section I discuss some of the various approaches to planning and some of the systems developed along the way. This is fonr by breaking this research down into four sections: planning as search, goal-based planning, planning as a temporal process, and planning as a learning mechanism.[2] The first two of these are germane to this work and are discussed in detail in this chapter.

2.1. Planning as search

The largest group of the programs that I describe falls into the category of "planning as search." This term describes those programs in which planning could be viewed as searching through

---

1– In this book we do not discuss the issue of choosing the primitive set of plans — it is enough that some bottom level exists. The reader should not assume that we consider this choice a simple task or a solved problem. Much of the past work in AI and cognitive science has been aimed at examining this issue. Suggestions for the set of primitives have ranged from small numbers (cf. Schank, 1972; Wilks, 1973) to statements that a vast number of primitives exist, all of them innate (cf. Fodor, 1978). The primary criterion used in the present work was expediency — the primitives are at the level needed to show the theoretical properties being discussed and no more.

2– These distinctions are defined as we go along, but the reader is warned that they are somewhat artificial: I drawing these distinctions in order to be able to categorize some of the differences in approaches. Most programs fall into multiple categories.

a space of alternatives. This space can be a network of tasks or an and-or tree of goal and task decompositions. Many of the results of this research have led to more general results in the field of "search," and many results from the search literature have been of use to the problem-solving researchers.

2.1.1. Means-ends analysis

The earliest work in problem-solving of this kind started as a direct application of the state/operator form described above. GPS (Newell, Shaw, & Simon, 1959; Ernst & Newell, 1969), or General Problem-Solver, used a technique, called *means-ends analysis*, which examined the goal state and looked to see what differences it manifested from the initial state. It then looked into a table that indexed the various operators by their effects. The differences that would be reduced by these effects were counted, and the operator producing the best results was applied. Applying this operator would create a new state, and this state would then be used as the new initial state. This would be repeated until all of the differences had been eliminated, and thus the goal state was reached.

GPS had profound repercussions in the psychological and search communities, and the technique of means-ends analysis and some of the programming techniques used to implement GPS, such as discrimination trees and pattern matching, have become standard tools of AI. However, GPS was designed to explore problem-solving at a very general level. As such, it did not define a specific representation to be used or suggest a particular set of operators for general problems. In GPS different formulations of the same problem can often have very different behaviors. This is important in the application of GPS as a psychological model (Simon, 1969), but causes problems to the researcher wishing to create computer problem-solvers.

Fikes and Nilsson (1971) used many of the ideas from GPS, specifically the notion of means-ends analysis, in a robot planner called STRIPS. STRIPS would handle a simple world consisting of several rooms, some boxes, and a robot. The world was represented in terms of predicate calculus assertions, and a resolution theorem-prover was used to determine what operators were to be applied when[3]. STRIPS also used an explicit notion of preconditions — each of the actions would require that specific states be met. For example, a precondition for the robot to push a box would be that the location of the robot was the same as the location of the box. Achieving the preconditions for an action would count as the set of subtasks to be solved next. Thus, pushing the box required being at the box which in turn engendered the goal of getting to that location. Again the process ended when it reached primitive conditions.

One problem that STRIPS had was the computational complexity of solving problems in terms of the specific operators and objects it knew. Presented with two states of the world, it would attempt to exhaustively examine all the differences between them and choose an operator based on all these differences.

To avoid this, Sacerdoti (1974) created a system called ABSTRIPS, which kept plans in what was called an abstraction hierarchy. When differences were examined they would have different levels of importance. Operators were designed to deal with these differences at the appropriate level of abstraction. Thus, if ABSTRIPS noticed a difference in the placement of a block it might use an operator such as MOVE-BLOCK. This plan would be represented something like

Move to the block.
Push the block to the new location.

Only later would it refine this to include moving through doors and around objects.

The STRIPS (and ABSTRIPS) formulation of problem-solving assumed "linearity" of plans. That is, the programs assumed that the subgoals of a plan could be independently achieved — order didn't matter. Thus, if we wished to push BLOCK1 to ROOM3 from ROOM2, and BLOCK2 from ROOM4 to ROOM1, it didn't matter which we did first. A set of projects followed from this which relaxed this assumption — planning in

---

3– The logic served the function that the operator-difference table served in GPS.

which the subgoals interacted.

2.1.2. Nonlinear planning

In 1974, several projects were developed that allowed certain amounts of nonlinearity in plans. Tate (1974) developed a system called INTERPLAN at the University of Edinburgh, Warren (1974), also at Edinburgh, created a system called WARPLAN, and Manna and Waldinger (1974) at SRI worked on a plan-based system for doing program synthesis. Each of these programs handled a small amount of nonlinearity — they were able to perform reordering on a set of otherwise linear plans.

Tate's system worked by performing a search to find the correct linear ordering of the subplans. It was able to reorder existing plans and to backtrack when contradictions arose. It did these by examining a table that represented interactions between goals that would be used conjunctively.

Warren and Manna and Waldinger used a different approach. Their systems built linear plans by adding each subtask to a plan in a nonsequential manner. As each is added, all those subtasks already in the plan are examined. If the present task would render an earlier task invalid, it would be placed later in the plan than that previous task. If, instead, it would be invalidated by an earlier task it would appear before that task in the plan. This system had the advantage of always adding new parts: It never had to remove a plan that already had been inserted.

However, these systems all had the drawback of dealing only with a certain level of nonlinearity. They all had to do computationally expensive search and often much backtracking to achieve the final result. The first work attempting to deal with fully nonlinear planning is Sussman's (1975) HACKER planning system. HACKER went along generating plans as if they were linear. However, a set of *critics* could be invoked by the program to check for and fix problems in plans caused by interactions. Each plan created by HACKER included information, called *comments*, which explained why that plan had been created. Each subplan contained comments. Whenever HACKER created new plans (i.e., used conjunctions of subplans) it went into a "careful mode" in which it examined these comments. These comments were made "active" as the plan was created. During the time that a comment was active its "purpose" was protected. If another comment became active during this interval, its purpose was compared to those of the previously activated comments. If a conflict was found the system went to a library of patches to see if something could be found to fix the problem. Once such a patch had been made, a version of the situation leading to the patch and information about the fix used were put into a library of critics. These critics were activated if a similar situation came along so that the same fix could be used if applicable.

This is made a lot clearer through an example. Figure 7 shows a simple Block's World problem and associated goal. Notice that if we try to execute (ON A B) ,then we will have to undo it to be able to achieve (ON B C). HACKER would try to solve this problem by generating a piece of code similar to:

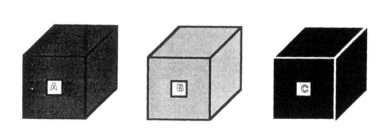

ACHIEVE: (AND (ON A B)
(ON B C))

Figure 7: A Block's World task.

```
(HPROG AND2
   ... (ACHIEVE (ON A B))
   ... (ACHIEVE (ON B C)))
```

Associated with this code would be some comments saying that the purpose of each of these achieve statements was the goal AND2. HACKER would then create the plan of putting A on B, taking A off B (so B could be moved), and putting B on C. In a linear planner we would now assume we were done, but HACKER would check the code in careful mode since it had made the linearity assumption. It would notice as it did this that the execution of the (ON B C) plan happened during the comment period of the (ON A B) plan (since they were in pursuit of the same goal). Since a precondition for achieving (ON B C) would require (CLEAR B), and since this would clobber (ON A B), the system noted a bug. It would then look in a patch generator and find that the fix for a precondition clobbering another goal would be to exchange the order of the goals. The system would thus change the code to

```
(HPROG AND2
   ... (ACHIEVE (ON B C))
   ... (ACHIEVE (ON A B)))
```

This plan would then be checked for further bugs. Since none are found it would run. Also, a critic would be created looking something like

```
(WATCH-FOR
      (ORDER (... (ACHIEVE (ON ?a ?b)) ...)
             (... (ACHIEVE (ON ?b ?c)) ...))
      (PRECONDITION-CLOBBERING ...
             (<reorder the achieve steps>)))
```

which would be activated whenever we tried to achieve a plan similar to the original AND2 program. This critic would cause the reordering of the achieve tasks.

The primary disadvantage of Sussman's system was that it sometimes did a lot of wasted work. The problem-solver would usually produce a correct plan, but only after first building a defective plan and then debugging it to form a new plan. This new plan might also have bugs, different from those in the first plan, and thus more replanning would be needed.

Sacerdoti (1977) proposed a solution to this problem in his NOAH (Nets Of Action Hierarchies) system. NOAH represented plans as *procedural networks* at various levels of detail. Each operation that it knew how to perform was represented as a set of other operations with known predecessors and successors. Each operation (or "node" in Sacerdoti's network terminology) had associated with it an add and delete list: a list of those changes to the world made by performing the operation associated with that node. Thus, in an example from Sacerdoti, if we wish to paint a ladder and to paint a ceiling we start with the single node plan of Figure 8a. This is broken down into two separate tasks that are split and later joined: Figure 8b. Each of these plans is next expanded into the component steps (Figure 8c)

At this point NOAH checks the add and delete lists for the various plan steps to see if they cause problematic interactions. This is done by the application of various constructive critics that can affect the plans. Applicable to the above plan would be a. RESOLVE CONFLICTS critic. This would notice that the above plan would have a conflict (since painting the ladder would disable using the ladder for climbing). Upon recognizing the conflict the critic orders plan steps so that the step containing the precondition being violated comes first. A different join statement is formed and the plan looks like Figure 8d.

Sacerdoti also had several other types of critics to do such things as *use existing objects* or *eliminate redundant preconditions*. Sacerdoti used a "table of multiple effects," based on Tate's form of difference tables, to make the critics more efficient.

One important feature of Sacerdoti's work was the use of a *least-commitment strategy* during planning. That is, critics were not applied until as late in the process as possible. Thus, plans were considered to run more or less in parallel until a low level of abstraction was reached. This allowed multiple effects to be noted and permitted the critics to make more comprehensive changes to the plans generated.

A)   Paint the Ceiling and Paint the Ladder

B)

C)

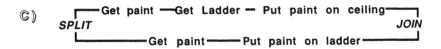

D)

Figure 8: NOAH paints a ladder.
The single node plan (A) is split into two subplans to be accomplished together (B). These plans are each expanded (C) and interaction between the plans are examined. When an interaction is found the plan can be altered to be more efficient (D).

Despite NOAH's least commitment strategy, however, choices made about the order in which actions should be added to plans could not easily be undone. Tate (1977) addressed this issue in his NONLIN planning system. NONLIN added an agenda with choice points to the NOAH scheme, thus allowing backup and reordering when necessary.

Yet another approach to nonlinear planning was that done by the MOLGEN project at Stanford (Martin, Friedland, King, &

Stefik, 1977; Stefik, 1980). As a mechanism for ordering plans, this system used constraints, which could be propagated during the planning session, and thus reordering and the like could occur.[4]

MOLGEN also used the notion of *meta-planning*. A set of rules and constraints were developed that applied to planning in general, rather than to the specific plans in the system. Instead of organizing its actions around a simple agenda, MOLGEN had three different levels of planning: the bottom level consisted of domain-specific knowledge, the middle layer had design (or planning) rules of the type found in NOAH, etc., and the top level had strategy rules including such things as *focus, resume, guess,* and *undo.* These strategies allowed MOLGEN to monitor the lower-level steps for specific intents. The control loop of MOLGEN chose strategies, these strategies planned the steps in design space, and the rules in the design space picked specific steps at the domain level to realize the current goals.

Most of the recent work in planning research of this type has focused on extending the models of these nonlinear planning systems, formalizing descriptions of their behaviors, and getting them to work for real-world problems. Perhaps the best known of these works is the DEVISER system (Vere, 1983; 1985), which extends the representational power of these systems into the domain of time and deals with the handling of multiple goals for a simulated satellite mission planning task. Instead of representing goals as "solve X," DEVISER represents goals as "solve X so that it is true after time T1 but before time T2 and is true for at least duration N." Such a temporal specification was called a *window.*

Events in DEVISER have associated durational information. Thus, much of the planning behavior in the DEVISER system involved setting up temporal constraints and comparing them to the durations.

4– Many of the ideas in MOLGEN are similar to, and sometimes based upon, a cognitive model being developed by Barbara and Frederick Hayes-Roth, which included the notions of abstraction spaces and opportunistic planning. See (Hayes-Roth & Hayes-Roth, 1979).

SIPE (Wilkins, 1983) dealt with special resource handling rules. It included information concerning the "expense" of various operations and rules to handle these expenses. It could also deal with such tasks as "boiling three pans on two burners" and other such resource limitations. Drummond (1985) extended the procedural networks of Sacerdoti into a more flexible format. Chapman's (1985) TWEAK system recasts much of the earlier work in a mathematically rigorous way. When TWEAK reaches a plan for an action, this formal treatment can show that plan to be a correct solution. Stuart (1985) and Georgeoff (1983) extend the Sacerodti format to the handling of multiple agents. These plans can coordinate the actions of several agents all cooperating to achieve a goal. Berlin (1985) developed a system called SPAN that integrated much of the work of Sussman, Sacerdoti, Tate, and Vere. SPAN created a coherent framework in which all of these varying techniques could be applied.

2.1.3. Plan interpreters

Along with the planning research just described, an AI tradition in rule-based systems was developing. This involved the work of three different communities: theorem proving (Moore, 1975; Nevins, 1974; Nilsson, 1971; Robinson, 1965), production systems (Newell, 1974; Rychener, 1975), and AI programming languages using pattern-directed invocation (Hewitt, 1972; Rulifson, Derkson, & Waldinger, 1972; Sussman & McDermott, 1972).

McDermott (1977), following the tradition of the latter, developed an AI language for plan description, and a planner to work with it, called NASL. McDermott explained:

> The main difference between this part of NOAH and NASL is that NOAH is a plan compiler, while NASL is an interpreter; that is, it expands and executes pieces of a plan as it goes. (p. 36)

NASL did not share the STRIPS-like assumption that the effects of all actions could be summarized as state changes, or that they could be fully explicated and stored in effect tables. It was unable therefore to take advantage of some of the simple algorithms developed by Sacerdoti for checking the interactions between subplans.

Charniak (1982; Charniak, Gavin & Hendler, 1983) developed a working version of NASL to run in his FRAIL system. In Chapter 1, Section 3.1, we described the control structure of NASL, so we do not reiterate it here. What is important to note is that the TO-ADD and TO-DEL statements of NASL serve the purpose of the add- and delete-lists of NOAH. Since these are retrieved on the fly and may be forward- or backward-chained, NASL's behavior can be changed by conditions of the environment. For example, we might have a different TO-ADD rule for a GOING action depending on whether or not the instrument of the going was a *car* or a *train*. NOAH and the other nonlinear programs did not have this ability.

The SIPE program of Wilkins (briefly mentioned earlier) to some extent bridged the gap between NASL and the NOAH style planners. SIPE, although basically a nonlinear planner, has an interactive facility that lets the user guide the planning process. The user can direct low-level planning operations (define which resources to bind to which variables), high-level interactions (the planner can be asked to do deeper planning if desired and to check plans being created for side effects caused by nonlinearity), or the interactions between the two (the planner can be asked to use a certain binding and then check and see if it would cause problems).

Another approach used for problem-solving, primarily in the domain of robot planning, has been the application of production rules. Sobek (1985) describes his FPS system, a goal-based problem-solver based on NOAH. FPS takes advantage of the production system architecture to allow planning to occur as a set of expansions. With each expansion various production rules can be fired, which act as critics. This system allows a certain measure of flexibility because these productions may depend upon features of the environment (represented as statements in a working memory).

2.2. Goal-based planning

A very different approach to planning grew out of research in the field of natural language understanding. Various work had attempted to develop a taxonomy of plans and goals needed for story understanding (Abelson, 1975; Charniak, 1975; Rieger, 1976; Schank and Ableson, 1977)

Meehan's (1976) TALESPIN program did story generation. It would establish a goal for a character and have it navigate through a simple world using a set of plans to achieve this goal. A sample output would be something like

> Once upon a time there was a nest in an ash tree. Wilma Bird lived in the nest. There was some water in a river. Wilma knew that the water was in the river. One day Wilma was very thirsty. Wilma wanted to get near some water. Wilma flew from her nest across a meadow through a valley to the river. Wilma drank the water. Wilma was not thirsty any more.

We can see from this that the TALESPIN program can, in some ways, be called a problem-solver. It understood how to satisfy goals and had a set of rules that could be used for this. It also contained various rules about social interactions between the characters based on the D-goals of Schank and Abelson (1977).[5] It was therefore able to generate stories with multiple characters and use such plans as *steal, lie, bribe, cooperate,* etc.

TALESPIN told stories one step at a time and didn't develop a complete plan for an action prior to generation. It was therefore subject to many problematical interactions that the nonlinear planners were designed to avoid. TALESPIN didn't worry about such problems, since describing the fixes that were developed often made for more interesting stories.[6]

Wilensky's PAM system (Wilensky, 1978) was designed to try to understand plans rather than to construct them. This work was important to the field of planning primarily in elucidating a new area of planning— so-called "human" planning. The stories read by the PAM program concerned such interactions involving more complicated domains than the Block's World-type problems being addressed by the nonlinear planning community. Even programs like DEVISER, which functioned in real-world

---

5– A set of proposed primitive concepts for various classes of human goals.

6– And for some very amusing mistakes. The interested reader should see the "Misspun tales" chapter of (Meehan, 1976) for an entertaining discussion of such issues.

applications, used well constrained and well understood domains for planning. Wilensky's work examined issues involving such goals as *hunger, loneliness, revenge* and other such difficult-to-formalize domains.

Wilensky didn't try to formalize the knowledge in these domains. Instead, he tried to categorize some of the issues involved in these real-world plans. Wilensky defined a terminology for dealing with multiple agent- and recurring-goal-planning, and developed and explored such concepts as *goal subsumption goal conflict, goal competition,* and *goal concord.*

The work of Jaime Carbonell Jr. (Carbonell, 1979) and of Schmidt and Sridharan (1978) was aimed at understanding stories that involved belief systems. Schmidt and Sridharan's work dealt with analyzing the goals of agents based on observed actions. A major portion of Carbonell's work was concerned with elucidating *counterplanning* strategies — agents planning either with or against each other.

Although these projects were not strictly speaking concerned with the design of problem-solvers, they added much to the vocabulary of planning research. Later work by Wilensky (1983) involved developing a planner to handle these issues. Wilensky's work, reflected in several systems built at the University of California at Berkeley, aimed at developing both planners and story comprehenders to deal with the domain of "common-sense" planning. These systems were based on a set of principles that included associating plans with goals in the system's memory, projecting future worlds based on a world model and a set of plans, detecting interactions between several plans and goals, using these interactions to influence other plans, and evaluating alternative scenarios of plans.

The planner based on these principles had four separate components. It first had a *goal detector* that could be used to determine when planning activity was needed. This was an important departure from the nonlinear planners in that no specific goal needed to be specified. The goal detector could recognize changes in the environment, the existence of other goals that could cause a new goal to come into effect, or problems in the present plans that would cause new plans to be invoked. Thus, for example, the goal detector might notice the following sorts of things: *becoming hungry* would engender a *get food* goal, this *get food* goal could cause a *go to restaurant* goal, and realizing this *go to restaurant* might need a *have money* step, which in turn could engender a *get money* goal.

A second component of the system was a *plan proposer*. This component would find stored plans that were indexed as being associated with various goals. When the plan proposer needed to expand an existing goal it was able to break that goal down into subplans. Thus this *plan proposer* was similar in function to the NASL planner discussed in Section 2.1.3.

A third component, and that most relevant to the present work, was a *plan projector*. This component would test the present set of plans by projecting the effects these plans would have on a world model. This mechanism differed in many ways from the add- and delete-lists of the nonlinear planners. Primary among these was the ability to take into account not merely the present set of plans and their interactions, but also the probable actions of other planners and the probable natural course of events.

The final component of Wilensky's system was the *executor*, responsible for carrying out the sequence of intended actions in the plan. As the executor carried out these plans, new facts were added to the world model.

Figure 9 shows the flow of control in Wilensky's planner. The goal detector looks at the world model to see if a goal is necessary. If a goal is found, it is added to a task network. The plan proposer proposes a plan to satisfy this goal. If this plan involves a specific action, the executor performs that act and uses it to create a new situation for the goal detector to examine. If the plan proposer suggests a more complex set of actions, the projector generates, from the present world model, a possible future state of the world. Again, this world can be examined by the goal detector and the process would continue.

This planner was used as the basis for a UNIX^TM Consultant developed by Wilensky. The advisor was able to generate plans based on this model and to generate advice on how to use such plans. This system could generate complex suggestions such as:

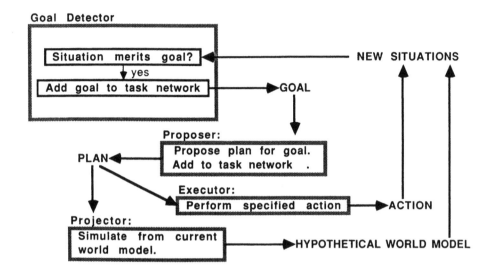

Figure 9: Wilensky's Planning System.
Based on (Wilensky, 1983).

USER: [trying to get space to save a file]
  I still don't have enough space.

CONSULTANT: Mail the file to yourself.
  Then ask the systems manager for
  more disk space.

In this case the system has recognized the goal of *saving a file*, realized the problem of *lack of disk space*, and generated a plan that consists of two parts: *temporarily storing the file without using disk space* [use mail], and *getting more space so it can be saved permanently* [ask systems manager for more space].

2.3. Planning as temporal reasoning

Another view of planning is that it is a temporal reasoning process — the representation of events in time replaces many of the nonlinear issues. Thus, instead of keeping a list of adds and deletes the system keeps track of what events are true and false at what time. Many of the issues relating to nonlinear planners and problem-solvers can be recast using temporal logics. The ideas of protection intervals, concurrency, and splits and joins are more easily dealt with when viewed as concerning states and actions with temporal durations.

Vere's DEVISER work was cast in such a framework. Other work concerned with representing temporal information can be found in Allen and Koomen (1983) and McDermott (1978). Recent work in developing planners based on this research can be found in the work of Yale's FORBIN project, specifically the work of Dean (1986). An overview of planning viewed as a temporal logic problem can be found in Charniak and McDermott (1985).

2.4. Planning as learning

Still another view of planning is that it is primarily a process of learning by example, or of extracting from earlier plans. In this work, simple plans are fleshed out into more complex plans, and these plans in turn are stored in such a way that they can be applied to other situations. An early version of this was described in Section 2.1.2 where we discussed how Sussman's HACKER system was able to create new planning critics. Recent work has expanded this approach into a basis for planning and problem-solving research (Alterman, 1985; Carbonell, 1983; Kolodner & Simpson, 1984).

3. Relationship of our model to past work

In an earlier Section (2.1.3), we cited McDermott's distinction between his NASL problem-solver and the NOAH planner. He pointed out that NASL functioned as an interpreter while NOAH functioned as a compiler. To see this more clearly let us contrast how NASL and NOAH might handle the example given in Chapter 1, Section 1.2, of planning the route of a hypothetical lunar robot. The robot was to make its way past a crater that had earlier been found to contain loose rocks. We gave this system the information that it must not carry a heavy object past such a crater.

NASL would attempt this by breaking the problem of transporting into several tasks: lift the atomic plant, go to the place to which it is to be taken, and put the plant down. Since the first task is to lift the plant, this would be done. NASL would now put an assertion into the database of the form (**CARRY ROBOT ATOMIC-PLANT**). The database would also contain the knowledge that (**ISA ATOMIC-PLANT HEAVY-OBJECT**).

The first step accomplished, the robot would now set out on its way. This would include expanding the plan for going to the base, which would involve subtasks such as: move to Tycho, turn left, move to base.[7] When the "move to Tycho" plan was executed the system would assert (**AT ROBOT TYCHO-CRATER**). At this point, however, it would notice that the statement (**LOOSE-ROCKS TYCHO-CRATER**) was also in the database, along with the rule that said not to go where loose rocks are if one is carrying a heavy object. At this point the planner would recognize the error and begin to replan. If it was lucky enough not to have slipped into the crater already, it would return to the original base and start again.

The NOAH type planner[8] would have no such problem. We would generate the same sort of starting plan as NASL did, but it would not be executed. Instead, the add and delete information for each of the steps would be used. We would find that lifting the power-plant added the information that a heavy object was being carried. As we expanded the second step (go to Tycho), an add-list object would be found that would observe the information about loose rocks being at Tycho. A critic would recognize the rule about not going near the crater. The planner would backtrack and attempt to generate a different route.

In both of these systems, work is done that could have been avoided if a more efficient choice had been made. A mechanism is

---

7– This is grossly simplified for the sake of this example. Those of you designing lunar robots should not try using this plan without suitable modifications.

8– For the sake of this example we are talking about a hypothetical nonlinear planner with all the capabilities of the systems NOAH, NONLIN, DEVISER, etc. Thus, the exact description may not match the behavior of any one of these.

needed that can help make better choices during planning. In the NASL model a better choice would make the robot exhibit a different behavior. Instead of heading off towards Tycho and then later coming back (or possibly not coming back — falls into craters do happen) the system heads off in the direction of a different route. In the NOAH model the outward behavior would be no different, but the robot would move in the correct direction sooner than before, since the planner would not have spent time working on an improper solution.

SCRAPS, as implemented, is an extension of Charniak's (1982) implementation of the NASL planner. Our reasons for choosing NASL as the planner to modify are not related to the work being described here; they relate both to theoretical issues involved in developing planning systems that work in dynamically changing domains (Hendler & Sanborn, 1987) and to pragmatic considerations having to do with availability and ease of reprogramming. This particular choice, however, is not essential to the ideas behind integrating the marker-passer and the problem-solver. SCRAPS is, in essence, an attempt to build the "better mousetrap" of planning — an efficient choice mechanism. Plans with a higher chance of success will be examined earlier; plans doomed to failure will never be expanded. This would be just as true in the choice mechanism of a NOAH-like planner as it is in NASL.

Many of the types of problems that SCRAPS is designed to deal with do not arise in the "clean" worlds that many past planning systems have been designed to deal with. They do, however, come up often in the "real-world" types of planning dealt with by Wilensky's systems. The examples in this book therefore deal with such domains; in fact, we use many of Wilensky's examples.

Wilensky's planner is able to move step by step in executing a plan, using the proposer and projector mechanisms to make sure that negative effects can be predicted and avoided. One problem with Wilensky's model is its failure to define how to build these components.

Another difficulty with the model proposed by Wilensky is how to examine the possible futures that the plan projector creates. If all possible worlds are created, and if all facts of importance in these worlds must be examined, the computational complexity gets as bad as or worse than that of the traditional nonlinear programs.

The primary difference between the SCRAPS system and the system that Wilensky proposed is the addition of the marker-passer to SCRAPS. The marker-passer/path evaluator mechanism can be thought of as replacing Wilensky's projector with a more efficient and "cleaner" algorithm. In the next chapter, I discuss how the marker-passer used by SCRAPS relates to previous work on such systems. Later chapters describe the algorithms used and the decisions made in their design.

CHAPTER 3

On Marker-Passing and Spreading Activation

One if by land, and two if by sea;
And I on the opposite shore will be,
Ready to ride and spread the alarm
Through every Middlesex village and farm.
— Henry Wadsworth Longfellow, *Paul Revere's Ride [1874]*

As mentioned previously, SCRAPS is an attempt to add a marker-passer to a problem-solver. In this chapter we describe this process and define the terms used to discuss it hereafter. We also review and discuss some previous work relating to the present theory.

1. Defining terms

In the introduction we compared marker-passing to hitting hockey pucks connected by springs. This metaphor can be pushed quite far. The amalgam of hockey pucks (*nodes*) and springs (*links*) is called an associative network, the process of hitting them is called *passing markers*, and the frictional damping is called *attenuation of marking*. During the process of passing markers, information is left at every node that is reached (all vibrating hockey pucks). This information is referred to as a *mark*. Marks can be single bits of information (making nodes *marked* or *unmarked*) or they can be structures of arbitrary complexity containing various other sorts of information.

The links connecting the nodes of the associative network carry information about the relationships between these nodes. These relationships may be uni- or bi-directional depending on type and implementation. One special link, the *ISA* link, is often distinguished from the others. The isa link defines a hierarchy of types within the network, and usually the semantics of these nets are such that properties from the node "higher" in the isa tree are

57

inherited by the lower nodes. The typical *parent* and *child* node terminology, borrowed from literature on "trees" in computer science, is usually used to describe these relations.

As mentioned in the introduction, in this book I generally use the term "marker-passing," but the term *spreading activation* is at times used synonymously. When we are using the spreading activation terminology, the following equivalences hold: marking of nodes is referred to as *activating* or *priming*, and marked nodes are called *activated* or *primed* nodes.

Several new pieces of marker-passing terminology are introduced in this book. The pieces of information left on nodes during the marker-passing process are referred to simply by the generic term *marks*. However, at times information is left by other processes so that the marker-passer can take advantage of it. We want this information to reside at a node in much the same way that a mark does, but we also want the placing of such information on a node not to cause the spreading of marks. This process is called *flagging* a node, and the information left by flagging is simply called a *flag*. The reasons for flagging, and the uses of flags, is discussed at length in Chapter 4.

We also use the term *zorch* to refer to the amount of activation energy associated with a mark.[1] Using this factor enables us to provide an elegant attenuation mechanism for our marker-passing algorithm. This too is described in Chapter 4.

2. Previous work

As will be discussed later in this chapter, this book is the first work to develop a computational model for integrating marker-passing with problem-solving. Just as it is not the first problem-solver by any means, it is also not the first system to use marker-

---

1– The notion of attenuation is quite prevalent in discussion of spreading activation. The term *zorch* is often used orally but rarely in writing. The earliest reference I can find to the word is a radio DJ in the San Francisco Bay area, who used the term to mean "high energy" during early 1950's radio broadcasts. Nowadays, the use of the term zorch to mean "an amount of energy" is prevalent at MIT. Perhaps one significant aspect of this book will be to bring "zorch" out of the closet and into the literature as a respected term. (More information on the MIT use of the word can be found in *The Hacker's Dictionary*, Steele et. al., 1983.)

passing algorithms for AI tasks. Previous work has involved developing marker-passing as an architecture for semantic tasks and using such a scheme for natural language processing and other such cognitive tasks.

2.1. Quillian

The first computational model of a spreading activation mechanism is M. Ross Quillian's (1966) *semantic memory* model. This work attempted to make a cognitive model of several memory processes concerned with word definitions and language tasks. This system handled these processes as a three-step operation: parsing input into an internal representation (stored in the early List-processing language IPL (Newell, 1963)), comparing and contrasting word concepts, and generating output in simplified English text. The second of these steps is the one of concern to us here.

Quillian's model kept word senses in an associative network form, and thus was able to compare and contrast meanings by expanding out from each concept a set of *activation tags*. Each tag contained two components: the name of the original parent node at which this set of activations began, and a pointer to the immediate parent. As each new node was activated it was checked to see if it already held an activation tag. If it had been activated from a different parent, then two paths were returned — the sets of nodes tracing back to each of the parents. If it had been activated from the same node as the present activation, then the system noted this and stopped tracing (thus preventing loops). If the node had not been previously activated, it would be tagged appropriately.

Using this scheme Quillian was able to generate a set of paths found by intersecting word concepts. Thus asked to compare, for example, "fire" and "burn," Quillian's program produced such output as "Fire is condition which burn," "To burn2 can be to destroy2 something by4 fire," and "Fire is a flame condition. This flame can be a gas tongue4. This gas is a gas which burn" (Quillian 1966; p. 45).

Quillian is probably better known for a later work derived from this earlier one. His Teachable Language Comprehender,

TLC (Quillian, 1969) was designed to handle natural language comprehension using this activation approach. Essentially, Quillian's system would spread actiavtion from each word of input as it was entered. This activation would be stopped when it was a certain "distance" from the initial concept — that is, when the breadth-first search had reached a certain depth limit — and the next word would then be processed. When a connection was found, this was considered to be a possible meaning of the words in combination and syntactic tests would be performed to see if this meaning could be used.

As an example of this process, consider how TLC handles the phrase *client's lawyer*. Activation markers are spread from *lawyer*, but since nothing has previously been activated, no paths are found. Activation is next spread from *client*, via a definition saying, in effect, *a client is someone who employs a professional*. This causes *employ* to be activated. Since nothing comes of this, the concept *professional* is activated. But this word, we discover, has been activated previously by *lawyer*. Thus, the proposal is made that the phrase has the meaning of *the professional (a lawyer) who is employed by this client*. However, notice that this same connection might have been found if *client* and *lawyer* had been in the same sentence but not in the same relationship (as in the sentence *My client was friendly with his father's lawyer*). This is checked for by a set of *form tests* that see whether the proposed property can be supported by the syntax of the sentence. In this case, the apostrophe followed by s (*'s*) identifies a syntactic relationship that matches the semantic relationship proposed by the sentence. The system would therefore accept this meaning.

2.2. Fahlman

Scott Fahlman (1979) designed NETL to be a hardware implementation of a marker-passing scheme (actually simulated in software). The network memory was similar to that of Quillian, but was realized quite differently. Each node in memory was replaced by a simple hardware device called a *node unit*, and each link became a hardware *link unit*. These devices were able to

propagate a set of markers in parallel throughout the network.[2]
The performance of these devices was controlled by a single serial
computer known as the *network controller*.

This led to a system that had some of the properties of
Quillian's, but with one major difference. According to Fahlman
(1979):

> The network system I am proposing is much more tightly discip-
> lined. The controller is not only able to specify, at every step of
> the propagation, exactly which types of links are to pass which
> markers in which directions; it is also able to use the presence of
> one type of marker at a link to enable or inhibit the passage of
> other markers.

NETL was designed to deal quickly with certain types of
knowledge-base issues: those concerning type hierarchies and
property inheritance. The system allowed two main kinds of
nodes, individual-nodes and type-nodes. Type-nodes served as the
templates for storing a set of properties about some class of
entities. The individual-nodes were each instances of some type
allowing inheritance. Thus, to use Fahlman's most famous
example, given *an elephant named Clyde* we would say that
CLYDE is an individual-node, which is an instance of the type-
node ELEPHANT. Inheritance works by storing properties at
various levels of a type hierarchy and having them inherited by all
those individuals associated with any type "lower" in the
hierarchy. Thus, if we knew *elephants are grey* and *mammals
lactate* then we would know that *Clyde is grey* and *Clyde lactates*.

NETL works by passing markers throughout the system via
the parallel architecture of the various node and link processors.[3]
Essentially, this proceeds by propagating several types of marks
through the network; the controller processor is able to query all
nodes to find how they've been marked. To see this, consider how
the question *what color is Clyde?* would be answered. The
network would look like that shown in Figure 10a. Marks of one

---

2– Fahlman claimed that eight to sixteen distinct markers would be the right number
for "human-like" performance, although he offered no evidence to support such a claim.

3– To describe the actual working of the parallel networks involved in NETL would
involve more complexity than we need for this book. The description here is somewhat
simplified — for details see Fahlman (1981).

type, call it *M1*, would propagate out starting at CLYDE. This would mark ELEPHANT and any other information we might have about CLYDE.[4] At the same time another marker, call it *M2*, would start propagating at COLOR. This would mark GREY, PINK, YELLOW, etc. The second iteration of marking would have mark GREY as *M1* by the link from ELEPHANT. Eventually, the controller asks all nodes that are marked as both *M1* and *M2* to report in. The node GREY, being the only node so marked, thus reports in.

An important feature of NETL was the existence of *cancellation links*. If we had *Clyde is a pink elephant* then we must not have CLYDE inherit the property GREY from the ELEPHANT node. This was done by having an explicit

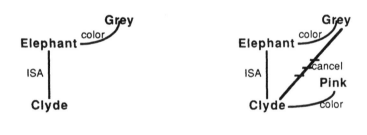

(a) Clyde is an elephant   (b) Clyde is a pink elephant

Figure 10: *Explicit cancellation.*
A) Clyde is an elephant, elephants are grey. B) Clyde is a pink elephant. An explicit cancellation link between Clyde and Grey is provided to block the inference made in (A).

4– For example, we might know that Clyde is also of type CIRCUS-PERFORMER.

cancellation from CLYDE to GREY and an explicit link from CLYDE to PINK (see Figure 10b). Cancellation during marking is done by using a different mark, call it $M3$, to spread up cancellation links and cause them to be considered "dead" for further marker propagation. Thus, for *Clyde is a pink elephant*, we would pass an $M1$ marker to ELEPHANT and PINK and an $M3$ marker to GREY. When ELEPHANT tries to mark GREY it finds that it is already marked by an $M3$ link and therefore it cannot be marked as an $M2$. Thus, when the controller asks for those nodes marked by $M1$ and $M2$, only PINK reports. Using similar types of marker-propagations, and various link types, NETL was able to handle set intersections, exclusive sets (such as LIVING and DEAD), scoping information, and other such inheritance hierarchy operations.[5]

It was an important property of NETL that it could efficiently produce answers to these various inheritance hierarchy questions. The set of nodes reported by NETL was to be the exclusive set of correct results for such operations. Thus, it was not considered correct to report that CLYDE was both GREY and PINK — he had to be one or the other. Unfortunately, it turns out that we cannot always guarantee this exclusivity. Touretsky (Touretsky, 1984) proved mathematically that marker-passing propagation algorithms of the type proposed by Fahlman have certain limitations. To state Touretsky's results informally, he shows that such a system cannot be made to handle cancellation links unambiguously.[6] Thus, Fahlman's system cannot be guaranteed to return only those nodes which are unambiguously correct answers.

Much recent research has been aimed at using massively parallel architectures to do inheritance and other such operations. These approaches, especially the *connectionist* approach, differ

---

5– The use of cancellation links, and many pitfalls concerning such use, has been discussed in many places. The interested reader is directed to Brachman (1985).

6– Touretsky's results actually go far beyond this. He provides a mathematical formulation of inheritance hierarchies, a formal mechanism for describing many of the operations performed therein, and proofs of several interesting properties about multiple-inheritance and cancellation.

significantly from the marker-passing approach advocated herein. On the other hand, some of the computational methods and ideas from this other work are germane to the present approach. We therefore discuss the relationship between these approaches and ours in Chapter 9.

2.3. Marker-passing and natural language

Recent work in the marker-passing paradigm has centered mostly around natural language processing. There is a fairly easy correspondence between certain typical problems in natural language and the types of information returned by activation-spreading algorithms. Prominent among these are context recognition, word sense disambiguation, noun-group semantics, and inference finding.

2.3.1. Work at Brown University

Charniak (1983) proposed a model in which the traditional parser of Figure 11a was turned into the system diagrammed in Figure 11b. This model uses a simple Quillian-style marker passer to do several natural language tasks. The idea was to take simple stories, such as the suicide/rope story mentioned in the introduction

Jack wanted to commit suicide. He found a rope.

and pass markers on each word as it came in. Paths found between words were examined by the deductive component, a *path checker*, which would check to see if they proposed a consistent context for the story. If they did, this context was used.[7]

Charniak also suggested the use of this marker-passing component to handle word sense disambiguation. This model would find connections between word senses by passing markers down all senses of a word. In a sentence such as:

The farmer bought the straw

the marker path between *farmer* and the *hay* meaning of *straw*

7– Since the marker-passer, which is in fact the same one used in the present book, is unable to check variable bindings and the like, we must use this mechanism. To see this, consider the case of a story like *Bill wanted to commit suicide. A rope fell down on Fred.*

(a) Traditional Parser

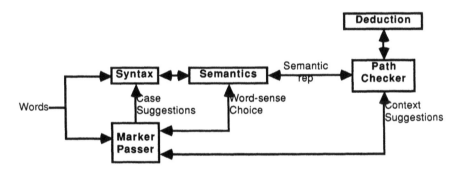

(b) Charniak's proposed parser

Figure 11: Adding marker-passing to a parser.
A) A traditional flow of control in a language processing system. B) The system proposed by Charniak (1983). The parser is augmented by a marker-passing system that helps in word sense disambiguation, case assignments and context recognition.

would account for the choice of this path over some other meaning, such as *drinking straw*. This would also account for confusion in sentences like

The astronomer married the star.

where the strong connection between *astronomer* and *star in the sky* makes finding the *movie star* meaning of *star* difficult to find.

Hirst (Hirst, 1983) used Charniak's approach (and, in fact, the same marker-passer) for doing word sense disambiguation in his *Polaroid Words* system. As each word came in marks were passed to all of its senses in parallel. Each word was disambiguated by a combination of the results of this marker-passing with syntactic information. Thus, once we concluded that a word could not be a verb those meanings associated with verbs would no longer be permitted. The correct meaning "developed" during the processing — prompting the name. Using this scheme Hirst's system was able to handle sentences such as

Nadia's plane taxied to the terminal.

by finding the connections between *taxi* and *plane* and between *plane* and *terminal*.[8]

Hirst, however, claimed that his system was not able to handle structural disambiguation via the marker-passer; and used another mechanism, a *semantic enquiry desk*, for this purpose. Charniak (forthcoming) has extended his marker-passer to handle this function. In fact, Charniak's system uses marker-passing as the unifying concept behind much of its natural language processing.

Charniak's new system, WIMP, attempts to provide a uniform treatment of natural language analysis. The basic idea is that a syntactic parser breaks sentences down into constituent pieces, which are then put together by the marker-passer. Charniak hypothesizes that the act of connecting these pieces into the semantic representation, via the marker-passer, subsumes many of the traditionally difficult parts of language processing.

We've already discussed how Charniak's system does word sense disambiguation (similar to Polaroid Words) and context finding (the suicide example). Let's consider some of the other issues. Again, let's use the example

Jack wanted to commit suicide. He found a rope.

Some of the things that the system must be able to do are: connect syntactic components to the semantic slots they fill,

---

8– We discuss Hirst's work in more detail in Chapter 9, Section 1.4.1.1.

handle the reference of *he*, and pick the *hang* context. We've already discussed the third of these earlier in this section; the second is done by finding the connection between the *he* and *John* using a marker-passing chain like

HE → (He represents) → Human-male → (John is Human-male)
→ John

The connection of objects to their slots is found by making the case-frames for verbs correspond to the slots in the frames for those events (see Hirst & Charniak, 1982, for a discussion of why this is done). We would now find paths such as this one

Jack → (isa Jack human) → human → (agent-of want human)
→ want → wanted

which enables us to connect JACK to the agent slot of the WANT frame. Similar such paths would be found to make SUICIDE the goal of the WANT frame, ROPE the object of the FIND frame, etc. Charniak's system also uses marker-passing to do noun grouping and prepositional phrase attachment via similar mechanisms.

Another important aspect of Charniak's work is its attempt to formalize some of the more *ad hoc* aspects of marker-passing. A considered examination of what it means to find a marker-passing path and how to reject false paths is found in (Charniak, fortcoming). This aspect of Charniak's work is described in greater detail in Chapter 5, where we describe some of the technical issues relating to the implementation of the SCRAPS system.

2.3.2. Other work

Several other natural language processing systems have been developed that do some form of marker-passing. A bidirectional breadth-first search methodology was used by Brian Phillips and myself (Hendler & Phillips, 1981; Phillips, 1984) in our system PATI, developed at Texas Instruments, Incorporated. This system would read abstracts from patents and try to create a conceptual representation for them in a semantic network system (Phillips, 1975).

The bidirectional search algorithm was used primarily for analyzing noun-groups and connecting them into the representation. For example, in a patent starting

> A modulator comprises two transistors each having collector, emitter, and base electrodes...

the noun group *collector, emitter, and base electrodes* would be handled by this mechanism. The head noun, in· this case *electrodes*, would be identified by the syntactic system. Detection of the modification of this head noun would be performed by the breadth-first bidirectional search from this word and each of those in the modifying group. Thus *base* would connect to *electrode* via a path through *transistor*. This mechanism was also used to connect this group into the conceptual structure being built. Thus, in the example above, the path from *electrodes* to *transistor* would be discovered via the search.

PATI was implemented using the object-oriented features of ZetaLisp (Weinreb & Moon, 1978) Thus, the network was programmed as a collection of objects of type *node*, each inheriting properties from the *node* class.[9]   The bidirectional spreading activation mechanism was programmed as a local decision process, much like that proposed by Fahlman.

A similar bidirectional search was used by Alterman (1985) in a system called NEXUS. This system constructed representations of the events described in some simple narrative texts. These representations were stored in a procedural logic form. NEXUS used a spreading activation program, implemented directly in the procedural logic, to do a bidirectional search. The inference paths found by this mechanism were checked by a second program to see if they obeyed certain semantic constraints. If they did, the path was accepted as a method of connecting the text.

Granger, Eiselt, and Holbrook (1984) developed a model that also used a separate mechanism for evaluating paths found by a

---

9– The present marker-passer is not implemented using flavors due to various portability constraints. It is thus a much more complex program for achieving the same result. I therefore find myself a strong proponent of the object-oriented programming technique, and strongly advise those wishing to implement marker-passing systems to consider this approach.

spreading activation mechanism. Their system, ATLAST, was able to make connections between text, similar to those in Charniak's suicide example, by use of a spreading activation mechanism. Figure 12 shows the organization of ATLAST's major components. One important feature of this system was that all of the components ran in parallel.

The ATLAST system used a mechanism like that proposed by Quillian. Marks spread out in a "wavefront" from a single

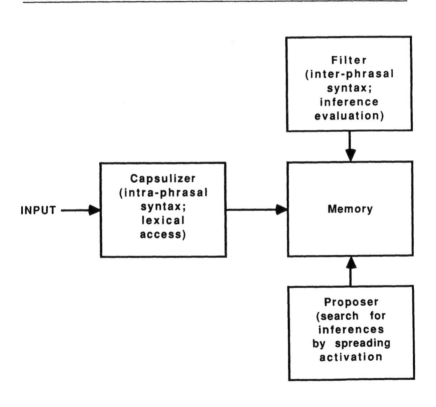

Figure 12: The ATLAST parser.
Based on (Granger et. al., 1984).

concept. Those nodes reached were marked as being primed. When another wavefront marked a node that was already primed, the path was found. The filter mechanism, which worked in parallel with the marker-passer, would evaluate these paths. If a valid path was found, the filter mechanism would cause the marker-passer to halt.

A similar two-part marker-passer/screening mechanism was used in a model developed by Norvig (1986). His system concentrated on the recovery of inferences from text.[10] Norvig's model had a two-pass filter for determining whether a path was relevant. First, some paths were ruled out quickly because the pattern of links could not lead to a plausible inference. Second, a matching procedure was used to determine if the information in a path was truly relevant to the present story. The lengths of the paths were limited so that this matching procedure could be kept efficient.

Riesbeck and Martin (1985) took a somewhat different approach. Their direct-memory access parsing system, DMAP-0, is based on Quillian's model, but builds form tests directly into the marker-passing algorithm. In this system, marker-passing isn't a simple "dumb" spreading-activation mechanism: the marker-passer uses information found at the nodes to determine how activation is to be spread. DMAP-0 used two types of markers: *activation* markers and *prediction* markers. It has a complex algorithm for the placement and removal of each type of marker.

Massively parallel architectures have also been put to use in the attempt to do natural language processing. Work that directly relates to the use of parallel processing in natural language systems can be found in the connectionist models of Pollack and Waltz (1982), Cottrell (1985), and Selman and Hirst (1985).

10– Norvig's work focuses on the classification and recovery of inferences during story comprehension. The marker-passing component was only one aspect of his model.

2.4. Other related work

Two other approaches to spreading activation should be mentioned in this section. The first is Anderson's (1983) ACT* model, which uses spreading activation as one of the bases for a cognitive model that has been computationally tested. This work uses a mathematical model to represent spreading activation in a production memory framework. The details of this work are presented in Chapter 8 where we discuss the work in cognitive psychology of relevance to our theory.

The second approach is the work of Pearl (1985), which attempts to do spreading-activation-type operations using Bayesian statistics in a weighted-link network. While this work is not directly relevant, it is interesting to note that Pearl's system makes it possible to do path-finding via probablistic algorithms. This is the first work to provide such "paths," and to use them for natural language issues, in such a probabilistic network.

3. How SCRAPS relates

As mentioned in the introduction, this book covers two essentially separable topics: integrating a marker-passer with a problem-solver and designing marker-passer systems. The present approach to both of these topics was influenced by, but is different from, the work reported in this chapter.

For SCRAPS to work it is necessary that the marker-passer be integrated with the problem-solver. This integration must occur in both directions. First, the marker-passer returns paths that the problem-solver can take advantage of. Thus, in the case of *planning to commit suicide while holding a gun*, the marker-passer must find the path between SUICIDE and GUN. This path is examined by the path examiner and information is left for the problem-solver to prefer the SHOOT frame. Second, the problem-solver must be able to leave information that the marker-passer can take advantage of.

The first part of this, enabling the problem-solver to take advantage of the marker-passing, is done via a combination of passing marks, returning paths, and evaluating these paths for content. The marker-passer itself derives from Quillian's model. It leaves marks similar to Quillian's activation tags, but borrows its control structure from the parallel ideas developed by Fahlman and implemented by Phillips and myself. (An earlier implementation of the same marker-passer was used by Hirst, and the present marker-passer is used by Charniak.)

The path evaluation component of SCRAPS is based on the model proposed by Charniak — that is, a second mechanism evaluates the paths returned by the marker-passer. This mechanism is similar to the one used by Norvig in that it uses a two-pass approach to path evaluation. First, paths are screened by some "syntactic" heuristics — their structure is examined for certain features. If these features are not found, the path can be trivially rejected. If they are found, a second set of heuristics is invoked to examine whether this path actually does provide useful information. Some of these later heuristics resemble the path checker developed by Alterman.

Having a deductive component leave information for the marker-passer is new to SCRAPS. Consider the following example

> I tell you that the air traffic controllers are on strike. You then must plan a trip to California[11].

The difficulty is to notice that the air traffic controllers' strike potentially rules out using the *flying* frame to achieve this goal. Notice that the information about the air traffic controllers must be added to our system in such a way that the marker-passer will later be able to take advantage of it.

Finally, C–SCRAPS is based on several processes running in parallel. The problem-solver, marker-passer, and plan evaluator all run at the same time, communicating via shared memory. The interactions between these components somewhat resembles that used by the ATLAST system. The primary difference is that C–SCRAPS tries to minimize communication wherever possible: ATLAST encouraged communication between components, C–SCRAPS discourages it. The design of C–SCRAPS is the subject of Chapter 7.

11– U.S. west coast readers should try to plan a trip to New York.

CHAPTER 4

Integrating Marker-Passing and Problem-Solving

You're either part of the solution or part of the problem.
— attributed to Eldridge Cleaver *[circa 1968]*

The diagram presented earlier of a system integrating a problem-solver and a marker-passer is reproduced here as Figure 13. To review: The basic flow of control is that the problem-solver attempts to achieve a goal given a set of initial conditions. As the problem is solved the marker-passer spreads activation from items being examined in the problem-solving effort. When paths among these items are found, they go to the path evaluator, which examines these paths looking for certain patterns. If these patterns are found, information is added to the memory to help direct the remainder of the problem-solving task. It is easiest to describe these steps as occurring in series, although better performance is of course achieved when they are performed in parallel. This chapter seeks to expand the description given so far and to present the details of this organizational scheme by presenting the program SCRAPS and explaining how it works. In essence, SCRAPS is viewed as the "working prototype" of this sort of system. This may cause a slight blurring of the distinction between the idea "integrating a problem-solver with a marker-passer" and the implementation "SCRAPS." Where this distinction is important, we will try to make it clear which we are referring to.

We present a breakdown of the components of SCRAPS and then discuss the classes of problems that SCRAPS handles. The latter includes a consideration of what sort of information gets marked under what conditions and how the marker-passer takes advantage of information previously discovered by a deductive mechanism for use during the problem-solving task.

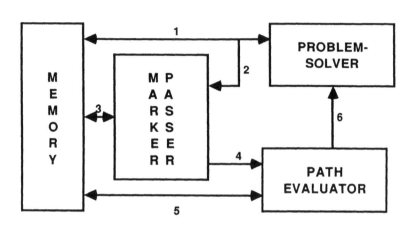

Figure 13: Flow of control in SCRAPS (yet again).
See Figure 5.

1. Inside SCRAPS

In this section each of the modules used in SCRAPS is described. These modules are discussed as "black boxes" — the input, output, and interactions are discussed in detail; the internals of the path evaluator are described in Chapter 5, and the marker-passer is described in detail in Chapter 6.

1.1. Inside SCRAPS — the memory

As mentioned in the introduction, SCRAPS' memory is the associative network built by the FRAIL system. While the details of the indexer that builds this network are not important to the present work, the types of statements entered and how they are stored do affect how SCRAPS works.

1.1.1. Network structure

After FRAIL reads in a frame description and turns it into predicate logic statements (as described in Chapter 1, Section 3.1), these statements must be stored in a format that can be used for marker-passing. This is done by storing the statements in an associative network. The basic scheme is fairly easy to envision — one simply makes the arguments into nodes, and uses the predicate for a link. Thus

(LIFT JACK CAT)

would be indexed into:

However, the actual scheme is more complex. First, the actual predicate used by FRAIL for the above would be

(LIFT JACK-15 CAT-23)

That is, some specific person named Jack lifts some specific cat, CAT-23. If we wish to retrieve this from memory we will probably not know which specifics are involved. We might wish to ask something like "who lifted a cat?" This question would be posed to FRAIL as a retrieve request such as

(RETRIEVE '(LIFT (PERSON ?x) (CAT ?y)))

If we used the simple indexing scheme proposed above, the associative network would not work. We must have some link from CAT-23 to CAT and from JACK-15 to PERSON. This is solved by storing such information in the form of INST statements. Thus, the network to store the information that JACK-15 lifts CAT-23 would be of the form

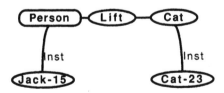

This is not quite enough, however: It would cover the objects in our database, but not the events. Just as CAT-23 is a specific

instance of a CAT, "Jack's lifting of this cat" is a specific instance of a LIFT event. Thus, we want knowledge of the form:

(LIFT-1 JACK-15 CAT-23)

to be represented as:

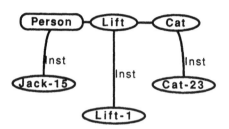

Notice that we also want to capture the knowledge of how JACK-15 and CAT-23 are related to LIFT-1. We need to capture the information that LIFT is a frame that contains slots, and that

---

(FRAME: LIFT   ;*lift is an action*
    ISA: ACTION
    SLOTS: (AGENT (PERSON)) ;*with a human agent*
           (PATIENT (THING))) ;*and some patient*

(FRAME: CAT ;*cat isa thing*
    ISA: THING)

(INST CAT-23 CAT) ;*cat-23 is a specific cat*
(INST JACK-15 PERSON) ;*Jack-15 is a specific person*

(INST LIFT-1 LIFT) ;*LIFT-1 is an instance of LIFT*
(:= '(AGENT LIFT-1) JACK-15) ;*Jack is the agent of LIFT-1*
(:= '(PATIENT LIFT-1) CAT-23) ;*Cat-23 is the patient of Lift-1*

Inset 3: FRAIL representation for LIFT.

Jack and the cat fill these slots. We need to note that JACK-15 is the AGENT of the LIFT and that CAT-23 is the PATIENT. We also want to capture the information that the AGENT of a LIFT must be a PERSON and that the PATIENT of a LIFT must be a THING[1]. This knowledge is represented to FRAIL as shown in Inset 3. The network form of this is shown in Figure 14.

LIFT is essentially a primitive act — it has no subacts. If it did, we would need to represent the bindings of the actions filling the slots of the subacts as well as the bindings of the act itself. To represent this knowledge we store correspondences. The frame knowledge

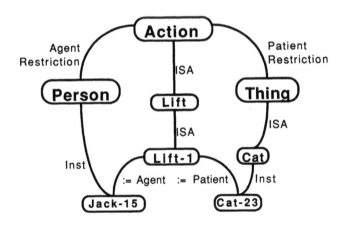

Figure 14: Jack lifts a cat.
The network corresponding to Jack's lifting of a (specific) cat.

1– THING is the node that roots our tree of objects. Thus PERSON, CAT, AN-IMAL, etc. are all THINGs.

```
(FRAME: RESTAURANT ?r ;restaurant isa action
    ISA: ACTION
    ACTS:
        ...        ;skipping some steps
        (LIFT-MENU-STEP    ;one step is that the
        (LIFT (AGENT (DINER ?r)) ;diner lifts up
            (PATIENT (MENU-OF ?r)))) ;the menu
        ...
)
```

tells FRAIL that one step of the restaurant frame is that the person eating (the DINER of this RESTAURANT event) lifts the specific menu being used. The correspondence from the DINER slot to the AGENT of the LIFT is shown in the part of the frame reading:

(LIFT (AGENT (DINER ?r)) ...

Rules that pertain to various parts of the frame are stored in the network associated with the frame and those things the rule pertains to. If we wish to have a rule saying that the act of eating can be accomplished by going to a restaurant, we would assert

(TO-DO (EAT (PERSON ?p))
(RESTAURANT (DINER ?p)))

which reads as "Person "?p" can EAT by fulfilling the DINER role in a RESTAURANT event." The network for this information, including all the information for the LIFT-MENU-STEP, is shown in Figure 15.

It is networks such as these over which the marker-passer spreads activation.

1.1.2. "Active" memory

Earlier in this book we alluded to the need for a deductive process to leave information that the marker-passer could take advantage of. Later in this section we give some examples in which we take advantage of this sort of information. At this point, however, we can discuss how this information is placed in the memory.

The Introduction (Section 3.1) discussed the forward- and backward-chaining rules available in FRAIL. A forward-chaining

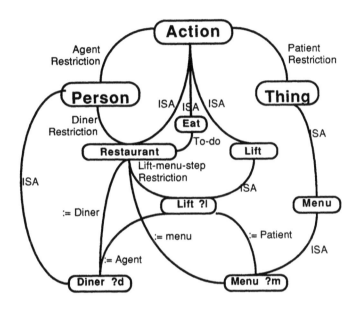

Figure 15: A portion of FRAIL's memory representation.
The network representing the information that a diner lifts a menu during a restaurant event.

rule of the form

$$(\rightarrow (\textbf{isa ?x dog) (barks ?x}))$$

was taken to mean that if some variable, to be bound to "?x," was asserted to be a dog, then we would add to the memory the information that "?x" barks. The backward-chaining rule

$$(\leftarrow (\textbf{barks ?x) (isa ?x dog}))$$

was taken to read as "if we wish to prove that "?x" barks, we can do so by showing that "?x" is a dog."

These two can be combined via a special predicate called "→G" which can be used to allow some backward-chaining to take place during forward-chaining. For example, the rule (Charniak, Gavin, & Hendler, 1983, p. 4.)

$$(\rightarrow \text{(isa ?x bird)} (\rightarrow\text{G (and (has-part ?x ?y)(isa ?y wing))}$$
$$\text{(uses-to-fly ?x ?y)))}$$

would mean that if we assert that "?x" is a bird we should look through the database for any part of "?x" that is a wing. If we find a wing, to be called "?y," we should assert that "?x" uses "?y" to fly with. Thus, the flying property of each wing is associated with the appropriate bird.

SCRAPS takes advantage of these three types of chaining rules. When we assert a fact into the memory, we sometimes wish for that information to be noticeable to the marker-passer — the appropriate hockey puck in memory is to be vibrated. This is done via a special FRAIL predicate called FLAG. When we assert that something is a flag it is put into memory with properties that the marker-passer can use. This does NOT activate any of the neighbors of this item. When we *flag* a node, it is activated, but it does not pass markers.

This FLAG predicate is used in conjunction with the chaining rules via assertions of the form

$$(\rightarrow \text{(on-strike ?x)}$$
$$(\rightarrow\text{G (job-of ?x ?y)}$$
$$\text{(flag ?y FAIL (striking ?x))))}$$

which reads "If some group, ?x, is on strike, then for each job, ?y, that that group performs, set a flag on ?y." This will flag all those nodes corresponding to the jobs of the striking group as being unavailable due to the strike. Thus, if we were to assert

```
(frame: sanitation-engineer
    isa: thing
    facts: (job-of (sanitation-engineer ?x)
                collecting-garbage))
```

and

(on-strike (sanitation-engineer ?x))
;all sanitation engineers are on strike

the above rule would flag the node "collecting-garbage" with the information that it will fail due to the sanitation-engineers' strike. If the marker-passer now encounters this node, it will report a path ending at the flag. The use of such is described later in this chapter.

1.2. Inside SCRAPS — the problem-solver

As previously discussed, the problem-solver used by SCRAPS is the NASL system. The problem-solving task involves invoking a situation with an initial task and a set of bindings. Thus, to return to our examples from the introduction, to invoke NASL to plan a suicide action we would use

(SOLVE 'Task1 '((INST task1 SUICIDE)
(:= (VICTIM task1) ME)))

NASL would now go through the problem-solving process (as described in the Section 3.1 of the Introduction) generating sets of tasks to fill, finding bindings, and solving the newly generated tasks.

SCRAPS uses NASL with only a few changes. The initial conditions are sent to the marker-passer. Each of the constants in these conditions is used to spread marks. In the example above, the marker-passer would be started spreading activation from the nodes SUICIDE, VICTIM, and ME.

As paths are found by the marker-passer they go to the path evaluator, which asserts RULE-IN or RULE-OUT statements that the problem-solver can use. The problem-solver uses these statements during the remainder of the planning task.

1.3. Inside SCRAPS — the marker-passer

It is the job of the marker-passer to spread activation from the nodes involved in the problem-solving effort. When activation from more than one origin is found at a node, a path is reported.

The marker-passer in SCRAPS is similar in design to that of Quillian (described in Chapter 3, Section 2.1). Each node is activated by leaving a MARK property on the atom associated with the node. This mark has several parts: origin, from-node, formula, zorch, and date. The *origin* records where this particular spread of activation started. *From-node* is the node immediately prior to this one in activation — the node that this one follows. *Formula* is the FRAIL statement that links the present node to the from-node. The other two, *zorch* and *date*, are used for attenuation of links and the eventual erasure thereof. (These are discussed in more detail in Chapter 6.)

As an example consider spreading activation starting from the node SUICIDE. SUICIDE requires an action of type KILL, so the node KILL gets marked. This in turn marks the methods of performing KILL. If we were to look at the MARK property of the node KILL we would find

```
(SUICIDE KILL
         (TO-DO (KILL ?KILL)
                (HANG (AGENT
                        (AGENT ?KILL))
                      (VICTIM
                        (VICTIM ?KILL)))))
```

which says the present activation started at SUICIDE and marked this node directly from KILL via the predicate

```
(TO-DO (KILL ?KILL)
       (HANG (AGENT
               (AGENT ?KILL))
             (VICTIM
               (VICTIM ?KILL))))
```

(which states that a method of killing someone is to hang that person).

The marker-passer is invoked with a starting strength (cf. Chapter 6) and a node of origin. As the marks are spread to neighboring nodes the marker-passer examines each node to see if it has already been marked from a different origin. If such a node is found, a path is returned. This path starts at one origin and ends at the other and is composed of the nodes and statements traversed by the marker-passer in each of the passes that resulted in the marking of this node. For example, the actual path for the

Introduction is shown in Inset 4.

When the connections between the nodes are fairly obvious, we will often omit them in describing the results of the marker-passing in order to save space. The path in this example would then be written as

suicide → kill → hang → noose → rope → ...

If the path that is found ends with a flag, the final nodes point to that specific flag. As an example, in the path above the node rope would be marked with what we call a PERCEPTUAL flag. Thus, the end of the path is

```
(SUICIDE
 (TO-DO (SUICIDE ?S)
     (ACHIEVE ?ACHIEVE3
             (AGENT
                 (AGENT (SUICIDE ?S)))
             (STATE-OF
                 (KILL ?KILL
                     (AGENT
                         (AGENT (SUICIDE ?S)))
                     (PATIENT
                         (AGENT (SUICIDE ?S)))))))))
 KILLING
 (TO-DO (KILL ?KILL)
         (HANG (AGENT (AGENT ?KILL))
             (VICTIM (VICTIM ?KILL))))
 HANG
 (RESTRICTION (H-INSTR (HANG ?S)) (NOOSE ?NOOSE1))
 NOOSE
 (MATERIAL-OF (NOOSE ?N) (ROPE ?r))
 ROPE
 ...
 )
```

Inset 4: The path from SUICIDE to ROPE.

```
(... → ROPE
   →(FLAG ROPE PERCEPTUAL
                 (POSSESS (AGENT ME)
                          (OBJECT ROPE))
   → FLAG)
```

signifying that this path ends at the origin "FLAG" and is reached because of perceptual information stemming from the possession of the rope by ME.

1.4. Inside SCRAPS — the path evaluator

The paths found by the marker-passer are passed to the path evaluator, whose job it is to examine these paths and extract information that can be useful to the problem-solver. This information is returned to the memory as of rules that NASL can take advantage of as during the solving of a problem.

The path evaluator functions through a set of "cascaded" heuristics. As each heuristic is used it does a quick check for a certain pattern; if that pattern is not found the path is passed on to the next heuristic.[2] The earliest heuristic is a screening mechanism for quickly rejecting those paths that unable to add information. It thus provides a functionality similar to that of the two-pass path evaluator of Norvig (1986). The rest of these heuristics extract information of specific types, and are described in detail in Chapter 5.

The information extracted from the paths is expressed in terms of RULE-IN and RULE-OUT predicates. These rules are conditionalized to apply only to the present problem-solving context. Thus, if some action couldn't be performed due to the sanitation engineers' strike, we might encounter a path of form

---

2– I describe this system as "cascaded" since the heuristics occur in a specific order. In actuality the system is designed so that the heuristics could run in parallel, as discussed in Chapter 7.

```
TAKE-OUT-GARBAGE
     → GARBAGE-COLLECTING
     → FLAG FAIL
          (STRIKING
               (SANITATION-ENGINEER ?s)))
     → FLAG
```

Assuming[3] that this path will result in a desire to rule out the present task, a "take out garbage" task, the system produces a rule-out rule conditionalized by the information in the flag, i.e.:

```
(← (RULE-OUT ?task
          (TAKE-OUT-GARBAGE ?action))
     (STRIKING (SANITATION-ENGINEER ?s)))
```

When the path evaluator creates a RULE-OUT predicate that cannot be conditionalized by some known fact (such as the strike in the example), it is conditionalized by the present problem-solving environment. This allows an action to be ruled out temporarily instead of permanently. Thus, if the lunar rover of past chapters could not traverse some path called path-1, the path evaluator would assert:

```
(← (RULE-OUT ?task
          (TRAVERSE ?action
               (PATH path-1)))
     (TOP-LEVEL-TASK TASK-27)
```

where task-27 was the task that NASL was invoked to handle.

Since the problem-solver checks for rule-out rules before trying any task, when the conditions expressed as antecedents of the backward-chaining rule (i.e. the strike in the first example, the appropriate task in the second) are satisfied the problem-solver either choses an alternate path, or fails at the present attempt if no alternative plans are available.

3– Until Chapter 5.

2. The integration of marker-passing and problem-solving

In the Introduction we described several types of problems in which the marker-passer could be used by the problem-solver. In this section we once again present problems of the type proposed in the introduction. This time, however, we describe the solutions in more detail, building on what we have just presented in Section 1 of this chapter.

2.1. What is being solved

Before presenting specific examples, let's take a moment to examine the set of problems that can be attacked by integrating a marker-passer into a problem-solving system. It will become clear that this approach transcends the few examples given in this book.

2.1.1. Examining the issue

Planning is a search problem. The search space, our knowledge base, is a network of plans. The connections in this network are subtasks, the steps of the plans, and branches corresponding to the various ways of achieving these plans.[4] Thus, our "hunger-solving" network would have plans such as restaurant, order, pay, and eat connected by subtask statements (for example **(Step-of Restaurant pay)**).

The fact that problem-solving corresponds to a search in this network causes a problem: Often a decision made early during the search is affected by information that will not be found until later during the process. This "early decision — late information" is of particular interest when the information that would allow a correct decision to be made is not accessible at the time of the decision.

Integrating marker-passing and problem-solving is one way to handle some aspects of this problem. We use the marker-passer to perform a fast breadth-first search of the tree looking for nodes with a special property — the property of having been previously

---

4– Primitives correspond to nodes that are singly linked into the planning network.

marked. When such a node is found the path evaluator is used to see if information that can affect present decisions is encountered. Thus, information later in the tree can be brought to bear at an earlier point. A rigorous look-ahead would be computationally complex, and thus the marker-passer serves, in essence, as a "quick and dirty" look-ahead mechanism that seeks to detect some of the potential problems the planner may encounter — this is the crux of marker-passing, particularly as used in this work!

Several concrete examples of this are given later in this section. Before we get to them, however, we digress to examine some alternate approaches to the "early decision — late information" paradox.

2.1.1.1. Digression I — preconditions.

Consider the following case

You should plan an eating event. By the way, you have lost your wallet and all your money.

It is clear that going to a restaurant would not be a particularly good way to approach this particular eating event because at some point in the restaurant frame we are forced to solve the subtask of paying — something we cannot do without money. The problem for a planning system is that at the point where we must make the choice (between the branches representing the choice of restaurant and those representing the other means of achieving eating), we have not yet encountered the information that no money is available.

The traditional AI approach to this problem has been to create a set of *preconditions* for each activity in the problem-solving domain. Thus, we'd have an explicit precondition for "restaurant" saying "you must have money prior to doing a restaurant-dining event." Now, when we make the choice we would check for money and discover the missing wallet and thus restaurant dining could be ruled out right away.

Unfortunately, a more careful analysis shows that preconditions will not solve this aspect of the "early decision — late information" bind. Consider the next case:

You should plan an eating event. Waitresses are on strike.

In this case it is clear that we again should not use the restaurant choice. The usual solution would be to add an "availability of waitresses" precondition to the restaurant frame. If, however, that was added we'd also need to add a precondition for each of the other agents in the frame (diner, maitre' d, cook, busboy, manager, parking attendant, etc.). Even now, however, all our problems are not solved. Supposing all the menus in the world disappeared, supposing you lost you ability to communicate, supposing chairs and tables ceased to exist, *etc., etc., etc.* The set of preconditions for a frame is exactly the frame itself!! Thus, the approach of using preconditions does not solve the problem.

We should make it clear here that, despite the difficulty with preconditions, it would certainly not serve usto abolish them. In certain situations preconditions are used for handling necessary constraints in the world (like the fact that to move a block in the Block's World, it must first have nothing on top of it). In other situations preconditions are used to capture the fact that certain violations are more common than others (it seems more useful to make "money" a precondition of "restaurant" than it is to make "existence of menus" one). We consider the approach outlined in this book as an adjunct to preconditions rather than a replacement.

2.1.1.2. Digression II — logical alternatives

A situation akin to the "early decision — late information" problem has also been encountered by AI researchers developing systems relying on deductive, logical inference mechanism. In this formulation the system is trying to decide whether some action can be done, and the database may or may not contain information that would contraindicate this action. For example, if we wish to know whether to cross the street, we must check the database to find out whether the light is red. The problem is that there are many conditions that could cause us to be unable to cross the street: A car could be coming, a siren could be heard approaching, etc.. If we have no information about one of these (i.e., we cannot find data in the knowledge base telling us whether a car is coming) we still must be able to decide whether the action should be undertaken. We must use some sort of default reasoning.

The usual solution is to use a non-monotonic logic predicate similar to the TH-NOT predicate of micro-planner (Sussman, Winograd & Charniak, 1970). The meaning of

(TH-NOT predicate1)

is that predicate1 cannot be proven from the present knowledge base. For the example above we would use TH-NOT in a chaining rule of the form

(← (CROSS STREET)
(TH-NOT (NOT (CROSS STREET)))))[5]

This can be read as "cross the street unless it can be proven that you cannot cross the street." If we now wish to know if we can cross, we try to retrieve the proposition **(CROSS STREET)**. The system now uses the chaining rule and thus will try to prove **(NOT (CROSS STREET))**. If this cannot be proven, then **(CROSS STREET)** will be assumed to be true.

We can now tell the system that various things would make the street crossing impossible by asserting them as forward-chaining rules that imply the consequent of of the TH-NOT. For example

(→ (RED LIGHT)
(NOT (CROSS STREET)))

(→ (IS-COMING CAR))
(NOT (CROSS STREET))

Thus, if **(RED LIGHT)** is in the knowledge base, then **(NOT (CROSS STREET))** is asserted. Since this is now in the knowledge base, the TH-NOT fails and we cannot prove **(CROSS STREET)** using this rule.

5– The logic in this section is simplified so as to include no variables, predicates that are "easy to read" rather than logically sound, and the like.

This situation gets more complicated if we wish to add more information to the database. Suppose we want to assert "you cannot cross the street if a hurricane is coming." This could be done by a rule of the form

$$(\rightarrow (\text{HURRICANE})$$
$$(\text{NOT (CROSS STREET)}))$$

This solution would not work well. Since a hurricane rules out doing many things, and since many things rule out crossing the street, the number of chaining rules in our system would grow very large. The assertion **(HURRICANE)** would therefore increase the size if our knowledge base enormously. Instead we would use a solution that includes a combination of backward- and forward-chaining. We could assert something like

$$(\leftarrow (\text{NOT (CROSS STREET)})) \textit{;you cannot cross the street}$$
$$(\text{NOT (BE OUTSIDE)}))) \quad \textit{;if you cannot go outside}$$

$$(\rightarrow (\text{HURRICANE}) \qquad \textit{;if there is a hurricane}$$
$$(\text{NOT (BE OUTSIDE)}))) \textit{;you cannot be outside}$$

This solution works in a world in which the number of chaining rules, backward and forward, can be kept small enough to prevent a combinatorial explosion during deduction. In a complex enough world, this becomes difficult, if not impossible, to do.

Consider some "real-world" examples of events caused by a hurricane. We need deductions that include not only not going outside but also things like "you cannot go to restaurants which have power outages caused by the storm," "you will not be able to buy 6 volt batteries after the storm (because so many of them are sold to people expecting to need to use lanterns)," "lines in the supermarket get very long because people are stocking up on food," "boat owners become somewhat irrational due to the stress of worrying," and so on. To get a logic system to notice many of these low-probability types of inferences (i.e. "you rule out restaurant in case of a hurricane") can require bringing large amounts of knowledge to bear at inappropriate times (checking to be sure no hurricane is coming before going to a restaurant or worrying about going to restaurants instead of preparing for the hurricane).

2.1.1 (continued) Examining the Issue

What I have been describing as the "early decision — late information" problem is one aspect of the far larger problem of "relevance"[6] — one of the major unsolved problems in artificial intelligence today. Briefly, this problem is the issue of deciding what information to bring to bear under which circumstances. If deciding whether or not to "ignore" some data takes longer than actually looking at that data, we have a serious problem. The planning issues addressed by integrating marker-passing and problem-solving, and thus those approached by SCRAPS, all fall into the category of "early decision — late information" and are therefore an attempt to attack one small part of the overall relevance problem.

To demonstrate the utility of the technique being proposed in this book, we look at some places where the "early decision — late information" problem arises during problem-solving. For each of these we develop an example in some detail and describe how the integrated marker-passer/problem-solver can approach that problem. (In Chapter 10 we show the detailed output of SCRAPS running on these same problems.)

2.1.2. Making a choice — the wrong one

When the problem-solver discovers an "or" branch in the tree it is choose one of the alternatives to use to solve the task. Some sort of choice heuristics are used to pick which task to start working on. Often the wrong choice is made, and either the planner fails or some sort of debugging (usually via backtracking) must be done.

6– Recent AI literature occasionally refers to this as the "frame problem," We use the more generic term due to an ambiguity in the term "frame problem" which is primarily used to describe a narrower problem relating to the temporal scope of events and potentially solved by use of non-monotonic logics.

As an example of this problem, consider again the case

You are told that the air traffic controllers (ATCs) are on strike.
At a later point you must plan a cross-country business trip.

We will assume that the planner has the following facts available
in the knowledge base

To travel cross country we can use: plane, train or bus.
We prefer (as a default) plane over train and train over bus.
The steps in a plane trip are:
  buy ticket, board, take-off, fly in the plane, disembark, get luggage
The take-off step involves:
  pilot asks for clearance, ATC does ATCING[7], ATC grants clearance.
The job of an ATC is to perform the ATCING action.

(This information is shown in "network" form as Figure 16.) We
also need to know that if the members of some occupation are on

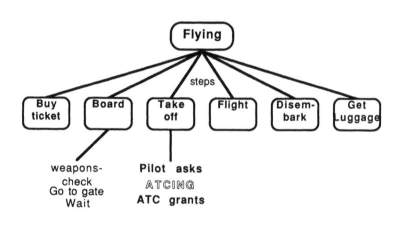

Figure 16: Taking an airplane trip.

7– ATCING here is being used as a short notation for a frame that involves looking
at the air traffic displays, checking various parameters, and whatever other special actions
the air traffic controllers do.

strike then we should flag this information. To do this we use the rule discussed in Section 1.1.2

$$(\rightarrow \text{(on-strike ?x)}$$
$$(\rightarrow\text{G (job-of ?x ?y)}$$
$$\text{(flag ?y FAIL (striking ?x))))}$$

This rule causes a flag for the marker-passer to be set if we assert that a strike is occuring. Thus, when we assert

(ON-STRIKE (ATC ?x))
;all air traffic controllers are on strike

the forward-chaining rule applies and, since the job of ATCs is to do ATCING, the node in memory for ATCING is flagged as of interest to the marker-passer. We are now ready to initiate the problem-solver's planning of the trip. To do this we would call the SOLVE function with the appropriate initial conditions, *viz.*

(SOLVE task1 '((INST task1 TAKE-TRIP)
(:= (DESTINATION-OF task1)
CALIFORNIA)
(:= (TRAVELER-OF task1)
***ME*)))**

The first thing SOLVE does is to bind the initial conditions to the slots in the TAKE-TRIP frame. This would cause marks to pass on each of the constants in this pattern: TAKE-TRIP, CALIFORNIA, *ME*. Marks would flow from TAKE-TRIP to each of the methods that could be used for trip taking (BUS, PLANE and TRAIN) and thence to each of the subtasks of these, etc. At some point the marker-passer would therefore be marking the GAIN-CLEARANCE step of PLANE and thence the ATCING node. At this point it recognizes the flag set on ATCING and returns the following path

TAKE-TRIP → PLANE → GET-CLEARANCE
→ ATCING → (FLAG FAIL (STRIKING (atc ?x)))
→ FLAG

The marker-passer also finds some other paths like

TAKE-TRIP
→ (DESTINATION-OF TAKE-TRIP *LOCATION*)
→ *LOCATION* → CALIFORNIA

TAKE-TRIP
→ (TRAVELER-OF TAKE-TRIP *HUMAN*
→ *HUMAN* → *ME*

All of these paths are now sent to the path evaluator to see if information of use to the problem-solver can be found.[8] The latter two are quickly rejected as uninteresting (cf. Chapter 5) since they can add no information for the planner.

The first path, from TAKE-TRIP to FLAG, is of more interest. Since it ends in a FLAG node, the path evaluator spends more time examining it. In this case the FLAG is of type FAIL, and the path has the required properties for adding information, so the path evaluator asserts a rule-out of the concerned frame

(← (RULE-OUT ?task (ATCING ?action))
(STRIKING (ATC ?x)))

The path evaluator also now examines the implicit and-or tree in the knowledge base to see if this frame is a subtask of another frame. If it is, that frame too can be ruled out. This process continues recursively until a frame is encountered that is one of a set of alternatives for some action. Thus, the path evaluator can now also assert

---

8– In C-SCRAPS much of this goes on concurrently. The paths are examined as found, rather than when they are all found, the problem solver continues while the marker-passer works, etc. These and other concurrency issues are discussed in Chapter 7.

$$(\leftarrow \text{(RULE-OUT ?task (CLEARANCING ?action))}$$
$$\text{(STRIKING (ATC ?x)))}$$

and

$$(\leftarrow \text{(RULE-OUT ?task (PLANE ?action))}$$
$$\text{(STRIKING (ATC ?x)))}$$

Control now returns to the problem-solver. It must make a choice between PLANE, TRAIN, and BUS. It does this by first checking to see if any of these are ruled out. Since the **(STRIKING (ATC ?x))** holds true, the RULE-OUT of PLANE holds. This means only TRAIN and BUS are still active. Using the rule that said TRAIN is preferred to BUS, the problem solver would now plan a TRAIN trip, thus avoiding the PLANE trip completely.

The advantage here is that the PLANE trip has never been expanded by a deductive mechanism. At no point did we need to consider who might have bought a ticket, what stewardess was on the plane, whether the traveler in this case would carry on a clothing bag, and all those other details that might have been considered before a traditional planner discovered the knowledge of the ATC strike. Only the marker-passer, which is a faster mechanism, has "examined" those branches.

2.1.3. Making a choice— a non-optimal choice

Another situation in which the choice mechanism can fall prey to the "early decision — late information" problem is when it makes a default choice and arrives at a non-optimal plan when information that could have led to a better solution was available. Consider the following situation

Plan a suicide. You are holding a gun.

Our knowledge base will contain the facts

SUICIDE is done by having an agent achieve the KILLING of that agent.
KILLING is done by any action that causes DEATH.
DEATH can be caused by: SHOOT and HANG,
SHOOT uses an instrument which is a GUN.
HANG is the default plan for SUICIDE.
HANG uses an instrument which is a ROPE.
ROPE can be purchased in a HARDWARE STORE.

(shown as a network in Figure 17).

In this situation, without the marker-passing component, our
planner would use the default path of HANG in choosing how to
commit suicide. Since it has a rule of where to get a rope, the
problem-solver now goes to the hardware store, purchases the
rope, and then commits suicide via hanging. At no point would it
take advantage of its possession of the gun.

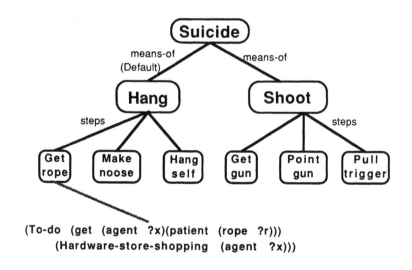

Figure 17: Plotting a suicide.

The integrated problem-solver/marker-passer deals with this situation by a method similar to that described in the previous example. In this case the gun is in the perceptual environment of the planner, so it is flagged.[9] This is done via a forward-chaining rule of the form

(→ (POSSESS ?x ?y)
    (FLAG ?y PERCEPTUAL (POSSESS ?x ?y)))

When we assert **(POSSESS *ME* GUN-1)** the system sets a flag on gun.

We now ask the system to solve the following

(SOLVE task2 '((inst task2 SUICIDE)
    (:= (AGENT task2) *ME*)))

Markers are passed on SUICIDE and *ME* and the paths found are shown in Inset 5.

These paths are once again passed to the path evaluator for analysis. As before, all those paths shown above ending in *ME* will be rejected as uninteresting and only the first one will be examined in detail (since it ends in at the FLAG node).

The path, with the variables included, looks like

SUICIDE
→(ACHIEVE (AGENT ?x) (DEATH (Victim ?x)))
    → DEATH
    → (CAUSES (KILLING (AGENT ?y)(VICTIM ?z))(DEATH ?z))
    → KILLING
    → (TO-DO (KILLING (AGENT ?a)(VICTIM ?b))
            (SHOOT (AGENT ?a)(VICTIM ?b)))
    → SHOOT
    → (INSTRUMENT SHOOT GUN)
    → GUN
    → (INST GUN GUN-1)
    → GUN-1
    → (FLAG PERCEPTUAL (POSSESS *ME* GUN-1))
    → FLAG

The path evaluator examines this path to see if the possessor of

---

9- We will for now that this is the right thing to do. This issue is discussed in Section 2.2.

SUICIDE → DEATH → KILLING
 → SHOOT → GUN → GUN-1
 → (FLAG PERCEPTUAL (POSSESS *ME* GUN-1))
 → FLAG

SUICIDE → (AGENT SUICIDE *HUMAN*)
 → *HUMAN* → *ME*

SUICIDE → DEATH → KILLING
 → (AGENT KILLING *HUMAN*)
 → *HUMAN* → *ME*

SUICIDE → DEATH → KILLING
 → SHOOT → (AGENT SHOOT *HUMAN*)
 → *HUMAN* → *ME*
;and others similar to this for HANG

Inset 5: Paths returned for suicide example.

---

the gun is the person committing suicide. Since the variables bind
appropriately,[2] the system realizes that one necessary component
of this frame has been found. It therefore proposes this as a good
alternative if a decision is to be made. This is done by the
assertion

(← (RULE-IN ?task (SHOOT ?action (AGENT *ME*)))
  (POSSESS *ME* GUN))

When the problem-solver is now resumed it must reach a
decision between which of the alternatives to use. It first checks
RULE-OUT rules. Since none are found it tries to rule in one of
the other alternatives. Since the POSSESS of GUN by *ME* still
holds true, the system rules in SHOOT as the method to try.

Notice that the system first has checked for rule-outs. If
some other feature (say, for example, my lack of bullets) had

---

2- ?x = ?y = ?a = *ME*.

caused SHOOT to be ruled out, this new RULE-IN would be ignored. Thus, the system will not be forced to take a bad alternative if information leading to its failure is already discoverable.

2.1.4. Demon invocation

Another situation in which appropriate information from later in a problem-solving task should be applied earlier is the case of "demon" invocation. The applications of one of these demons should occur as early as possible, particularly when this can involve the suitable modification of a plan. To see this, consider the following example (from Wilensky, 1983)

You wish to get the newspaper on a rainy day.

In this case we want to modify the GET-NEWSPAPER frame so that a step which includes carrying an umbrella is added. We'd like to add this step prior to going outside and getting wet. Indeed, we'd like to add this step as close to the start of the plan as possible so as to be able to eliminate wasted effort (i.e., getting a coat and then going back to the closet for the umbrella would be redundant). Once again we will be able to use the combined marker-passing/problem-solving system for this example.

The knowledge base (also shown as a network in Figure 18) includes the following information

Getting a newspaper involves: get coat, open door, go to the location of the newspaper, pick it up, return home, close door.
Newspaper-1 is at location-1.
It is raining at location-1.

We also wish to assert a special form of rule, a demon, to assert that an umbrella should be carried in the rain. This rule is of the form

```
(DEMON (AND (AT (PERSON ?p)
            (LOCATION ?location))
        (CLIMATE ?location RAINING))
    (ADD-PRIOR-REQ
        (AND (CARRY (AGENT ?p)
                (PATIENT ?object))
            (INST ?object UMBRELLA))))
```

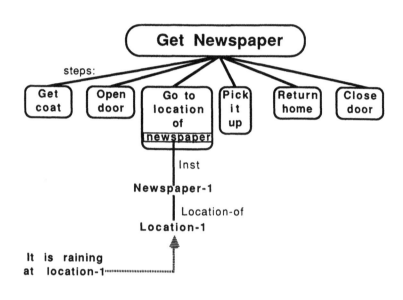

Figure 18: Getting a newspaper on a rainy day.

which reads: IF some action causes a person to be at some location, AND IF it is raining at that location, THEN modify that act to include a CARRY frame which has that person carry an object, which is an umbrella.[11] The predicate ADD-PRIOR-REQ is used by SCRAPS to guarantee that this CARRY frame must occur before the conditions that cause the invocation of the demon — in this case, before the action causing the AT predicate to be asserted.

Once again we start by assuming a perceptual flag — this time on the "raining" frame. In the "ultimate" system this would be done by having the visual component directly note, and flag,

---

11– The actual binding of this "umbrella" to some specific umbrella is done by NASL during the problem-solving process.

this information. We simulate this by simply asserting the flag

(FLAG LOCATION-1 PERCEPTUAL
                     (CLIMATE LOCATION-1 RAINING))

We now start the problem-solver with the initial information

(SOLVE task3 '((INST task3 GET-NEWSPAPER)
               (:= (AGENT task3) *ME*)
               (:= (NEWSPAPER-OF task3)
                  NEWSPAPER-1)
               (:= (LOCATION-OF NEWSPAPER-1)
                  LOCATION-1)))

Markers are therefore passed starting at the frames GET-NEWSPAPER, *ME*, NEWSPAPER-1, and LOCATION-1.

The marker-passer returns the paths shown in Inset 6 which are passed to the path evaluator.

The latter two are rejected as uninteresting. The path from NEWSPAPER-1 to FLAG is examined (since it ends in a FLAG). However, as shown in more detail in Chapter 5, this path proves

---

```
GET-NEWSPAPER → GO-TO → AT
   → (DEMON ... AT ... RAINING ...) → RAINING
   → LOCATION-1
   → (FLAG PERCEPTUAL (CLIMATE LOCATION-1 RAINING)
   → FLAG

NEWSPAPER-1 → LOCATION-1 → (FLAG ...) → FLAG

GET-NEWSPAPER → (AGENT GET-NEWSPAPER *HUMAN*)
   → *HUMAN* → *ME*

GET-NEWSPAPER → GO-TO → (AGENT GO-TO *HUMAN*)
   → *HUMAN* → *ME*
```

Inset 6: Paths returned for newspaper example.

to add no information and nothing is asserted. The first path is also examined because of the flag rule. While examining this path the path evaluator discovers the DEMON. Checking variables, it discovers that this rule would be applicable (since the location of the rain is the location of the newspaper in the GET-NEWSPAPER action). It therefore makes suitable assertions to alter the GET-NEWSPAPER task:

(← (SUBTASK GET-NEWSPAPER-1 CARRY-STEP-1)
    (CLIMATE LOCATION-1 RAINING))
and
    (INST CARRY-STEP-1 CARRY)
    (:= (AGENT CARRY-STEP1) *ME*)
    (:= (OBJECT CARRY-STEP1) ?object)
    (INST ?object UMBRELLA)
    (BEFORE CARRY-STEP-1
        (GET-COAT-STEP GET-NEWSPAPER-1))[12]

The problem-solver now regains control and plans the action. The new first step is to get the umbrella and this would be done.

2.1.5. Interactions within plans

The final "early decision — late information" issue to be illustrated here arises when information in different parts of plans interacts to cause problems: specifically, when something to be used at one point in a plan might cause another subplan to fail. In this way it is similar to the problems described in the nonlinear planning literature as "subgoal conflicts." As an example of the type of intra-plan interactions that marker-passing/problem-solvers can handle, consider the following case

You are on a business trip (in a distant city). You wish to purchase a cleaver.

The knowledge base (network in Figure 19) contains the following facts

---

12– All of this can be read as saying "create a new subtask of GET-NEWSPAPER to include carrying an umbrella. Put this step before the step at which one gets the coat (the previous first step)." The backward-chaining rule in the first assertion in the group says that this is all done because it is raining where we are going.

To BUY something you: enter store, exchange money for
    the item, leave the store, take the item to
    the place it is to be used.
To get home you must use FLYING (shown earlier in Figure 16)
    or take the BUS.
The BOARDING step of the PLANE frame includes going through a
    WEAPONS-CHECK.[13]
If you go through a WEAPONS-CHECK with a WEAPON you will
    be ARRESTED.
A CLEAVER has two common uses: KITCHEN TOOL and WEAPON.
(Being ARRESTED is a bad thing.)

We ask the system to solve the following

(SOLVE task4 '((INST task4 BUYING)
           (:= (AGENT task4) *ME*)
           (:= (OBJECT task4) CLEAVER-27)
           (:= (INST CLEAVER-27) CLEAVER)))

Once again the system will start by passing markers. In this
case the markers will flow from BUYING, *ME*, and CLEAVER-
27. (Since the task of buying, as described above, involves getting
what is bought to its intended place of use, the system will pass
markers through the various options of how to take a trip.) The
following path of potential interest will be found

    BUYING → TAKE-TRIP
      → PLANE → BOARDING
      → WEAPONS-CHECK
      → IF you go through WEAPONS-CHECK
          with a WEAPON
            you get arrested
      → WEAPON → CLEAVER
      → CLEAVER-1

In this case it is more difficult to recognize that this is an
interesting path. It is found by means of a pattern-matching-type
heuristic that looks for paths which include chaining rule

13– I am well aware that "checking luggage" enters into this problem in a big way,
but choose to open that whole can of worms in the Conclusion where it is described, along
with some potential complications, as "future work."

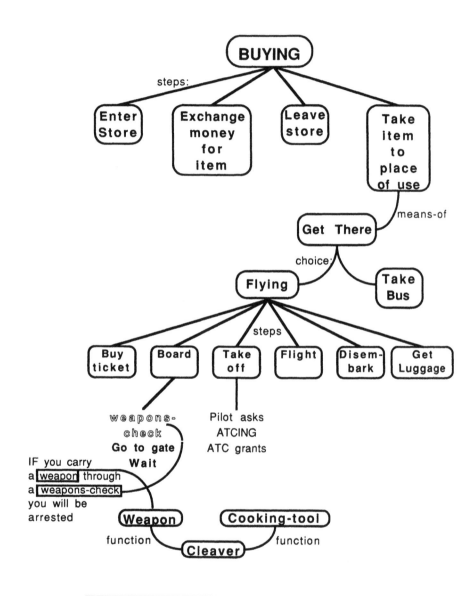

Figure 19: Why you can't carry a cleaver on an airplane.

predicates[14]. In this case it will be discovered that the AGENT of the BUYING, *ME*, binds with the person to whom the arrest applies. Since being arrested is a "bad thing," the system decides to rule out the frame that causes it. It asserts

> (← (RULE-OUT ?task
> 　　　　　　(WEAPONS-CHECKING ?action))
> 　(TOP-LEVEL-TASK task4)[15])

In a matter analogous to the ruling out of PLANE from the rejection of ATCING in Section 2.1.2, the system then asserts:

> (← (RULE-OUT ?task (BOARDING ?action))
> 　(TOP-LEVEL-TASK task4))
> and
> (← (RULE-OUT ?task (PLANE ?action))
> 　(TOP-LEVEL-TASK task4))

The problem-solver now regains control of the situation and plans the buying event up until the TAKE-HOME step. At this point it rejects PLANE because of the new RULE-OUT statement. One of the alternate plans (BUS or TRAIN) will be used.

The example above turns out to have some other interesting ramifications. Note that being on a business trip might well rule out both train and bus (because we already have the airplane ticket, or perhaps because we are in a hurry to get home). Now all the paths for TAKE-HOME are ruled out. At this point the system would back up and decide not to buy the cleaver. The system would need to do some backing up, but this is better than the alternative: to buy the cleaver and end up being arrested.[16]

14– This heuristic is presented in detail in Chapter 5.

15– In this case the rule is only conditionalized by a match of the top-level task since it is unclear, at this point, exactly what caused this interaction. It might be conditionalized better as (HAVE *ME* CLEAVER), but this is a situation not yet in existence at the time this rule-out is asserted! The system has not yet performed the BUY event, it is only starting to plan it.

16– It would obviously be better if SCRAPS were able to debug the error, rather than simply ruling-out the path. Such an extension is described in the Future Directions Section of Chapter 11.

2.2. Tying up a loose end

By now the basic overview of the integrated marker-passing/problem-solving technique and the basic organization of the SCRAPS program should be fairly clear to the reader. Three very loose ends, however, still remain

(1)   How does the path evaluator work? Can we eliminate the hand-waving and really say "here are the heuristics used"?

(2)   How does the marker-passer really work? What parameters affect its operation?

(3)   When do things get flagged and when don't they?

The first two loose ends are tied up in Chapters 5 and 6, respectively. The goal of this section is to deal with the third. Specifically, we will deal with (a) why flags exist and (b) when they are used.

2.2.1. Why do flags exist?

One of the primary differences between the SCRAPS system and the other marker-passing systems described in Chapter 3 is the existence of flags. Why do we need flags for problem-solving? To understand this we must consider why things get marked in the first place.

Consider what happens when we start marking at some node in memory. We mark this node and each of its children, and each of their children, etc. At this point some subset of our knowledge base is "vibrating" (to use our old hockey pucks analogy). What does this vibration mean?

It would seem at first that the fact that a node is activated has some meaning outside of the marker-passing context. In fact, however, this is not the case in SCRAPS. Nodes such as "cooking," "food," "terrorism," "injury," and "physical object" will also be active. It is not until a different origin node is used to propagate marks that any paths are found. It is the *paths* that are important, not the *marks*.

In a planning program we are starting from a single problem, usually with a small number of initial conditions. As we saw in the first three examples above (Sections 2.1.2 – 2.1.4), the paths generated solely from the initial conditions often did not include the critical nodes. It is knowledge external to the problem-solver that we wish to catch. We must have some way for deductive mechanisms to "leave notes" for our marker passer — which is what the examples required. Flags provide this property.

An obvious question might be "Why use flags at all?" Why not just have the deductive mechanisms call the marker-passer directly and leave those marks around with a new origin? For example, in the air traffic controllers' strike of Section 2.1.2 why could we not just pass markers starting at ATC?

The reason this won't work has to do with the question "When are marks removed?" Consider the air traffic controllers' strike. This example was prompted by a real example in which the time between the assertion that the strike was occurring and the time at which the trip was to be planned was a matter of weeks. For our system to work, however, marks from one problem-solving run must not interfere with another.

This leads us to a contradiction if we are to use marks to deal with planning in the ATC case. The marks placed by the marker-passer need only last as long as the problem is being solved. They are activated during problem-solving by the marker-passer and are removed when the goal has been reached. The mark on ATCING, however, is activated outside the context of the problem-solver and its persistence is not scoped by any particular problem — we do not want the problem-solver to remove it.

A similar effect occurs in the case of the gun, which needs to remain marked as long as it is possessed, and the umbrella which is needed only as long as it is raining. A system that interacts with our knowledge base is necessary to place and remove certain types of marks—those which last for the duration of an event external to the present problem-solving context. This is the defining characteristic of flags.

2.2.2. When are flags used

At present we have identified two situations in which flags are necessary. The first is where a fact invalidates an expected state of the world. In this case we set a flag when an assertion should make us cease believing one of the default rules in our system.

This is the justification for the flagging in the strike rule — the strike causes us to cease believing the default expectation that air traffic controllers will be available. Rules of this form are chained in via rules such as

```
(→ (on-strike ?x)
    (→G (job-of ?x ?y)
        (flag ?y 'fail '(on-strike ,?x))))
```

The second time a flag is set is when an object or predicate is in the perceptual environment of the planning agent. This is the rule that motivates the "suicide/gun" and "raining/newspaper" flags of Section 2.1.3 and 2.1.4. These flags are placed by forward-chaining rules such as

```
(→ (POSSESS ?x ?y)
    (PERCEIVES ?x ?y))
```

```
(→ (PERCEIVES ?x ?y)
    (FLAG ?y PERCEPTUAL (PERCEIVES ?x ?y)))
```

We have also seen that one might like to place a flag when a situation can cause harm (mental or physical) to the "cleaver" example. Instead, a chaining rule was used to convey the fact that going through a weapons check with a weapon would lead to arrest. The reason for this strategy is that there is not a single node on which to leave a mark, and thus, one would need to mark an entire pattern — going through a weapons check while holding a weapon. If we could we would use a second order rule such as

```
(→ (CAUSES ?situation ?state))
    (→G (HARMS ?state (PERSON ?agent))
        (FLAG <the arguments in ?situation>
              FAIL
              (HARMS (STATE-OF ?state)
                     (PERSON ?agent)))))
```

we could then represent the weapons checking rule as:

```
(CAUSES (AND (POSSESS (PERSON ?p)
                      (WEAPON ?w))
             (WEAPONS-CHECKING ?wc
                               (CHECKEE ?p)))
        (ARREST ?arrest
                (ARRESTEE ?p)))

(HARMS (ARREST ?arrest (ARRESTEE ?person))
       ?person)[17]
```

Unfortunately, this is beyond the scope of our present system. In a representation framework that allowed higher-order rules, the latter would be used.

The path evaluator is able to take advantage of each of these types of flags. In the next chapter we discuss the exact heuristics used to do this, as well as those used to evaluate paths which do not end in flags.

17– This could also be done via a set of backward-chaining rules such as "being arrested leads to social disgrace and monetary loss" and "social disgrace (or monetary loss) is a form of harm."

CHAPTER 5

Inside the Path Evaluator

> The reason that I thought we ought to talk this morning is because in our conversations I have the impression that you don't know everything I know and it makes it very difficult for you to make judgments that only you can make on some of these things.
> — John W. Dean III[1]

In Chapter 3 we discussed two different approachs to marker-passing. The first, based on Quillian's model, uses marker-passing as a "dumb" mechanism that returns all the paths that can be found.[2] The second, more like Fahlman's scheme, makes marker-passing "smarter" — the goal is for only correct paths to be reported. The mechanism in SCRAPS, and the mechanism I advocate here, is the former.

Since we allow this marker-passer to return all the paths it finds, we must use a path evaluator to examine the paths found. The path evaluator extracts information from those paths which have certain features. To do this the program must have two features: It must reject as quickly as possible paths that can add no information, and it must find the appropriate data in paths that can.

In this chapter we discuss how plan evaluation works in general as well as the specific heuristics used in the SCRAPS system. Following this we discuss a formal basis for such heuristics (developed by Eugene Charniak) and show its relation to the heuristics used by SCRAPS.

1- Said to President Richard Nixon 3/21/73 (as recorded in "Transcripts Submitted to the Committee on the Judiciary of the House of Representatives by President Richard Nixon").

2- Taking into account some sort of attenuation mechanism.

1. Path evaluation

For a path evaluator to work efficiently it must be capable of
quickly rejecting those paths which can add no information[3].
These paths can occur in two ways. First, a path may be of such
a form as to be "meaningless." In this case the path returned by
the marker-passer would correspond to an illegal deduction if
followed. If I have a situation with a perceptual flag on "GUN"
via **(POSSESS JOHN GUN)** and am asked to plan a
"SUICIDE" with the agent set to "BILL," the marker-passer
would find a path like

> **SUICIDE-1 → SUICIDE(BILL) → KILLING
> → SHOOT → GUN →
> (FLAG PERCEPTUAL (POSSESS JOHN GUN)
> → FLAG**

If we tried to use this information we would discover that this
path implies that JOHN and BILL must unify with the same
variable — a situation not logically permissible.

A second type of rejection is of those paths that hold no
inherent contradictions, but rather add no information that the
problem-solver could use. If our friend Leslie, who is an air traffic
controller, wished to plan a trip during the ATC strike we would
find a path of the form

> **LESLIE → (INST LESLIE ATC) → ATC
> → (FUNCTION (ATC ?x) (ATCING ?y)
> → ATCING
> → (FLAG FAIL (ON-STRIKE (ATC ?x)))
> → FLAG**

The variables of this path would unify correctly but would add
the information that "Leslie is on strike" — of no particular
interest to the problem-solver.

The most efficient way to program the path evaluator is as a
set of heuristics that first eliminate those easily found paths which

---

3- The marker-passer used in SCRAPS will eliminate certain paths (as shown in
Chapter 6). Even so, a large proportion of the paths coming along will be meaningless.

cannot add information. We then use heuristics which first test for a pattern to be found in a path and pass it on if the path is not found. We thus have the following schema for each heuristic

Check for some specific pattern in the path.
   If it is not found,
      pass this path on to the next heuristic.
   If it is found,
      check the variables in this path for unification.
      If they unify,
         assert the appropriate rule.
      If not,
         pass this path on to the next heuristic.

We use one of these rules for each of situations that an integrated problem-solver/marker-passer can handle (as described in the previous chapter.)

2. Path evaluation in SCRAPS

The path evaluator in SCRAPS is designed to be a set of heuristics as described above. Instead of discussing these in an abstract form we describe the form used in the program. The rules are shown in the specific knowledge representation of FRAIL. We do, however, try to make the rules as independent of the representation as possible.

2.1. Heuristic 0 — quick rejection

The first rule used by SCRAPS corresponds to the sort of "first pass rejection" used in (Norvig, 1986) and (Alterman, 1985). In this case we reject certain classes of paths.

First we can reject paths we have already examined. Paths found by the marker-passer are not necessarily unique. In certain instances the same path is found with two different points of intersection (the node marked from both origins). The path evaluator adds each path examined to a list and checks this list with each new path. New paths found to be in this list already are rejected.[4]

Second, we can eliminate paths that are "ISA plateau"'s. When a path meets at an intersection via two "ISA" predicates, it is not a path that can add information for marker-passing. Consider for example a path connecting ROPE and SUICIDE such as

> **ROPE → NOOSE → HANG**
> **→ (ISA HANG ACTION)**
> **→ ACTION → (ISA SUICIDE ACTION)**
> **→ SUICIDE**

In SCRAPS it is easy to do this rejection efficiently. We take advantage of the fact that in our representation some nodes are used far more often than others. These "promiscuous" nodes are those that head up large subtrees of the ISA hierarchy and are often those used in the slot restriction predicates. These include nodes such as *person, animate, thing, action,* etc. By examining the intersection point of the path we can see if it meets at one of these nodes. If it does, it is very rarely the case that the path could give us useful information — it is far more likely that the path corresponds to a "plateau." We therefore eliminate those paths meeting at such a node.

If the path does not meet at such a node, we can examine the predicates on both sides of the intersection point. If they are both ISA predicates, with the appropriate syntactic forms, then we again can eliminate such a path. We do this after the above test, since it is slightly less efficient.

These two checks together make up the first rule applied by SCRAPS; they constitute a "first-pass" rejection that eliminates many false paths from consideration.

4— A shortcoming of most Lisps is the inability to put properties on lists. An early version of SCRAPS used hash tables for this operation. It was found that the list of examined paths is typically short and that the overhead of hashing just about equalled the time for the MEMBER operation to be applied. SCRAPS now simply uses the lists as described above although a larger system would need to use a more efficient scheme.

2.2. Heuristic 1 — dealing with demon rules

The rest of the heuristics used by SCRAPS have the form described in section 1. They first examine the path for a pattern, then check the variables for consistency, and finally add the information for the problem-solver if appropriate.[5] The first heuristic tried is the check for a demon. This rule uses a simple pattern match looking for a predicate in the path matching the form of a demon. If such a predicate is not found, control passes to the next heuristic. If the match succeeds, the variables in the DEMON are unified with the variables in the predicates next to it in the path; these then unify with those next to them, etc. until we reach the endpoints of the path. If all the variables can be consistently bound, then the path is considered "meaningful" and the path evaluator will use the demon to give new information to the problem-solver. If the unifying of the variables fails then we proceed to the next rule.

A demon rule has the form

> (DEMON
>   (AND <condition1> <condition2> ... <condition-n>)
>   . <action1> <action2> ... <action-m>))[6]

meaning that if all the conditions hold true the actions should be run. For example, consider the "umbrella demon" of Chapter 4, Section 2.1.4

5– Although SCRAPS applies these rules in the order described here, they are essentially independent and in a concurrent system could be run in parallel as discussed in Chapter 7.

6– This demon is stored in FRAIL as a frame with two slots: an antecedent, which contains the conditions, and a consequent, which contains the actions to be taken when the demon is invoked.

```
(DEMON (AND (AT (PERSON ?p)
                (LOCATION ?location))
            (CLIMATE ?location RAINING))
       (ADD-PRIOR-REQ
            (AND (CARRY (AGENT ?p)
                        (PATIENT ?object))
                 (INST ?object UMBRELLA))))[7]
```

When we find a path through this demon, and if we can unify the variables in the path consistently, we know that two of the conditions have been marked.[8] If the rule is binary, with only these two conditions, then we can perform the actions conditionalized by the present task. These actions are performed by running a program associated with the predicate of the action using the assertions in the predicate as arguments. Thus, for the umbrella rule, we would run the program associated with "ADD-REQ" on the assertions

(CARRY (AGENT ?p) (PATIENT ?object))
and
(INST ?object UMBRELLA)

The program associated with ADD-REQ then asserts the information necessary for the planner to add this step (see Chapter 4, Section 2.1.4).

If more than the two marked conditions are involved, we retrieve from the knowledge base the other conditions (with the same variable bindings used in the two conditions already found). If these also hold, then we can perform the actions in the same manner as with the binary rule.

7– As you'll recall, this is taken to mean "If a person goes to a location and it is raining at that location, then add a requirement to the dominating frame that this person carry an umbrella."

8– The demon rules are indexed by their conditions, not by their actions. Thus, for a path to meet at a demon at least two conditions must have been marked.

2.3. Heuristic 2 — dealing with "perceptual" flags

The next rule examines the path for perceptual flags that do not involve demons. This is done by checking the path for a final node which is a flag. If such a node is found, and if the variables unify, the path will imply that the action preceding the flag should be ruled in. This RULE-IN rule is conditionalized by the predicate that caused the flag (found in the formula immediately proceeding the flag in path). Thus, in the path for suicide/gun

> SUICIDE → KILLING → SHOOT → GUN
> → (FLAG PERCEPTUAL (POSSESS JOHN GUN))
> → FLAG

the evaluator would assert a rule-in of the SHOOT task conditionalized by John's possession of the gun:

> (← (RULE-IN ?task (SHOOTING ?action))
>   (POSSESS JOHN GUN))

We now work backward along the path looking at each of the constants. For any of these which is an action frame we wish to see if the immediately proceeding action appears as a subtask. If it does we should rule this action in as well. If not, we stop. In the example this would do nothing; in the next section we examine an example in which this backward checking yields data.

If this heuristic is successful the path evaluator goes on to the next step. Otherwise it is passed on to the next heuristic.

2.4. Heuristic 3 — dealing with "fail" flags

The next heuristic used is similar to heuristic 2 (and in the actual implementation these two heuristics share various tests and code in common). Again we check to see if the path ends in a FLAG — this time, however, checking to see if the flag is of type FAIL. If we find such a flag, we again check the variable bindings to see if the path is consistent. If it is we wish to assert a RULE-OUT of those subtasks which caused us to encounter the flag. As in heuristic 2, this new rule will be conditionalized by the predicate associated with the flag. After this, we once again work backwards along the path, this time ruling out any action frames that dominate the existing frame.

To get a better feel for this checking of dominating frames, consider the case of the air traffic controllers' strike. A path of the form

$$\text{TAKE-TRIP} \rightarrow \text{PLANE} \rightarrow \text{CLEARANCE} \rightarrow \text{ATCING}$$
$$\rightarrow (\text{FLAG FAIL (ON-STRIKE (ATC ?x)))}$$
$$\rightarrow \text{FLAG}$$

would cause us to rule out ATCING by backward-chaining from the condition of the strike. We would then proceed backwards along the path looking for action frames. We would find in order ATCING, CLEARANCE, PLANE, TAKE-TRIP. We cannot, however, just rule all of these out: We need to make sure that each one is a subtask of the one preceding it in the path. We discover that ATCING is a subtask of CLEARANCE, so we can rule out CLEARANCE. CLEARANCE, in turn, is a subtask of PLANE so we rule out PLANE. PLANE, however, is not a subtask of TAKE-TRIP; rather, it is one of a set of alternative methods for achieving this goal. We therefore do not rule it out (and stop checking the frames).

2.5. Heuristic 4 (em dealing with intra-plan interactions

The final heuristic applied by the SCRAPS system checks for paths that can cause harm or benefit to the planner via unexpected interactions. It is this rule that handles situations like the "pacemaker" case in the Introduction and the "cleaver" problem of Chapter 4.

This rule looks similar to the others. It starts by searching for a pattern in the rule — in this case, a certain form of backward-chaining rule. It then tries unifying the variables and, if this can be done, asserts appropriate rule-in or rule-out rules. The first check is for a backward-chaining rule as one of the predicates in the path. If one of these is found we try the unification step.

At this point things get a little more complex. Since this chaining rule has been marked we know that it is a possible situation for the consequent part of the rule to be applicable. We need to see what happens if this consequent does occur. We do this by asserting this consequent and examining the database for new assertions that result in harm or benefit to the planner. In the "cleaver" example, we discover that this rule being true would result in our arrest. We assert this "arrest" clause and decide that this is of harm to the planner. We therefore wish to rule out the conditions that would cause this harm. (If, on the other hand, anyone walking on a plane with a cleaver was given a million dollars, we would recognize this as of benefit to the planner and try to rule in the plane option.)[9]

Once we have determined that this consequent is harmful (or beneficial) we wish to avoid (or achieve) the antecedent. This is done by ruling out (or in) the appropriate frame. This frame is recognized in the chaining rule. (In the cleaver case this would be the "weapons-check" subtask.) We then work backwards from the rule, as was done in heuristics 2 and 3, to find which other frames in the path are necessarily affected. Each of these is changed in the same manner as the frame in the rule.

3. Digression — a formal footing

The heuristic rules in SCRAPS are not quite as *ad hoc* as they might at first seem. Charniak (1986) has developed a formal explanation of marker-passing paths that can be said to "motivate" the rules used in SCRAPS. To demonstrate this we describe Charniak's technique and relate it to SCRAPS' path evaluation heuristics.[10]

When a path is found between two nodes in a knowledge base by the marker-passer, this means more than that some mechanism has found a connection. The nodes must be connected by some form of inference path, and the semantics of the network define the meaning of the inference. In some cases this inference

---

9– One of the weaker points of the present SCRAPS system is how this sort of consequent is recognized. It is accomplished by asserting the consequent of the chaining rule and then trying to prove "BAD-THINGS-HAPPEN-TO" from the knowledge base. Positive effects are found by retrieving "GOOD-THINGS-HAPPEN-TO." The state of the AI art at the moment makes a more elegant solution to this problem a book in itself. As such I simply do what is done in many text-books and leave it as an exercise for the reader.

10– In this discussion I do not assume that the reader is familiar with the intricacies of logic and resolution, I thus simplify some of nitty-gritty details of the logic. The reader interested in a more formal approach should look out for the aforementioned Charniak paper.

path will be of interest to a problem-solver (or story comprehender), in others it won't. If the underlying associative network has no unifying semantics, this is as far as we can go in formalizing this notion.

Luckily, however, most networks have some form of meaning and therefore the inferences in the paths found by the marker-passer can be checked for meaning. Charniak has shown that when the basis of the associative network is first-order logic, as it is in the FRAIL system, we can go further than this.

In a system such as FRAIL, the nodes in the database represent arguments to predicates, the links represent the predicates. Thus, if a path is found between two nodes we have found a set of logic statements connecting them. In the path from suicide to rope shown in Inset 7, we see that the constant "suicide-1" is linked to the constant "rope-1" via the set of predicates

```
(INST ROPE-1 ROPE)
(MATERIAL-OF NOOSE ROPE)
(RESTRICTION (H-INSTR (HANG ?S))
                      (NOOSE ?NOOSE1))
(CAUSES (HANG ?HANG1
             (AGENT ?X) (PATIENT ?Y))
          (KILLING ?KILLING3
             (AGENT ?X) (PATIENT ?Y)))
(TO-DO (SUICIDE ?S)
          (ACHIEVE ?ACHIEVE3
             (AGENT (AGENT (SUICIDE ?S)))
             (STATE-OF (KILLING ?KILLING1
                      (AGENT
                        (AGENT (SUICIDE ?S)))
                      (PATIENT
                        (AGENT (SUICIDE ?S)))))))))
       (INST SUICIDE-1 SUICIDE)
```

If these patterns contained no variables, the inference path from "ROPE-1" to "SUICIDE-1" would be easily obtained. It is finding a consistent set of variable bindings that makes this task difficult. (In the path above we do find such a set of bindings so we conclude that this path is a legitimate inference path between these constants.)

```
(ROPE-1
  (INST ROPE-1 ROPE)
  ROPE
  (MATERIAL-OF NOOSE ROPE)
  NOOSE
  (RESTRICTION (H-INSTR (HANG ?S)) (NOOSE ?NOOSE1))
  HANG
  (CAUSES (HANG ?HANG1 (AGENT ?X) (PATIENT ?Y))
          (KILLING ?KILLING3 (AGENT ?X) (PATIENT ?Y)))
  KILLING
  (TO-DO (SUICIDE ?S)
      (ACHIEVE ?ACHIEVE3
          (AGENT (AGENT (SUICIDE ?S)))
          (STATE-OF (KILLING ?KILLING1
                  (AGENT (AGENT (SUICIDE ?S)))
                  (PATIENT (AGENT (SUICIDE ?S)))))))
  SUICIDE
  (INST SUICIDE-1 SUICIDE)
  SUICIDE-1)
```

Inset 7: Path from ROPE-1 to SUICIDE-1.

Viewed in this way, the inference path corresponds to a logical proof. That is, if the path is able to connect the two constants in a manner consistent with the rest of the knowledge in our database, and such that the variables within the path unify consistently, then the path can be viewed as a deductive procedure, or proof, connecting the two items. If, however, the items cannot be connected in such a manner, there must be something in the path that invalidates such a proof.

One way of testing paths for such conditions would be to use a resolution device as the basis of our evaluator. This requires reformulating the logical statements in a normal form. For FRAIL this is done primarily by replacing the slot restrictions with disjunction and negation. Thus, a statement like

(restriction (h-instr (hanging ?hang)) noose)

becomes

$$\neg[(\text{ISA } ?X \ (\text{H-INSTR } (\text{HANGING } ?\text{HANG})))$$
$$\Lambda$$
$$\neg(\text{ISA } ?X \text{ NOOSE})]$$

which in turn becomes

$$\neg(\text{ISA } ?X \ (\text{H-INSTR } (\text{HANGING } ?\text{HANG})))$$
$$V$$
$$(\text{ISA } ?\text{x NOOSE}).$$

Once we have the data base in normal form, we can test a path by resolving the first statements on each end (e.g. those using the constants at the ends of the path) against the rest of the facts in this path. This resolution yields a set of predicates that must be consistent with our existing knowledge base if this path is going to be true.[11]

If we make one change to the resolver we will get a significant result. We now insist that at each stage of resolution new predicates being added to the set already generated must unify[12] with one of the predicates in the set; if this fails we will consider the resolution to fail. The result of this change is that certain paths will fail to resolve. These paths will be exactly those in which the path requires an inconsistent binding or for which some variable would not be bound. (The former would be the case if we flagged PAYING from BILL HAS NO MONEY and then tried to plan JOHN GOES TO THE RESTAURANT.) The latter would result from paths that went through ISA plateaus and certain other plateau situations.[13]

11– It actually generates the negation of these predicates as a disjunct. To avoid the problem of talking in double negatives we change this, conversationally, into the associated conjunct of predicates that are not negated.

12– I am actually pulling a logical rabbit out of a hat here, since I am talking about "abductive unification" in this case, not traditional unification. The interested reader should see (Charniak, 1986) for a description of this form of unification and a mechanism for performing it.

13– Alterman's system used a rule which recognized ISA plateaus and also "CAUSAL" plateaus — situations in which A causes C and B causes C. Charniak's resolution procedure finds both of these situations and certain others with similar semantic properties.

3.1. Using this formal basis in SCRAPS

There are two reasons we have not used Charniak's resolution idea directly in SCRAPS. The primary reason is the necessity that the database be in disjunctive-normal form. Although the FRAIL database is stored as a set of logical predicates, they are not stored in normal form. Doing the translation, and making the appropriate changes to the NASL and SCRAPS programs is beyond the scope of the present work. A second reason arises from the use of the abductive unifier in the resolution procedure. Abductive unification is a new technique, not as well understood as traditional unification, a drawback for practical use.[14]

Instead of applying the resolution procedure directly, we use it to motivate the heuristics in SCRAPS. They are essentially heuristic approximations to information that the resolution process would generate.

To see this we must consider the two major purposes of our heuristics: screening out paths that will fail due to unification conflicts and adding information when unification succeeds. When resolution works, negations of the end points of the path must be resolved against all the predicates in the path to produce a null set. The set of variable bindings necessary to make this occur corresponds to a correct unification of the variables in our paths. When the variables within paths will not unify, the formal resolution technique would also fail. Thus, the paths failing unification in heuristics 1–4 would not be accepted by the resolution mechanism and also fail in our system. The heuristic 0 rules, those screening out paths with plateau states, also correspond to paths that would not resolve. To see this, consider the following partial path

---

14– For example, abductive unification can be shown to have a possible worst-case nonterminating behavior. The situation that can cause this situation however, will not arise in Charniak's system (personal communication) which uses abductive unification. We are presently exploring the technique and use it in the latest versions of NASL and SCRAPS.

```
DOG
(ISA DOG ANIMAL)
ANIMAL
(ISA CAT ANIMAL)
CAT
```

To produce the null set we will be forced to resolve (ISA DOG ANIMAL) and (ISA CAT ANIMAL) with elements in the resolution set. The only way this could work, however, would be if we were able to assert that DOG and CAT could be unified with each other. Since this cannot occur, the resolution would fail.

On the other hand, when we succeed in performing the resolution, we are left with the set of predicates that must be added to the knowledge base for the present path to hold true. Among these predicates would be found the various flags, demons, and chaining rules[15] that the heuristics in SCRAPS look for. Once these are found the heuristics proceed as described in the previous section. The resolution technique thus serves as the model on which the heuristics are based, rather than being applied directly.

Despite the speed of these heuristic techniques used for evaluating plans, it still takes time. Thus, it is important to keep the number of false paths found by the marker-passer as low as possible. This is done via both an attenuation mechanism and and by designing certain types of low-level path elimination heuristics directly into the marker-passer. These are discussed in the next chapter.

15– These chaining rules would actually not be directly in the set of predicates, since chaining rules are changed when put into normal form. The information in the antecedent and consequent, however, would be included in the set.

CHAPTER 6

Designing a Marker-Passer

Do not move the markers on the border of the fields
— Amenemope, *The Instruction of Amenemope*, (*circa* Eleventh
Century B.C.E.)

In implementing a marker-passing system, one is forced to address
many issues. Some of these are design-level decisions involving the
type of marker-passer to write. Others involve issues that arise
from the general process of marker-passing, rather than from any
specific design. In this chapter we examine both of these types of
issues and discuss some of the ramifications of each. We then
discuss the actual marker-passer implemented in SCRAPS and
show how it deals with both sorts of issues.

1. Design issues

Marker-passing systems can be roughly categorized in terms of
three design decisions: what is returned, the correctness of this
return, and whether the processing is based on a parallel or serial
model. In this section we describe these issues.

1.1. What is returned

One decision to be made by the designer of a marker-passer is
what it is to return. Should it, like Quillian's program, return a
set of paths linking nodes of origin? Or should it return a set of
nodes representing the intersections of the origins, as Fahlman's
system did?

If the marker-passer is viewed as a system that "answers a
specific question," returning a set of nodes may be all that is
necessary. Fahlman's NETL system, for example, was designed to
answer questions like "what color is Clyde?" When the system
returned "Gray," there was no reason to examine the path
between "Clyde" and "color-of."

If, on the other hand, the marker-passer is viewed as returning inference paths between concepts, a set of nodes is insufficient. It is not enough to know that "suicide and "rope" meet at "hang." We must know whether the existence of this path is telling us that a rope is available, in which case "hang" should be chosen, or whether one is not available, in which case this frame must be avoided. We need to examine the whole path, not just the node of intersection.

Keeping track of the paths is expensive, however, in terms of memory space. At a minimum, each node which is marked must store a pointer to the place of origin and a pointer to the immediately preceding node. Further, if multiple paths are allowed between nodes, as is the case in FRAIL and most semantic network systems, we must keep a pointer to the specific link that was traversed for this mark. This means that at the least each node that is marked must carry three pieces of information, rather than a single one. In a large network in which many nodes are marked at a given time, it is expensive to carry this information.

Returning paths also has a cost in terms of computation time. For a marker-passer to return only the nodes of intersection requires a marking time solely proportional to the number of nodes marked. In a concurrent formulation this time becomes proportional to the length of the longest path found, a smaller number. If paths are to be returned, then as each node of intersection is found the return path must be computed. The time for the marker-passer to run is thus increased by a time proportional to the product of the number of paths found and their lengths. If great care is not taken to ensure that the number of paths found is small, the marker-passer's performance can degrade quickly.

1.2. Correctness

Since performance can degrade quickly as the number of paths increases, it is incumbent upon the designer of the marker-passing system to keep the number of paths returned by the marker-passer small. Ideally, only paths useful to the system using the marker-passer would be returned. One way of achieving this is to make the system take advantage of features of the underlying representation scheme — to have the marking differ depending on the links between nodes. NETL (cf. Chapter 3, Section 2.2) is an example of a system that passes markers differently, depending on the links being traversed. For example, the marking algorithm normally uses two different marks, one from each endpoint. When, however, a cancellation link, is encountered a third mark is used.

We shall call the changing of marks and marking procedures based on the links traversed *smart marker-passing*. The goal of a smart marker-passing scheme is to make sure that the system returns only correct information. If we're returning a set of nodes, each element of the set will be, in essence, a correct answer to the question that invokes marker-passing. (For example, it would be correct to return "pink" when marking from "Clyde" and "elephant" in the case in which Clyde was pink. If the system returned the set "pink, gray" it would be considered an error.) When the smart marker-passer returns paths, these paths should all be of use to whatever mechanism is evaluating them — any other paths are considered to be an error.[1]

In contrast to this is a technique in which the marker-passing algorithm does not take into consideration the semantics of the nodes being traversed — so-called "dumb" marker-passing. In a dumb marker-passing scheme the links being traversed have little or no effect on the algorithm. This type of marker-passer will find all paths between the nodes being marked, regardless of how meaningful they are.

One of the key differences between these two formulations of marker-passing is the treatment of variables. In a smart marker-passing scheme we must take into account the bindings, in the dumb marker-passing scheme we needn't. Thus, the smart marker-passer would not find a path between "Bill going to the restaurant" and "John losing a wallet," while the dumb marker-

---

1– The present system closest to a smart marker-passer that returns paths would probably be Riesbeck and Martin's DMAP-0 system (described in Chapter 3, Section 2.3.2). This system uses the semantics of the underlying system to move around a small set of marks. The nodes marked at the end of a pass roughly correspond to what we have been calling a path.

passer would.

This ability to take variables into account must be "paid for." In a sequential implementation this payment comes in the form of time. The marker-passer itself will need to use some form of pattern-matching and binding during the marking process. If this is done, the time for such matching must be taken into account, and the marker-passer becomes less efficient in comparison to the deductive mechanism.[2] In a parallel system one can do the variable binding and checking without such time delays. This, however, can only be accomplished at the expense of more "control" mechanisms and the accompanying need for more hardware complexity.

A marker-passer can treat some links differently, can have some limited amount of binding knowledge, can do some screening of paths, etc. Thus, the decision between "smart" and "dumb" is not deciding between two poles, but rather picking a point on a spectrum. At one end are the very dumb marker-passers that return a large number of nodes or paths, many of them incorrect; at the other end are systems that return small sets of correct paths. Most marker-passers, including that used by SCRAPS, fall somewhere in between.

1.3. Parallel *vs.* serial

Since Fahlman's work, marker-passing has generally been viewed as a parallel process — Quillian's model is too computationally inefficient to run on a traditional serial machine. This does not, however, have to be the case. Some marking programs, for example Riesbeck and Martin's DMAP-0, have a different and often serial formulation. In these models marks pass outwards in more or less discrete steps, and the order of these marks is important. In other models it is important that paths of length N be found before paths of length $N+1$. Both of these designs impose some serial constraints on the marker-passing algorithms.

2- Given the prevalence of time-space trade offs in computer science, it is possible that we could find a way to avoid this time by using extra links. A limited example of this would again be the cancellation links in NETL, which allow certain paths to be avoided at the expense of extra links.

The most parallel formulation of marker-passing views activation spreading as a massively parallel process. The programs for marking a node are formulated to be "local" algorithms — algorithms that can be performed by a fairly simple processor located at the node and knowing only of itself and its connection to its neighbors. This imposes a severe constraint on the marker-passing algorithm: It may not take into account "global" effects.[3] Mechanisms for allowing local algorithms to perform complex control problems involving seemingly global effects are currently an active research area. (See, for example, our discussion of the work of Shastri, 1985, in Chapter 9.)

Adding parallelism to the marker-passer affects the design decision mentioned above. The gain in efficiency from parallelism can make up for some of the extra time needed to return paths or to make the algorithm smarter. A smart, serial marker-passer returning paths would be the slowest formulation but the one needing the least "post processing" (by a path evaluator or the like). A massively parallel, dumb algorithm returning only nodes would be the most efficient, but also the least useful. The marker-passer in SCRAPS is designed to fall somewhere in the middle, sort of a "semi-smart," massively parallel, path-returning algorithm.

2. Marker-passing issues

Whatever formulation of marker-passing is used (in the range smart, serial to dumb, parallel), there is a set of issues that must be attended to. In this section we discuss these issues and describe some of the approaches used in past systems.

2.1. Attenuation

The most important issue involved in marker-passing is attenuation of the marking. Consider our hockey pucks analogy introduced in Chapter 1. What happens if the hockey pucks vibrate with no frictional damping? If we strike one puck the

---

[3]- The algorithm used by the marker-passer of SCRAPS is formulated to be a local algorithm and to run on a fictitious massively parallel machine. Details of this algorithm appear in Section 3.3.1 of this chapter.

entire network starts to move — we activate all the concepts in our net. If we now strike another puck the set of nodes vibrating from both is still the whole network. Clearly this is not useful and we must add this friction by some mechanism.

One type of limitation is simply to use a smart marker-passing algorithm. In this case we do not pass to all the neighbors of each node marked, but rather only to some distinguished ones. The NETL system, for example, marked all the nodes in the direct ISA hierarchy above a selected node, but only under certain conditions were the other nodes this node was linked to marked. Thus NETL had no explicit attenuation mechanism, since the algorithm was designed so as not to need it.

In a dumber marker-passer the attenuation mechanism can be built into the algorithm in the form of a length limitation. In a complex network all the nodes are connected to each other. Some of these paths are long and tortuous — they require that a large number of inferences hold true. If one holds the breadth of activation spreading to a set limit, these long paths can be avoided. Quillian's system, and most of the systems based on it, use such a limitation.

A limitation on length is not enough, however, since many paths that add no information are quite short. Consider the following paths from SUICIDE to ROPE

(1) SUICIDE → KILL → HANG → NOOSE → ROPE

(2) SUICIDE → ACTION → HANG → NOOSE → ROPE[4]

These paths have the same length, and yet the first is more useful for inferencing than the second. The reason for this is that the node ACTION serves as the ISA hierarchy root for a large proportion of the frames in our system and paths through such nodes as this are likely not to be useful. Further, allowing marks to flow through nodes such as ACTION will cause a tremendous proliferation of paths being found. This will be a problem

---

4- SUICIDE and HANG are both actions.

especially to those marker-passers that return a set of paths, since the efficiency of marking is proportional to the number of paths found in such a system.

Charniak (1983) suggested dealing with this problem by checking the outbranching of nodes during marker-passing. Those "promiscuous" nodes which have an outbranching greater than some predefined constant will not propagate marks. They can be marked, but they cannot pass marks through. There are two major objections to this scheme.

The first drawback is that while it eliminates those paths that would be found by passing through a promiscuous node, it will not eliminate those paths that meet at such a node. Thus, if we start marking from two frames that are both of type OBJECT, the first one will mark OBJECT and then stop. The second frame will do the same. However, at this point OBJECT will have been marked from each of the two nodes and thus will report a path. A solution to this is to amend Charniak's scheme so that promiscuous nodes not only serve as dead-ends to the marker-passer but also are not themselves marked.

The second drawback is shared by both the length and promiscuity limitations. When we use such limitations, our marking becomes very dependent on the form of the knowledge we are representing, not on the meaning. To see this, consider two ways to represent the relation between various frames concerning animals (Figure 20). In the first case the paths from COW and MOOSE to ANIMAL are short but go through a node with high branchout. In the second the paths are longer, but the nodes are less promiscuous. If we used a promiscuity limitation the second path might be found and the first might not; if we used a length limitation the reverse might be true.

Ideally an attenuation mechanism should combine information about length and promiscuity so that longer paths are allowed if they involve little outbranching, and short paths that go through somewhat promiscuous nodes are also allowed. One simple mechanism for doing this is to set some standard total number of marks which are to be passed each time the marker-passer is invoked. We simply start by setting this number, decrement it by one each time we mark another node, and

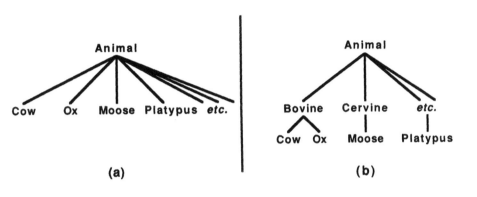

Figure 20: Not all networks are created equal.
a) A simple hierarchy, broad but shallow. (b) A more complex hierarchy with some extra nodes—Deeper and less broad.

conclude marking when we reach zero.

The decision to use a mechanism that counts marks interacts with the design decision to have a parallel mechanism. If one desires local computations only, a number register cannot be shared by all the nodes during marking. If a central mechanism is needed to keep track of the count, we lose our ability to take the advantage of the massive parallelism needed for efficiency.

The attenuation mechanism used by SCRAPS is designed to limit both length and branchout of the paths found without violating the locality constraints needed for massively parallel computing. This is done by using a numerical constant, called *zorch*, to start marker-passing and dividing it by outbranching as we proceed.[5] If we start at a highly branching node, it and all of

---

5– The *Program Notes* column of *IEEE Spectrum* (April, 1985) described this as "the death and taxes algorithm." Zorch is viewed as an ancestor node   which dies, pays a small inheritance tax, and then divides its monetary inheritance among its children. Each of these children then pays the same small tax and lets their children inherit. This goes on down each branch of the "family tree" until a point is reached where the family is bankrupt and can no longer pay the tax.

its first set of descendants can be marked, but the zorch runs out quickly. If, however, we hit such a promiscuous node late in processing, its descendants are not marked since we do not have enough zorch left.

A major problem with using a limitation such as number of nodes or zorch is finding a means to pick the original starting number. It turns out, however, that this number can be chosen empirically depending upon only the average length of the longest paths that the marker-passer will be allowed to return. Informally, the idea is that the marks spreading out form a "circle" of activation around the origin. When we mark from two origins all of the paths found have intersection nodes that fall in the area where the two circles overlap. The longest paths found are those paths that meet at points on the circumference of both circles. The initial zorch can be found by deciding how long we want these longest paths to be and computing a zorch number which will cause the radius of each circle to be roughly half that length.

Let us call the average outbranching factor in our network B and the average maximum length of paths to be returned L (L corresponds to the number of nodes in a path whose intersection point falls on the circumference of both of the circles described above). Each path is made up of a component from an origin to an intersection node p_1, that node itself, and a component from the intersection to a different origin p_2. On the average path, $p1 = p2$, so the average intersection point will occur at a depth of $d = (L-1)/2$ (where depth is equivalent to the radius of one circle in terms of the number of nodes marked). To pick the constant in a number-limited scheme, then, we note that to mark to depth d requires an average of

$$1 + B + B^2 + ... + B^d$$

marks. Therefore the starting constant that will deliver the average length is

$$B + B^2 + ... + B^{(L-1)/2}.$$

When we use a zorch factor we note that we are dividing at each branch and therefore that getting to a depth of d requires a starting zorch of B^d. Thus, the starting zorch for achieving average path length of L is $B^{(L-1)/2}$.

Using the above, we see that if we want an average maximum path length of 7 and the average branching in our network is 10, we would set an initial zorch number of
$$10^{(7-1)/2} = 1000$$
or an initial constant number of marks at
$$1+10^2+10^{(7-1)/2} = 1111.$$

When we view the zorch mechanism in the context of a parallel system we discover that it can also serve other purposes. In a system in which the marker-passer runs in parallel with the problem-solver the zorch number can be viewed as a feedback mechanism letting the problem solver control the number of paths requiring consideration. (Such a mechanism is discussed in Chapter 7, Section 1.4.) Further, when we examine the issues involved in creating certain kinds of massively parallel marker-passing systems we discover that this form of attenuation has important properties in regard to temporal aspects of marker-passing. We shall return to this later in this chapter.

2.2. Marks

Another decision to be made is how much information to leave on a mark. The simplest form of mark is a tag bit on a node, set to 1 if the node is marked. This type of marker tells us if a node has been marked but not anything about when it was marked or from what origin. Other schemes use very complicated marks that include more information at the cost of space. A list of the types of information a mark can contain follows:

(1)   *Point of origin.* We may wish to record a pointer to the node of origin for a set of marking. This enables us to tell, upon encountering a node already marked, the source of that marking. This is essential in a marker-passer that returns paths.

(2)   *A pointer to preceding nodes.* If the marker-passer is to return a path it must be able to follow back pointers to the node of origin. To do this a mark must contain a pointer to the immediately preceding node.

(3)   *Path information.* If the marker-passer in question is to return paths as opposed to just nodes of intersection, it is useful to keep track of the links that are traversed. The

simplest way of doing this is to include in the mark a pointer to the link leading back to the previous node. A more complex way is to encode the entire path traversed so far. This is expensive in terms of space (since much redundant information is encoded), but increases the efficiency of the path-finding algorithm.[6]

(4)   *Weight.* Some schemes entail an activation that decays over time. Others involve being able to compute a strength of a path to be returned. In these cases we need to encode information about the strength of marking.

(5)   *Time and date.* Later in this chapter we discuss several schemes for avoiding marker-passing problems that require information about when a mark occurs. We'll use the term "time" to refer to a property corresponding to an actual system clock time.[7] A property that is set by the system on all marks in a given set of mark propagations will be called a "date."

2.3. Link types

One simple form of "smarts" that can be added to a marker-passer is the ability to handle some types of links differently from others. Two ways to do this are adding one-way links and adding weights to the links.

2.3.1. One-way links

The marker-passer can be limited by treating certain links in the network as "one-way links" — markers can be passed over them in only one direction. As an example consider the marking of ISA links. A node like MAMMAL will have a very large set of nodes connected via ISA links (cat, dog, moose, platypus, etc., etc.). If

---

6– In the simplest formulation the algorithm would now run in constant time by simply merging the paths back to each origin from a point of intersection. Later in this chapter, however, we will show some examples where this algorithm wouldn't work and a more complex one is needed. In the latter case efficiency is still improved, but not as greatly.

7– Or any other means of making available to parallel processors uniquely identified, monotonically increasing time units.

we mark one of these exemplars, we'd like to mark MAMMAL and also to mark the properties of MAMMAL that might be important during inferencing (lactates, live-bearing, etc.). We would probably not, however, like to mark all the other exemplars, since this would require marking many nodes.

This type of thing cannot be handled simply by our attenuation mechanism. A node like MAMMAL is likely to be tagged as a promiscuous node (or to have a high enough outbranching that zorch cannot flow through). We will therefore not mark any of its neighbors. To be able to mark the appropriate "important" properties we need to eliminate the alternate exemplars from the nodes considered during marker-passing.

The simplest way to do this is to treat specially certain links, such as ISA. When we count the neighbors of the node we should not include those that are "down" ISA links. We do, however, want to include nodes that are "up" ISA links (for example, the link from DOG to MAMMAL). When we mark the neighbors we mark only those which have the correct relation (in this example, the parent but not the children).

One problem with such an approach is controlling whether certain links are always one-way links, or whether they are sometimes used in other directions. ISA links, for example, might wish to be traversed in the opposite direction from that described above if we were using the marker-passer to help a system performing a categorization task. If these one-way links are allowed to change directionality, a mechanism for performing this must be built into the marker-passing algorithm.

2.3.2. Weighted links

Another way to influence the behavior of the marker-passer is to give each link in our network a different weight. When marks are passed, those nodes having greater weight get activated "more." This method only works either in the presence of an attenuation mechanism such as the zorch scheme of SCRAPS or when the paths returned by the marker-passer are ordered by strength.

There are two ways that such weights can be assigned: Each link can have its own weight, or each type of link can be given a value. For the former we could say, for example, (ISA A B) has weight X while (ISA C D) has weight Y. For the latter we would say all ISA links have weight X. Whichever way is used, the marker-passer takes advantage of this information during marker-passing and spreads activation accordingly.

One possible use for weighted links would be to add "learning" to a marker-passing scheme. In such a system, each time a path returned by the marker-passer was used by the rest of the program the links in that path would be given slightly greater weight. The more often such a path was used, the more preferred it would become. While a system like this is relatively easy to implement, it is difficult to predict its learning behavior over time. The issue is further complicated by decisions as to what happens to weights over time, how the unused links are to be treated, and how the weights are to be set.

The primary problem with using weighted links is finding a way to assign the values — one hopes to be able to assign these links in something other than an *ad hoc* manner, and yet finding a rational basis is difficult. For this reason SCRAPS does not use weighted links.

2.4. Loops and multiple paths

When markers are passed over an associative net, the network structure of the representation causes a difficulty. Wherever a loop occurs, the marker-passer can have problematic behaviors, which we discuss in this section.

2.4.1. Loops during marking

Consider the network of Figure 21, which represents the following facts

```
(FRAME: ANIMAL
    ...
  SLOTS: (HEAD-OF (HEAD))
   ;the head of an animal is some type of head
)

(FRAME: ELEPHANT
    ISA: ANIMAL
  SLOTS: (HEAD-OF (ELEPHANT-HEAD))
   ;an elephant has a specific kind of head
)

(FRAME: ELEPHANT-HEAD
    ISA: HEAD
  SLOTS: (NOSE-OF (TRUNK))
    ;an elephant's nose is a trunk
  )
```

Consider what happens when we pass marks starting at ELEPHANT. The first nodes marked from ELEPHANT are ANIMAL (via the ISA link) and ELEPHANT-HEAD (via the slot restriction). Marks then flow from ANIMAL to HEAD, from ELEPHANT-HEAD to HEAD, and from ELEPHANT-HEAD to TRUNK. We continue to pass markers and mark ANIMAL and ELEPHANT-HEAD from HEAD. The next step then marks ELEPHANT from both ANIMAL and ELEPHANT-HEAD. If marking now continues we repeat this whole process, since we are starting at ELEPHANT once again. This continues until we reach the attenuation limit and stop. We need a scheme to eliminate this redundant work.

The traditional way of handling this (*a la* Quillian, 1967) is to leave a trace of each origin; if we come to a node marked from the same origin, we stop marking. Thus, in the example above we would not mark ELEPHANT-HEAD from HEAD since it has already been marked from ELEPHANT.

While this method eliminates loops that occur during marking, it can cause problems in systems in which the marker-passer returns multiple paths (such as the one in SCRAPS). This issue is discussed in the following section.

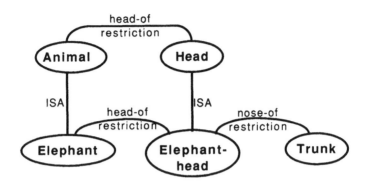

Figure 21: A network with a loop.
One common place that loops show up in frame systems is when ISA relations include slots—for example, ANIMALs have HEADs, while ELEPHANTs have "ELEPHANT-HEAD"s which are more specific.

2.4.2. Multiple paths

Consider what happens in the example above when an activation from another origin encounters one of the nodes we have marked during looping. If an intersection were found at the node TRUNK, say, the set of paths returned would be those shown in Inset 8, a potentially infinite set.

If we use the scheme discussed in the previous section, we eliminate all but the first path. However, path 2 provides certain information that path 1 does not, and this information may be important to the system invoking the marker-passer. We have thus eliminated the looping paths (3 and on) at the cost of losing a path we need. To avoid this a more complex mechanism must be designed.

In one such mechanism, each mark keeps track of its origin as before. This time, however, when we encounter a node marked from the same origin we do not stop; instead, we update the information found at that node to allow two backtraces. Thus, if

ELEPHANT-HEAD is asked to report a path back to ELEPHANT, it will report both subpaths. These subpaths are then combined by the path return mechanism.

This solution works in the situation above, but may not always work in a parallel environment, since path 1 may be reported before the mark from HEAD reaches ELEPHANT-HEAD. In this case the new information is updated on ELEPHANT-HEAD but the marking then stops. Nothing now encounters TRUNK again, and therefore path 2 is not returned. The set of paths returned is thus determined by the exact characteristics of the parallel system, in some we would get path 2, in some we wouldn't — a race condition decides.

A solution for this problem is to use a scheme in which an extra property is put on each node. Each time a path through a

---

(1) ELEPHANT → ELEPHANT-HEAD → TRUNK

(2) ELEPHANT → ANIMAL → HEAD
 → ELEPHANT-HEAD → TRUNK

(3) ELEPHANT → ELEPHANT-HEAD
 → HEAD → ANIMAL → ELEPHANT
 → <Path 1>

(4) ELEPHANT → ELEPHANT-HEAD → HEAD
 → ANIMAL → ELEPHANT
 → <Path 2>

(5) ELEPHANT → ELEPHANT-HEAD → HEAD
 → ANIMAL → ELEPHANT → ELEPHANT-HEAD
 → HEAD → ANIMAL → ELEPHANT
 → (<Path 1> or <path 2>)

etc.

Inset 8: Paths intersecting at TRUNK.

node is found, a time stamp is put on this property of the node. When we mark a node for a second time from the same origin we check to see if a path has come through at an earlier time. If it has not, we add the back pointer to the set of marks and pass no more marks from this node. If a path has come through, we allow marker-passing to continue.

To see how this works, consider our example once again. First, consider the case in which we find the path from TRUNK to ELEPHANT before the marking of ELEPHANT-HEAD from HEAD. As the path is found we set the property on ELEPHANT-HEAD to show that a path came through at time $T1$. We now come to mark from HEAD. Since the path property is already set, we know that we must continue marker-passing. The markers propagate once again and TRUNK is marked. We now follow the path back from trunk to ELEPHANT. Since ELEPHANT-HEAD contains two paths back to ELEPHANT, both paths can be found.

If, instead, we had reached TRUNK after the second marking of ELEPHANT-HEAD, the situation would be different. In this case the mark from HEAD comes to ELEPHANT-HEAD but the path property has not been set. We therefore mark ELEPHANT-HEAD with information leading back to both origins and mark no further. (so as to eliminate loops in marking — see previous section). At a later time the path from TRUNK to ELEPHANT is computed, and since both paths are recorded at ELEPHANT-HEAD paths 1 and 2 are both reported.

The scheme as outlined so far has one remaining bug: When the TRUNK node was found before the second marking of ELEPHANT-HEAD, path 1 was returned twice. This is solved by using the time stamp associated with the property. If a time stamp is associated with each mark on a node we need only report paths through marks that came later in time than the last path through. In this way we would mark ELEPHANT-HEAD from ELEPHANT at time T_i, put a path property on ELEPHANT-HEAD at time T_j, and mark ELEPHANT-HEAD from HEAD at time T_k (where $i<j<k$). When we once again compute a path from TRUNK we would report only those paths containing nodes marked later than T_j and thus do not report the redundant

information.

2.4.3. Follow-on

Another problem that arises during marker-passing is that of "follow-on." What do we do when we encounter a node marked from a different origin? We certainly wish to report the path found, but do we continue marking? Consider the example in the previous section: When we mark TRUNK from ELEPHANT-HEAD, do we continue marking? If so, we may find redundant paths, since TRUNK may have been marked from some other origin, say NOSE. In this case the first path reported would be

(6) ELEPHANT → ELEPHANT-HEAD → TRUNK → NOSE

If marks continued the next marker-pass would activate NOSE from TRUNK. Since this is already marked, a path would be returned. This path, however, would be the same as path 6. If the path from NOSE to TRUNK involved intermediate nodes, path 6 would be reported as any of these nodes was encountered, since each would have been previously marked from the node NOSE. Eliminating redundant paths from the return keeps the path evaluator (or whatever program calls the marker-passer) from needing to examine them, but the time necessary merely to compute them can easily swamp the marker-passing.

Again, an apparently simple solution is just to stop marker-passing at the point at which a path is returned. Certain aberrant conditions, however, can occur in an attenuating system. Consider the case shown in Figure 22. Let us assume that we start marking from A and that B is the last point marked (due to attenuation). If we now start marking from C we will reach B and report the path from A. Consider, however, that we may still have activation energy left. If we stop marking (since a path has been found), we will not try to mark node D. It may be the case, however, that D has been marked (either from A or some other origin) and a legal path, perhaps a necessary one, will not be reported.

A solution to this is to extend the time stamps used as a solution to the loop detection problem. Instead of just noting a time, we also keep track of where the back path originated. Follow-on is now allowed, thus avoiding the problem of missing

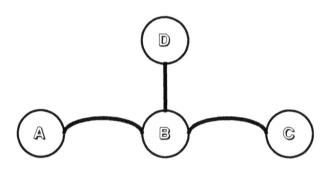

Figure 22: Some nodes.

paths. To keep from reporting redundant paths we have the marker-passer check the path property of a node before a path meeting at that node is reported. If the path would be redundant it is not reported.

Let us make this clearer by once again using the example in Figure 22. We mark starting at A and proceed to mark B. The attenuation limit is reached so we stop marking. We now start marking at C and reach B, finding the mark from A. A path is computed and the marker-passer adds

$$A \rightarrow B \rightarrow C$$

to the list of paths to return. As this path is computed A, B, and C are stamped with path properties reporting a connection between A and C. We now continue the marking and both A and D are checked.

At this point we find the information that A has already been marked (from itself) and therefore we check, by looking at A's path property, to see if a path should be reported. Since we have already reported a path from C to A, no new path is reported.

If, on the other hand, D had been marked (either from A or a different origin) no path property would be found. When it is marked from C the check for such a property fails and the system reports the new path. This would update the path property on B to include the earlier path to A and the new path to D. If yet another node were to come along and wish to mark B, both of these nodes are listed, so as to prevent redundant paths back to each of these nodes.

2.4.4. Loops in paths

One other type of loop occurs in marker-passing systems. These loops occur during path reporting when two nodes mark each other from the same origin. As an example of this, consider what happens if we add a link from A to D in Figure 22. If we pass marks from A, both B and D will be marked at the first step. At the second step B is marked from D and D is marked from B, both with origin A. C is also marked from B.

If C had previously been marked from another origin, a problem would now arise. As the path-reporting algorithm tries to find all paths from C to A, it follows the link from B to D and adds to the subpath found so far all paths back to the origin A. Unfortunately, one of the paths from D back to A is through B. Thus a loop arises as B goes to D and D goes to B — our path-finder never stops.

This sort of loop is easy to detect, however. If the same node occurs twice in a path we know that some sort of loop has occurred. We simply have the path-checking algorithm check whether the node it is presently examining is an element of the path found so far. If it is, the path-finder is in a loop and can terminate this path.

2.5. Erasing marks

If the marker-passer is used by another system, or several other systems for that matter, it will eventually get full of marks. The issue of erasing the marks thus arises. There are essentially two ways of doing mark erasure: erasing them all and having marks degrade. In a system like SCRAPS, where the marker-passer is called for the solution of a specific problem, we can define discrete marker-passing "events." At the end of one of these, we can erase all previous marks and begin a new round of marking. Thus, erasing marks requires no more than a message broadcast to all nodes asking that marks be removed.

More interesting is the case where a system uses the marker-passer continuously.[8] In this situation the marks in the system must be erased over time. Charniak (forthcoming) and Norvig (1986) use a time stamping system and exponential decay of marks. Each mark has both a date slot (which keeps track of when the mark was added to its node) and a number representing the present weight of that mark. As time passes this weight is decreased, and when it falls below a certain threshold the mark is removed.[9]

2.6. Path ordering

When the return from the marker-passer is to be processed by another program, such as SCRAPS' path evaluator, it is useful to have some heuristics for judging the strength of a path. In one model, the second program rates the returns of the marker-passer, ordering the paths returned. In a second model the marker-passer judges the paths and orders its own return using some heuristic evaluation.

Past systems (Hirst, 1983; Norvig, 1986) have used heuristics for judging the strength of paths returned by the marker-passer via a heuristic taking into account the length of the path and some function of the outbranching of the nodes along it. The exact formulation of the heuristic however, has been left to be decided by experimentation and *post hoc* comparison.

In the second model, paths are given a strength rating according to properties of the nodes and links traversed during marker-passing. If this rating falls below a certain threshold the

---

8–For example, Charniak's natural language system or the long-term planner, discussed in the Conclusion (Section 3.4).

9– Charniak implements this via the zorch mechanism of his marker-passer. When path strength is computed the system uses "effective zorch" rather than the actual zorch mwhere the "effective zorch" on a node is found by dividing the zorch with which it was marked by 2 to the (present date/date of marking) power.

path is not returned. Paths with strengths above this threshold are ordered by strength so that the evaluator examines "better" paths first.[10] Path strength is not equivalent to equal semantic utility: it is quite possible for a strong path to be returned in which, for example, variables would not unify or an ISA plateau is encountered. Path strength does, however, correlate well with semantic use, since stronger paths will usually require fewer inferences for realization.

3. How SCRAPS does it

This section discusses the design of the marker-passer implemented in SCRAPS in terms of the issues discussed previously. We will examine the format of the marks used in the system, the ordering of the paths returned, the marking and path-reporting algorithms, and finally some miscellany of interest.

3.1. SCRAPS — marks in detail

The marker-passer in SCRAPS marks each node with a list of records. Each of these records contains elements corresponding to one of the types of information listed in Section 2.2 (as shown in Inset 9).

Each time a node is activated during marker-passing a record containing these elements is added to the lists of marks. These marks are examined at various points during the marking algorithm, but are not accessible to any other component of the system.

3.2. SCRAPS — ordering the return

The marker-passer in SCRAPS uses the zorch attenuation mechanism described in Section 2.1. We have thus been able to develop a path strength mechanism that allows the marker-passer to eliminate certain paths and to order the others (cf. Section

---

10– Details of a scheme for doing this are described in Section 3.2 where we discuss the path strength formula used by SCRAPS.

11– SCRAPS does not presently use this decay feature. It is included since this same marker-passer is used in Charniak's WIMP system. WIMP does do exponential decay.

---

(1)   ORIGIN The node from which the present set of activations started.

(2)   FROMNODE The node that immediately preceded this one in the path.

(3)   FORMULA The predicate logic formula (corresponding to a link) that led from the fromnode to this node.

(4)   ZORCH The amount of zorch the node received at the time it was marked.

(5)   DATE Each time the marker-passer is invoked date is updated; used to implement exponential decay of marks.[11]

(6)   TIME System clock time at which this node was activated; used for loop avoidance and follow-on detection, as discussed in Sections 2.4.1–2.4.3.

Inset 9: The marks used by SCRAPS.

2.6).[12]

The formula for computing the path strength is generated by examining how the zorch mechanism works. We start by passing marks from a node with an initial zorch Z. This node will have some number $B1$ of neighboring nodes. We divide Z by this number $B1$ and mark each of the neighbors with this new zorch. These neighbors then compute the number of their neighbors and each divides its zorch by that number and the process continues. This goes on repeatedly until a node is reached for which the number of neighbors is greater than the present zorch.

If at some point we reached some node $Node_i$ that has already been marked from a different origin, the present zorch is

---

12– This method of computing path strength via the zorch mechanism was first suggested by Charniak (personal communication, 1984).

$$\frac{Z}{B_1 \times B_2 \times ... \times B_{i\text{-}1}}$$

(where $B_{i\text{-}1}$ is the branching factor of the node immediately preceding this one in the marking process). This node, however, has also been marked from another origin with a zorch on the mark computed in the same manner from the other origin. If we multiply these two zorches we get

$$\frac{Z^2}{B_1 \times B_2 \times ... \times B_l \;\; (not\ including\ B_i)}$$

If we consider a network in which the average branching is B and the average path length returned is L, this formula can be approximated by

$$\frac{Z^2}{B^{L\text{-}1}}$$

where L is the average length of paths found.

This formula has two important aspects. The first is that the initial zorch, Z, is a constant for the system and thus the numerator of the equation remains constant. Our initial zorch setting affects only the actual value of this formula, not the relative weighting. Second, we note that the denominator involves taking the branching factor to the power of the length of the path. Thus, if the network is fairly uniform (i.e., if the deviation of outbranching from the average is small) the number returned by this formula is inversely related to the path length.

These properties are quite desirable for a path strength formula. The most intuitive heuristic to use is to have path strength equal path length. With the present formula, this is true in cases where the outbranching of the nodes in the path is fairly constant. The present formula is also quite simple to compute: We simply multiply the two zorches together.

There is still one weakness, however: We have not taken into account the outbranching of the node of intersection. If two paths meet at a promiscuous node, the total path strength should go down. To make the formula complete we need only multiply in the outbranching of the node of intersection and set the path strength to be

$$\frac{Z^2}{B_1 \times B_2 \times ... \times B_l}$$

(this time including B_i.)

Using this path strength we can make an interesting observation. Due to the way zorch works, we can guarantee that the first formula (the one not including B_i) will always have a value ≥ 1. (Remember that zorch stops at the point at which the product of outbranchings is greater than Z. Thus, the two products multiplied together must have a value $\leq Z^2$. The numerator of our equation will therefore be $\geq$ than the denominator and the value will be ≥ 1.) When we include the outbranching of the node of intersection in the denominator, however, the value can go below one.

Consider what it means for the path value to go below one: This only happens when the combined amount of "left over" zorch at each of the nodes before the intersection (the i-1 nodes) would not be enough to pass through the intersection node. If we squared the initial zorch and started marking from one origin, we would reach the attenuation limit before marking the other. By using the equation above for computing path strength, the marker-passer can eliminate any paths for which the value falls below one.

SCRAPS computes a path strength for each path it finds during marker-passing. If during this process a path strength falls below one, that path is eliminated from consideration. Those paths remaining are returned. Using this mechanism ensures that we eliminate many paths of low strength at the marker-passer level (thus saving the plan evaluator from having to examine them). A higher strength is given to short paths than long ones, and greater path strength is associated with thin paths than is associated with paths that have large outbranching.

3.3. SCRAPS — nitty-gritty

The algorithms used by SCRAPS to do marker-passing and path reporting are formulated to be local computations — each node can do its work knowing nothing beyond for its own internal state, the addresses of its neighbors, and the TIME and DATE information. The present marker-passer is implemented in a LISP macro package language called NISP (McDermott, 1983) and runs as compiled code on each of several different machines.[13] It currently uses a serial implementation with queues to simulate the concurrency available in a parallel environment.

The marker-passer used in SCRAPS is a relatively "dumb" marker-passing algorithm that returns paths. It does not have weighted links (cf. Section 2.3.2) but does handle certain links in special ways (to be discussed later). Implemented in the program are mechanisms for dealing with the features of marker-passing discussed in this chapter. These include

> An attenuation mechanism— dividing an initial
> zorch setting (cf. Section 2.1).
> Loop avoidance via the PATH
> property (cf. Section 2.4.1).
> Redundant path elimination via the PATH
> property (cf. Section 2.4.4).
> A DATE property for erasing
> marks (cf. Section 2.5).
> Path strength computation (cf. Section 2.6).

The next section provides a pseudocode-level description of the marker-passer and discusses certain "smart" features of this marker-passer.

3.3.1. Pseudocode for the marker-passing algorithms:

13– The present machines on which SCRAPS can run include: Apollo Workstations running T, VAXen running Berkeley UNIX and Franz Lisp, and Symbolics and Texas Instruments Lisp Machines running Zetalisp. NISP also runs under CommonLisp — FRAIL and the marker-passer have been run in this environment.

RETURN-PATHS is a global variable   *;used to contain the*
                                ;paths returned by the marker-passer.
DATE is a global variable   *;holds the "date" of marking*
ZORCH is a global variable   *;initial attenuation number*

;The top-level function used
PASS-MARKERS(NODES)
DATE = *DATE* + 1   *;set a new date*
LOOP For each NODE in NODES
    IN-PARALLEL: *;pseudocode for parallel calls, see note 1 below.*
    MARK(NODE, NODE,'ORIGIN, NIL,*ZORCH*)   *;calls mark for each origin*
END LOOP
IF there are any paths in ***RETURN-PATHS***
THEN sort ***RETURN-PATHS*** (based on path strength) *;sort the paths and*
     RETURN the sorted list.   *;return them*

Pseudocode for the marker-passer

(comments·in italics)

;The actual marking function
    MARK(NODE,ORIGIN1,FROMNODE,FORMULA,ZORCH) *;mark algorithm*
      TIME = the time on the system clock   *;set a new time*
      Local variable NEW-MARK = a record of: *;to be used in the algorithm*
                (ORIGIN,FROMNODE,FORMULA,ZORCH,DATE,TIME)
;STEP 1: Check for previous marks. If we find them from the same origin
; check for loops and follow-on. If we find them from other origins
; the report the appropriate paths
    Check the MARKER property of NODE   *;check for previous marks*
      LOOP for each MARKER do:
        IF marked from the same origin
        THEN IF the old fromnode and formula
                are the same as the present ones
              THEN STOP!! *;we are about to enter a loop: stop MARK*
              ELSE IF the PATH property denotes a path
                    from ORIGIN1 to any node at a time < TIME
              THEN add NEW-MARK to the list of marks
                  and STOP!! *;no need to do any more: stop MARK.*
              ELSE go to NEXT MARKER
        ELSE IF marked from a different origin (ORIGIN2)
          THEN IF the PATH property denotes a previous path
              between ORIGIN1 and ORIGIN2
              THEN go to NEXT MARKER   *;path is redundant*
              ELSE REPORT(NODE,MARKER,NEW-MARK)
                ;this will allow path reporting
    END LOOP.
;STEP 2: Check zorch and outbranching. If enough zorch to continue
; then mark the neighbors of this node. Otherwise just stop
    local variable NEIGHBORS# = number from NEIGHBORS property of NODE
    local variable NEW-ZORCH = ZORCH divided by NEIGHBORS#
    IF NEW-ZORCH $\geq$ 1 T
    THEN LOOP for each NEIGHBOR in the NEIGHBORS property
      IN-PARALLEL:
      MARK(NODE-OF(NEIGHBOR),ORIGIN1,NODE,
                  LINK-TO(NEIGHBOR),NEW-ZORCH)
    ELSE STOP!!

```
;the report function
; this function will collect two sets of paths, one back to each origin,
; and merge them together if there is enough path strength to do so.
; the return is then added to the global variable collecting the return paths
 REPORT(NODE,MARK1,MARK2)
   local variables REPORT1,REPORT2
   local variable NEIGHBORS# = number from NEIGHBORS property of NODE
   local variable START-PATH is a record with
     PATH: NIL
     STRENGTH: *ZORCH*-squared / NEIGHBORS#    ;see note 4 below
   IN PARALLEL:
   REPORT1 =
      REPORT-TO(MARK1,START-PATH,NODE)
   REPORT2 = REPORT-TO(MARK2,START-PATH,NODE)
   LOOP FOR REP1 IN REPORT1
    IF REP1
    THEN LOOP FOR REP2 IN REPORT2
           IF REP2
           THEN
             local variable PATH-STRENGTH =
                        PATH-STR(REP1,REP2,NEIGHBORS#)
             IF PATH-STRENGTH ≥ 1
             THEN add a path to *RETURN-PATH*
                with strength: PATH-STRENGTH
                and path: REV-PATH(REP1) → NODE → PATH(REP2)
                    ;see note 2 below
           NEXT REP2
         END LOOP
    NEXT REP1
   END LOOP
```

```
;REPORT-TO is the local function used for parallel reporting of paths.
; in a parallel system this would be done by the processor at
; the node herein called FROMNODE(MARK)
  REPORT-TO(MARK,PATH-SO-FAR,RETURN-NODE)
; add the information from the previous mark to the path
; which will eventually be returned
  local variable NODE = FROMNODE(MARK)
  local variable TIME = time on system clock
  local variable NEW-PATH-SO-FAR = a record with
        PATH: NODE and FORMULA(MARK) added to PATH-SO-FAR
        STRENGTH: 1/ ZORCH(MARK) × STRENGTH(PATH-SO-FAR)
;set up the PATH property with the appropriate TIME
  put a list of MARK and RIME on the PATH property of NODE
; check to see if this node is already in the path.  If it is
; we can stop
  IF NODE is a member of PATH(PATH-SO-FAR)
  THEN non-local-return NIL to RETURN-NODE ;see note 3
; if the path-strength gets too low then we can stop
  IF STRENGTH(NEW-PATH-SO-FAR) < 1
  THEN non-local-return NIL to RETURN-NODE ;see note 3
; if this node is the origin the path is done
  IF NODE = ORIGIN
  THEN non-local-return NEW-PATH-SO-FAR to RETURN-NODE ; see note 3
; otherwise find all paths back to the same origin recursively
  ELSE LOOP FOR MARKER in MARKER property of NODE
      IN PARALLEL:
              IF ORIGIN(MARKER) = ORIGIN(MARK)
              THEN REPORT-TO
                      (MARKER,NEW-PATH-SO-FAR,RETURN-NODE)
          NEXT MARKER
          END LOOP.
```

;*a computation of the path strength of a merged path*
  PATH-STR(PATH1,PATH2,NUMBER)
    return
      ZORCH-squared / STRENGTH(PATH1) $\times$
                              STRENGTH (PATH2) $\times$ NUMBER

NOTES:

(1)   IN-PARALLEL means that the operations in the loop are done concurrently. In actual implementation this means they are added to a QUEUE so as to perform in a breadth-first (rather than depth-first) manner.

(2)   REV-PATH just reverses the path. This is added so paths are returned with the origins as the endpoints (not shown).

(3)   REPORT-TO assumes that a nonlocal return is possible, as in a system providing continuation message passing. This would be needed in a fully parallel implementation of this algorithm. At present the system simply uses traditional function returns.

(4)   *ZORCH*-squared is the square of the original zorch number, computed once and made global (not shown).

3.3 (continued) SCRAPS — Nitty Gritty

Certain features of SCRAPS do not appear explicitly in the above pseudocode. Specfically, some of the setup for the marker-passer is done via extensions to the indexing scheme of FRAIL. A data-driven component is added to the indexer that allows the NEIGHBORS property used by the code above to be set up correctly.

Each node in the system is set up to contain a property that tells what other nodes it is connected to and via what links. This is done by making the NEIGHBORS property a record containing two pieces of information: A number set to be the number of neighbors to which the present node is connected, and a list composed of records containing a node and a formula that links this node to that neighbor. For example, the ELEPHANT-HEAD node of Section 2.4.3 would have the following NEIGHBORS property

```
NEIGHBORS(ELEPHANT-HEAD):
   NUMBER: 3
   LINKS:( (ELEPHANT
        (RESTRICTION
          (HEAD-OF (ELEPHANT ?X))
               (ELEPHANT-HEAD ?Y)))
        (HEAD (ISA ELEPHANT-HEAD HEAD))
        (TRUNK (RESTRICTION
               (NOSE-OF (ELEPHANT-HEAD ?X))
                  TRUNK)) )
```

When an assertion is made to FRAIL, the indexer looks at a special property of the main predicate and adds this statement as a link in the NEIGHBORS property of each of the appropriate nodes. It is this that allows SCRAPS' marker-passer to handle one-way links and to have certain special handlers for some predicates. For example, the predicate ISA will add to the NEIGHBORS property of the second element in the predicate, but not the third. If we assert **(ISA ELEPHANT-HEAD HEAD)** this is added as a link from ELEPHANT-HEAD to HEAD, but no change is made in the NEIGHBORS property of the node HEAD. During marker-passing this corresponds to a "one-way" link (cf. Section 2.3.1) on ISA properties. No mechanism is provided for allowing links to change directionality except at assertion time.

3.4. Massively-parallel marker-passing

The pseudocode for the marker-passer in SCRAPS is designed to facilitate using this algorithm on an idealized massively parallel processor. This processor is a "theoretical" machine in which there are as many nodes as needed, where each node has a processor and as much memory as needed, where each node can broadcast to many other nodes simultaneously, and in which all the recipients of a message broadcast from a single node receive that message simultaneously. (We discuss this machine again in Chapter 7, Section 1.3.3.)

On such a machine we assume that each node in our memory corresponds to a single processor in a machine. Each of these processors would know how to respond to the following messages:

(1) **MARK(from, formula, zorch, date)** Check for intersections and send report messages to the appropriate neighbors. Send mark messages to each neighbor.

(2) **REPORT-TO(mark,return-node)** Add a component of a path from a marked node to an origin. If this node is the origin it reports to the return-node; otherwise it passes a continuation to the next node on a path back to the origin.

(3) **DECAY()** Lower the strength of all marks, erase those falling below a certain threshold. Decay messages are broadcast to all nodes by a central control processor.

With this model of marker-passing we can make an interesting observation: Let us presume that to pass a marker a processor computes some information about each of the nodes it is connected to, and then broadcasts a mark message to each of these nodes.[14] Thus, the time it takes for a processor to complete a mark operation is proportional to the number of neighbors it has. In such a system we can do away with the path strength computation. This is because, under these assumptions, path

---

14– As we've defined our machine, these messages are received simultaneously by these neighbors.

strength will be equivalent to return order — a path that would have higher strength will be returned sooner than one with a lower strength.

To see this, consider the case where we have already passed marks from one origin. As we pass marks we are dividing until we reach an attenuation limit, at which point we stop. The nodes already marked form a metaphorical "circle" around the origin with a radius of $(L-1)/2$ (where L is the average length of the paths returned by the marker-passer). Those points within the circumference are already marked, those without are not. Each of the points at this border are related by the path strength needed to reach them — they are all as close as possible to the original number for zorch. The path strength needed to reach a node is the initial zorch divided by the cumulative branchout. The points on the border, therefore, are those as far as possible before the dividing of branchout reaches zero — they are the points at which path strength would be roughly equal to one.[15]

At this point we start marking from another origin. If this point of origin is within the original circle, it is already marked and the path is reported right away. Thus, paths within the circle — those in which the path strength back to the original node was high — are reported right away.

If the point of origin is not within the original circle, we note that the points of intersection will be those on the perimeter of the original marking. These points, however, are roughly a constant distance from the first node of origin (and therefore roughly a constant path-strength from the original node), and they will each therefore add a roughly constant component to the path strength. The first of these points to be marked will be those closest to the new origin, where "closeness" is now defined in terms of how long it takes marks to reach them. This closeness, however, will exactly correspond to branchout under the

---

15– The only exception to this rule will be the points at which the path stops at a promiscuous node. In these cases, however, marks coming through this node from another origin will be computed in time proportional to the branchout of the promiscuous node. These paths will take a long time to compute, so that the argument to be made in the following paragraph holds.

assumptions previously stated — the less cumulative branchout, the sooner the node is reached. Thus, the order these paths are returned corresponds to our previous definition of path strength.[16]

On the basis of the preceeding, we notice one more interesting property. Each of the points on the circumference of the original circle is marked at about the same time — their cumulative branchout is about equal and under the assumptions above this causes them to be reached at about the same time (since the neighbors of a node are marked at a time proportional to branchout). In such a system, zorch, as we've used it, becomes equivalent to time taken to reach a node. The attenuation limit, therefore, need no longer be an actual number passed among the nodes. Instead, we can compare the clock time at which a node is marked to the clock time at the point where marker-passing started. The zorch limit now corresponds to the maximum time a set of markers will be allowed to propagate.

In the next chapter we discuss the properties of a concurrent implementation of SCRAPS. In this discussion we assume that the marker-passer is a separate process. Ideally this marker-passer would be a massively parallel system for efficiency reasons. As we shall see, however, the model is not dependant on this: Several formulations of marker-passing systems are discussed.

16– This argument only holds in cases where we do not allow one-way links or use any sort of link weighting. In each of these latter cases anomalous situations can arrive that would cause a path of lower strength to be reported earlier than another.

CHAPTER 7

C-SCRAPS — Adding Concurrency

> The buddy system matches two divers together for
> mutual enjoyment and safety in the water... Even though
> the buddy system seems to inhibit a diver's mobility, it
> does so only to guarantee the safe completion of the dive
> for both buddies... Well-matched divers find no difficulty
> in cooperating with each other because each is trying to
> accomplish the dive objective for both.
> — Lou Fead, *Easy Diver [1977]*

Classification of existing parallel machines is usually based on the
number of processors they contain and various attributes of the
interactions and memory sharing of these processors. Based
purely on processor number, these mchines fall into roughly three
groups: *coarse grained* machines, with between two and about
one hundred processors, *medium grained* machines with between
one hundred and about 10,000 processors, and *fine grained*
machines with more than that. In this chapter we examine an
existing implementation of a concurrent version of SCRAPS
running on a simulated coarse grained machine (using multiple
processes and shared memory communication), and then describe
designs for running this system on three different existing
machines with various different parallel capabilities.

1. Why concurrency?

Up to this point we have discussed functionality issues in adding a
marker-passer to a problem-solver. It is now time to examine the
efficiency issues. We start once again by examining the flow-of-
control diagram for SCRAPS (Figure 23). We observe that if we
leave out the memory component (Figure 24), the flow of control
becomes a loop in which the problem-solver invokes the marker-
passer, the marker-passer returns paths to the path evaluator, and
the path evaluator adds information to the problem-solver. This

159

loop resumes each time the problem-solver invokes the passing of markers.

If each of these steps happens in series the problem-solver must wait until the marker-passer and path evaluator have finished. If the marker-passer finds no paths or if the path evaluator makes no relevant assertions, the problem-solver has waited for nothing; instead of making it more efficient we have impaired its performance.

The argument can be made that even if the overall behavior of the planner is slower its performance has been improved. Consider the "suicide while holding a gun" example in which the problem-solver chooses a better solution than it would if it used

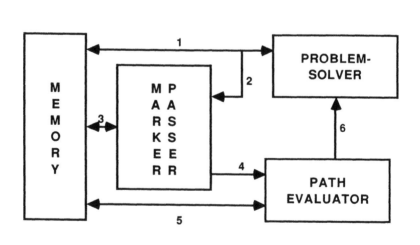

Figure 23: The flow of control in SCRAPS (last time).
See Figure 5.

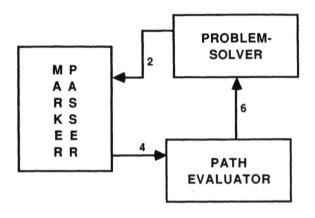

Figure 24: Flow of control, not including memory.
Information passes in a loop from the problem-solver to the marker-passer to the path evaluator and back to the problem solver.

the default approach.[1] However, we have not shown that our intended suicide will not die of old age before deciding to shoot himself. We must design a system that is computationally viable.

Another argument is that the time saved in backtracking is worth the time spent in marker-passing. Proving this would require examining the exact behaviors of both the problem-solver and marker-passer, finding average-case results based on the size of the knowledge base and the number of paths found, and examining the complete problem space of planning to see how often backtracking will occur. It might then be possible to demonstrate the benefit of a system such as SCRAPS in terms of overall performance. Unfortunately, while I believe this proposition to be true, such an analysis is far beyond the scope of

---

1– Likewise, consider the case from the Introduction in which the lunar rover doesn't fall in the crater — not losing the rover is worth a degradation of performance.

this book. While we might be able to mathematically compare the deductive behavior of the problem-solver with the "dumb" behavior of a marker-passer, such an endeavor would inevitably prove fruitless because much of this behavior is dependent on the exact form of the underlying data and the exact set of frames in the knowledge base.

A way to make the system computationally viable is to change the design so that it can clearly be demonstrated that the system's overall performance is not slowed down *at all* by the addition of the new component. The worst case should be equal to the time the problem-solver would take alone. I hereby make this extravagant claim, with one qualification: I wish to use multiple processes. A concurrent formulation of SCRAPS will not slow down the problem-solver. In this chapter we describe the program C-SCRAPS, a concurrent implementation of SCRAPS.

1.1. The implementation

Concurrent-SCRAPS realizes the basic flow-of-control diagram of Figure 23 via separate processes corresponding to the elements in this diagram. This involves having problem-solver, marker-passer, and path evaluator processes that can communicate with each other. All of these processes interact with a single memory. The closest realization of this is to use a simple parallel scheme in which we set up three separate modules communicating via shared memory.

The present implementation of C-SCRAPS uses exactly that scheme, taking advantage of the multiple processing capabilities of our Lisp workstations. Three windows are created, one for each of the processes. A typical C-SCRAPS screen is shown in Figure 25.

The problem-solver window runs the same version of NASL as non-concurrent SCRAPS. It simply goes along solving the problem after invoking the marker-passer. The only difference is that in C-SCRAPS it does not wait for results: constants are simply added to a control queue used by the marker-passer, no return is expected or awaited.

The marker-passer is no longer invoked via a function call, but stays in a permanent loop examining the head of the previously mentioned control queue. Whenever a value is found at

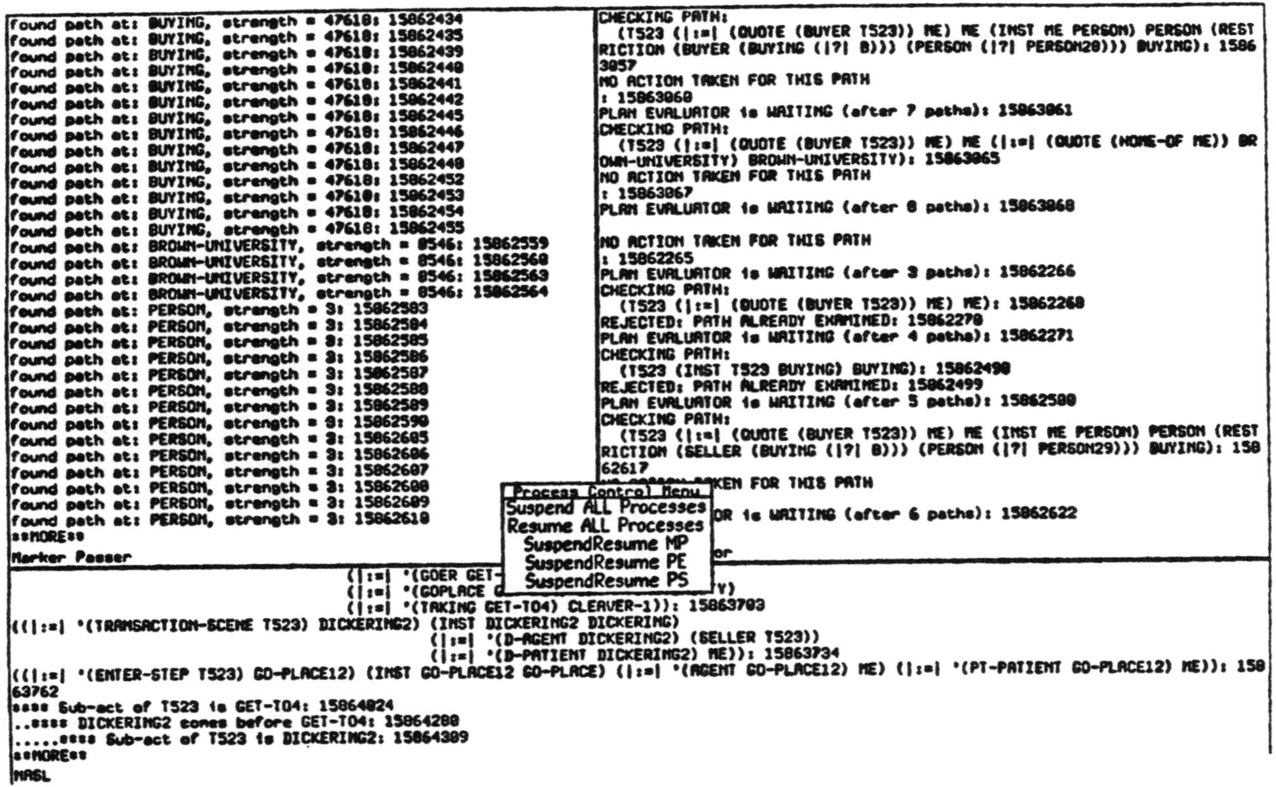

Figure 25: Example of the output of C-SCRAPS.

C-SCRAPS, running on a Symbolics Lisp Machine, runs as a set of three interacting processes communicating through a shared memory.

the front of this queue that node is marked.

The control queue allows us to simulate the passing around in parallel of a set of activations, rather than the successive activation of sets of nodes around a single origin. This behavior is accomplished by having each node that is marked add its neighbors to the tail of the QUEUE. Each new set of activations desired by the problem-solver is achieved by adding a node to the head of the same queue.

To understand this better, consider an example. Let us once again use the "elephant and trunk" example of Chapter 6 (Figure 26). The nodes in this system, and their neighbors, are

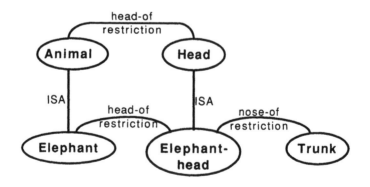

Figure 26: A network with a loop (again).
See Figure 21.

NODE:	NEIGHBORS:
Animal	Elephant Head
Elephant	Animal Elephant-head
Elephant-head	Elephant Head Trunk
Head	Animal Elephant-head
Trunk	Elephant-head

In the non-concurrent version of SCRAPS we would mark from ELEPHANT and pass markers outward until the limit was reached. We would then pass markers from TRUNK until an intersection was found. In the new version we will pass markers from both ELEPHANT and TRUNK simultaneously.

The system is started when the problem-solver asks that a node be marked

QUEUE: [ ]
to be added: ELEPHANT

As the problem-solver asks that nodes be marked, each of these nodes is added to the head of the queue. Each item in the queue has associated with it an indication of its origin. Thus, the situation becomes

QUEUE:[(ELEPHANT from ELEPHANT)]
to be added:

ELEPHANT is marked — it is removed from the queue and its neighbors are added

QUEUE: [(ANIMAL from ELEPHANT)
**   (ELEPHANT-HEAD from ELEPHANT)]**
to be added:

So far there is no difference from the way the marker-passer works in the non-concurrent version of SCRAPS. At this point, however, the problem-solver may wish another node to be marked

QUEUE: [(ANIMAL from ELEPHANT)
**   (ELEPHANT-HEAD from ELEPHANT)]**
to be added: TRUNK

Since this is a new origin it is put at the start of the queue

QUEUE: [(TRUNK from TRUNK)
        (ANIMAL from ELEPHANT)
        (ELEPHANT-HEAD from ELEPHANT)]
to be added:

The marker-passer now takes the head of the queue, TRUNK, and marks it. This causes the neighbors of this node to be enqueued

QUEUE: [(ANIMAL from ELEPHANT)
        (ELEPHANT-HEAD from ELEPHANT)
        (NOSE from TRUNK)
        (ELEPHANT-HEAD from TRUNK)]
to be added:

ANIMAL now heads the queue, so it will be marked and its neighbors added to the end of the queue. These will be tagged from the same origin, producing the situation

QUEUE: [(ELEPHANT-HEAD from ELEPHANT)
        (NOSE from TRUNK)
        (ELEPHANT-HEAD from TRUNK)
        (HEAD from ELEPHANT)]
to be added:

If we now continue the marking process, marking and adding nodes to the queue, we will mark ELEPHANT-HEAD twice, once from the enqueueing from ELEPHANT and once from TRUNK. When ELEPHANT-HEAD is marked the second time the path reporting works as before.

This change makes no difference in terms of what is returned by the marker-passer. It does, however, change the total time until paths start to be returned: The time until the first path is found is reduced because we no longer need to wait for the complete marking from the first origin before the second set of marking starts. In the above example, then, the node HEAD is not marked until the nodes previously enqueued from TRUNK are processed. The path through ELEPHANT-HEAD is found before this marking.

This is important because the path evaluator is also in a loop similar to the one being used by the marker-passer. It is waiting for paths to be found so that they can be analyzed. As each path is found by the marker-passer it is added to the end of a list in the shared memory. Whenever this list is non-empty the path evaluator takes the first element and applies the heuristics described in Chapter 5. As rule-in and rule-out assertions are made they are added to the memory so that the problem-solver (which has been proceeding in parallel with this process) can use them if necessary.

1.2. Efficiency

It should be clear that this scheme satisfies the claim made earlier: The worst-case efficiency of the integrated system is the same as that of the problem-solver running alone. If the marker-passer/path evaluator combination adds no information to the memory, the system performs as if the problem-solver were running alone. There is still one hypothetical case we must explore: We must show that the performance is sometimes enhanced. If the problem-solver always reached its goals before the other processes had finished we would not be able to demonstrate that we have improved matters.

Unfortunately, there is no principled way to demonstrate that this does not occur — the marker-passer and path evaluator must be designed in such a way as to be faster than the problem-solver. In Chapter 10 we show examples in which C-SCRAPS does add information to memory prior to its being needed by the problem-solver. Here we justify this empirical evidence by analysing the system's behavior.

As mentioned previously, the primary reason that the marker-passer/path evaluator methodology is able to stay ahead of the problem-solver is the relative inefficiency of memory retrieval and variable binding in the associative network scheme as compared with the "dumb" behavior of the marker-passer and the heuristics of the path evaluator. The marker-passer used in SCRAPS is an efficient search mechanism — as discussed in Chapter 6, it need not consider variable binding. It simply follows links between constants. The heuristics used by the path evaluator were designed to eliminate false paths quickly, only taking time to check variable bindings when other information indicated a possible use. The problem-solver, on the other hand, is a deductive mechanism, and must do variable binding at each step to make sure a consistent plan is being generated.

Even given this difference in performance, it is not always the case that the marker-passer and path evaluator have added all the information they can before the first choice is made by the problem-solver. The reason for this is that the first choice point can be reached before marker-paths are evaluated. Consider the case of planning a trip during the air traffic controllers' strike (the example of Chapter 4, Section 2.1.2) — the problem-solver may choose the PLANE frame before it reaches the information that this frame should be ruled out.

A solution to this problem is to give the path evaluator the ability to alter the behavior of the problem-solver. In C-SCRAPS this is achieved by extending NASL to leave a trace in memory of each of the frames it is pursuing. If the path evaluator wishes to rule out a frame that is already being executed, it leaves a message in memory telling the problem-solver to fail and take the appropriate actions — backtracking and undoing past behavior in a system that provides for backup, printing appropriate failure messages in a system that doesn't. If the problem-solver has not yet reached the point of failure on its own, it will back up when it finds this information; if, on the other hand, the problem-solver has already reached the point of failure predicted by the path evaluator, it will ignore the now redundant failure message.

This approach neatly solves the problem of what to do when the problem solver has made a choice that the path evaluator will later rule out. It does not, however, help when the planner makes a choice prior to a RULE-IN or executes an action before a modification occurs. These latter two cases are less straightforward to deal with.

Suppose, as is the case in the "suicide while holding a rope" example (Chapter 4, Section 2.1.3), the path evaluator rules in an alternative. When this occurs the problem-solver may have already passed the choice point at which this rule-in would be valid (the HANG frame may have already been chosen). There are two alternatives. One is just to let the problem-solver continue on its way. If the improper choice fails, the system will back up and then have to make a second choice; at this point the rule-in information will be available and the system will succeed. If the original choice does not fail, the system generates a correct plan, and therefore the original goal is solved.

The other alternative is to have the path evaluator interact more directly with the agenda mechanism used by the problem-solver. Now, when a RULE-IN is asserted, we add the ruled in frame to the agenda at the appropriate place. The path evaluator then causes the problem-solver to stop its present course, save the state, and return to the choice point. It then takes the new choice and continues on. If this choice later fails (the gun has no bullets) the system will back up, return to the frame originally chosen, restore the state, and continue.

The C–SCRAPS system uses this second alternative, but in a limited form. The NASL problem-solver, as a plan interpreter (cf. Chapter 2, Section 2.1.3), is unable to do backtracking. To back up it would have to restore the state of the world prior to any actions it took and these actions often cannot be easily undone. For example, consider the case of the "get-to" frame. One of the side-effects of this frame is that the agent is no longer at the location she/he was at prior to the going. To undo this we must recompute where the agent was and restore him/her to that place. We must also undo all the other side-effects of the trip: the purchase of the plane ticket, the change of location of the pilot, stewardess, and other passengers, etc. The amount of work required is quite large. SCRAPS uses the second approach, but when the problem-solver is already pursuing a plan known to lead to failure, SCRAPS causes it to quit and assert FAILURE — earlier than it would have done otherwise (an example of this behavior is given in Chapter 10, Section 3.2).

A final question arises: What happens when a plan is modified after it is already in action? Consider the case of the "getting a newspaper on a rainy day" example from Chapter 4, Section 2.1.4. We may decide that the first step of "fetch newspaper" should be to get an umbrella. Unfortunately, we may make this decision after the frame has started to execute — the information has come in too late.

One solution to this problem requires adding a certain "intimacy" between the problem-solver and the path evaluator.

The path evaluator must have access to information on where in the problem-solving task the planner presently is. The new step to be executed is added at the first appropriate place that is yet to be reached by the planning system. Thus, if we had reached the point of getting a coat but had not yet opened the front door, the path evaluator would add the "get umbrella" step prior to the door opening. If the planner has already reached the point of applying the DEMON rule on its own, the Path Evaluator need not take any action at all.

The problem with the above solution is that it requires giving the path evaluator the ability to check the *current* state of the problem-solver. By the time the path evaluator adds the new step to the frame, the problem-solver may once again have passed it. The only solution is to let the path evaluator suspend the problem-solver, check the state, add the information to the frame, and then continue the problem solving process. This, however, will violate our assumption that these two are completely separate, concurrent processes. We are back to the original problem of guaranteeing that the problem-solver is not stopped longer than it would take the original process to encounter the DEMON rule.

C-SCRAPS uses a different approach that takes advantage of a non-deterministic feature of NASL's design. The new step can be added at the latest point prior to a DEMON that the function associated with the DEMON allows (cf. Chapter 5, Section 2.2.). Thus, instead of specifying that the umbrella should be retrieved first, the rule in C-SCRAPS would ask that the CARRY frame be invoked prior to the OPEN-DOOR frame. The mechanism used by NASL performs the steps of a frame in a non-deterministic order unless specific order information is given. If we assert

> **(BEFORE (CARRY-UMBRELLA-STEP**
> **(GET-NEWSPAPER ?action))**
> **(GO-OUTSIDE-STEP ?action))**

the system will perform the carrying of the umbrella at some point constrained only to be prior to going outside. If we are already past the latter step the system will encounter the DEMON rule on its own, so this information would become redundant. This solution works quite well in NASL, but it is not a general solution for all planning systems — some systems do not allow this type of nondeterminism in the ordering of subacts.

1.3. Future versions

What we have been discussing up till now is the present version of C-SCRAPS, which has been implemented; examples of its output are shown in Chapter 10. More recently, however, we have been exploring how SCRAPS can benefit by use of several different types of parallelism. In this section we describe three different designs for running different parts of SCRAPS on present-day parallel systems. First, we examine a version of C–SCRAPS designed to run on a machine containing several processors with no shared memory and discrete communications. We then examine how we might run a system like SCRAPS on a machine with a large number of shared memory processors using a Lisp dialect designed to exploit such parallelism. Finally, we discuss how a machine with a large number of simple processors can be made to look like the idealized, massively-parallel, marker-passing machine mentioned in Chapter 6, and how such a machine could be tied into C–SCRAPS.

1.3.1. SCRAPS for a few communicating processors

The first type of parallelism we shall explore is that of a a machine consisting of several linked processors, each possessing its own memory. An example of such a machine is the MCMOB, formerly ZMOB, machine developed at the University of Maryland (Weiser et.al., 1985).

ZMOB is a non-shared MIMD machine using a "conveyer belt" interprocessor communication system. Each Zmob processor has a Z-80 microprocessor, floating-point hardware, 64k ram, and serial and parallel ports. (The Computer Science Department at the University of Maryland completed a 128 processor ZMOB in 1985.) MCMOB replaces the Z-80 with an mc68010 processor and one megabyte of memory but retains the conveyer-belt message-passing architecture. A sixteen processor McMob became operational in July 1986.

While the present implementation of C-SCRAPS uses a shared memory, it has in fact been designed so that shared memory is not necessary. A loosely coupled set of processors, each functioning independently, has advantages over a set of processors contending to share the same memory: Each processor uses its own memory, so access time is shorter than it is when memory contention may be occurring.

We are now ready to propose the design for a parallel, loosely coupled version of SCRAPS using a small number of processors (Figure 27). The flow of control is similar to that used in C-

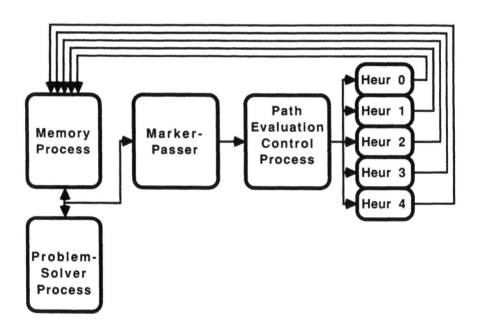

Figure 27: The design of C^+-SCRAPS.
C-SCRAPS as it would be augmented to run on a small number of processors without shared memory.

SCRAPS. The marker-passer is run on one processor, serving as a knowledge base for the problem-solver, which runs on a separate processor. As paths are found they are evaluated by a concurrent version of the path evaluator, and the resulting information (RULE-INS, RULE-OUTS, etc.) is returned to the knowledge base.

This approach takes advantage of a design feature of the path evaluator used in C-SCRAPS. The heuristics involved in path evaluation are designed to run independently and concurrently. Each heuristic does a pattern-matching step followed by a more complex test if the match succeeds. Each of these rules can run in parallel — none depends on the result of the others.

This system starts as does the present version of C-SCRAPS: The problem-solver is invoked to achieve a goal. The initial conditions statement is passed both to a memory process which uses which does standard deduction and a marker-passing memory the other which contains the marker-passer. While the problem-solver receives information from the standard memory, the marker-passer sweeps through the second memory performing the appropriate activations and generating paths. As each of these paths is found it is sent to the path evaluator which runs the quick check heuristics to look for redundant paths and ISA-plateaus. Those paths not rejected are piped to the four other heuristics in parallel. Each of these evaluates the paths found, as discussed in Chapter 5, and returns any new rules that should be added to the standard memory. The problem-solver can take advantage of these rules in the ways discussed earlier in this chapter.

This version is designed so as to take advantage of MCMOB's version of parallelism. The primary problem with loosely coupled architectures is avoiding memory contention and long latency periods. The model here assumes that each of the processors contains a fair amount of local memory and sends very specific types of messages to other parts of the system. The problem-solver sends single nodes to the marker-passer, the marker-passer returns paths to the path evaluator, and the path evaluators return assertions to the knowledge base.

1.3.2. A *Future* C–SCRAPS

A very different model of the use of parallelism allows the user to specify when parallel evaluation may occur, but not how it is to occur. In such a model the user does not have explicit control of the processors, as in the MCMOB system, but rather uses an evaluation scheme that allows various parts of programs to be run on any processor that becomes available. One such system is Butterfly Lisp (Scott et. al., 1986) designed to run on the BBN Butterfly, a medium grained parallel machine with 128 or more processors which communicate via a shared memory. In this section we look at a design for C–SCRAPS that takes advantage of this approach to parallelism. (This design has not yet been implemented at the time of this writing.)

The primary mechanism used for concurrency in Butterfly LISP is a programming construct called a *future* (Baker & Hewitt, 1977). Essentially, a future is a LISP expression that is not evaluated when called, but rather is put on a queue and evaluated as soon as a processor becomes available. To view the result of this evaluation one uses the TOUCH function, which returns a value if the object has already been evaluated. If the object has not yet been evaluated the system halts until such time as a processor becomes free to perform this evaluation.

One weakness of using futures as a concurrency mechanism is that when a process creates many futures, and then very soon after touches them, it may lose some of the benefit of the parallelism. The longer the time between the creation of a future and the touching of it, the better the chance of its having already been evaluated. Thus, systems gain the most from this form of parallelism when they interleave the creation and examination of various different types of futures.

C–SCRAPS is formulated in such a way that it can do this form of interleaving. Instead of creating different processes for each of our modules (problem-solver, marker-passer, and path evaluator) as we did in the MCMOB version of C–SCRAPS, we create a single process that interleaves the working of the problem-solver with the marker-passing and path evaluation functions. Thus, the resultant system is somewhat of a cross between SCRAPS and C–SCRAPS. The resulting algorithm is shown in Inset 10. The staggering of path evaluation and problem-solving allows the marker-passing paths greater time to be evaluated.

This scheme is expected to speed up problem-solving primarily in that the time taken by our form of marker-passer tends to be dominated by the computing of the paths, not by the passing of marks (as discussed in Chapter 6). Using this algorithm we can compute the faster part and then leave the path computations to come later. Since the paths returned are kept in a queue, later paths found have a longer time until being touched by the path evaluator.

The staggering of problem solving and path evaluation allows more time to pass before the evaluation of paths occurs. The danger of such an approach, however, is that, as could happen in C–SCRAPS, the problem-solver may make a choice prior to the particular path that would invalidate that path being found by

======================================

BUTTERFLY–SCRAPS [task, initial-conditions]:

(1)   The problem-solver is started as usual, various initializations are performed.

(2)   The initial conditions go to marker-passer. Marker-passer spreads marks, but doesn't compute return paths. Instead, a form to evaluate (i.e., a future that, when evaluated, computes the path) for each path found is added to a queue.

(3)   The problem solver is started up. It computes for a set period of time. If the problem is solved we stop (and are done).

(4)   If there are paths to be evaluated, the path evaluator is invoked. Paths are taken from the queue and run through the evaluation heuristics. This continues for a set period of time.

(5)   Return to step 3.

Inset 10: Algorithm for SCRAPS using *futures*.

======================================

the path evaluator. As discussed previously, we fixed that
problem in C–SCRAPS by letting the path evaluator keep track
of the progress of the problem-solver and leaving information what
would let it recognize the failure. The same solution works for us
here.

1.3.3. Massive parallelism

The third machine examined in the design of our system is the
Connection Machine (Hillis, 1985), a fine grained, single instruction
multiple data machine with a high-bandwidth general
interconnection scheme. It is composed of 2^{16} processors, each of
which has several thousand bits of local memory. A single
instruction stream is used, and the instructions are broadcast to
all other machines. A router is used to allow any processor to
send a message to any other processor. A host machine is used to
control the Connection Machine, usually a high performance Lisp
workstation.

Our present design for the use of such a machine
concentrates on using the connection machine as a marker-passing
memory. In essence, we propose to duplicate the present multiple
tasking version of C–SCRAPS with the connection machine taking
the place of memory and the control of this occuring where our
former marker-passing process was. The resulting system is shown
in Figure 28. As items are retrieved from memory by the problem
solver, running on the Lisp Machine, marks flow through the
processors of the connection machine finding the paths to be
reported to the path evaluator.

Our present design involves using the "CM controller"
process to simulate the idealized machine discussed in Chapter 6,
Section 3.4. As discussed, this involves getting the connection
machine to simulate the properties of a machine in which

(1) There are many processors each with as much processing
power and memory as needed for marker passing.
(2) Each node can broadcast to many other nodes simultaneously.
(3) In which all the recipients of a message broadcast from a
single node receive that message simultaneously.

Our contention that we can simulate this machine on the present
connection machine architecture is based on three factors: the

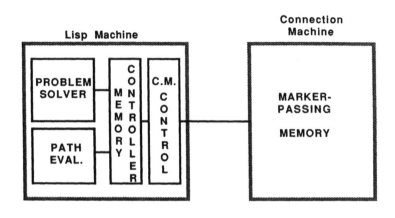

Figure 28: The design of CM-SCRAPS.
C-SCRAPS as designed for a connection machine architecture: a large number of independent processors each with its own memory.

ability to provide locality of reference in the indexing scheme of a language such as FRAIL, the ability to create a local implementation of marker-passing, and the connection machine's capability of having processors route messages to other processors in parallel.

The first of these, the locality of reference of the indexing scheme of a language such as FRAIL, is described in Charniak (1985). Roughly speaking, we index the known propositions about some frame in a particular area of memory corresponding to that frame. Thus, the statement (ISA CLYDE ELEPHANT) is stored in memory areas corresponding to CLYDE and ELEPHANT. To find all those things which fit the pattern (ISA ?x ELEPHANT) we look in the ELEPHANT area (implemented as a set of properties on the atom) for assertions that start with ISA. A unifier is then used for variable binding.

On a connection machine, this locality of information is important because it enables us to have a single "virtual" processor, which can store the information corresponding to the assertions we know about an object. This "virtual" processor is implemented using a small set of connection machine processors for efficiency's sake. The address of one of the nodes in this virtual processor is used for indexing. Thus, to represent (ISA CLYDE ELEPHANT) we put into the memory of the virtual processors for CLYDE and ELEPHANT a bit string corresponding to a code for ISA, the address of CLYDE, and the address of ELEPHANT. Finally, each virtual processor contains a memory structure corresponding to the list of addresses to be sent a marking message, some memory structures for keeping track of marks already received, and some control bits set when the object in question has been marked, needs to compute a path, or is ready to mark its neighbors.

To simulate the timing of sending messages that arrive simultaneously at a set of neighbors, a "routing cycle" is used for message-passing. This cycle provides a small number of machine cycles to allow messages to be sent and to arrive. These routing cycles are varied with compute cycles that provide the processors time to compute the neighbors that are to be routed messages. Thus, the algorithm for marker-passing is to have a set of compute cycles in that all processors which have been marked compute their neighbors for marking and examine their "mark" area to see if they should return a path. If a path is to be returned the appropriate control bits are set. If, as a node is computing the neighbors to be marked, it reaches a flag corresponding to the end of the information about neighbors, some control bits are set to cause marks to flow.

At the end of a compute cycle, two routing cycles occur. In the first, those nodes wishing to return paths send the appropriate messages to other nodes (which will perform their part of the path computation in successive path-returning cycles). In the second cycle, those nodes ready to mark their neighbors send the appropriate messages. The system now returns to the compute cycle. This loop of "path return," "mark," and "compute" cycles continues for a set amount of time.

We can now make the following observation: The time for a node to compute its list of neighbors becomes proportional to the branchout of the node — nodes with small branchout are ready to mark their neighbors sooner than nodes with high branchout. When this fact is coupled with the behavior of the system described, simulating our ideal machine, we have created a system meeting the requirements described in Chapter 6. In such a configuration path zorch and time correspond as proven earlier. Thus, we no longer need an explicit zorch factor for path computation, and paths are returned in an order corresponding to path strength. Further, the initial zorch number now corresponds to the amount of time for which the cycle above is repeated.

This uses the connection machine for a marker-passing memory, not as a serious adjunct to the planning or path evaluation mechanisms. In Chapter 9 we review work in the field of connectionism and discuss some attempts to use more of the parallelism in the actual planning tasks.

1.4. Zorch revisited

In the serial implementation of marker-passing we introduced the zorch mechanism for providing the attenuation necessary for causing marker-passing to terminate. In Chapter 6 we showed that this number could be picked empirically based on the "average longest path" desired by the designer of the system. Thus, we had reduced a seemingly random factor to a desired system behavior. Still, the setting of the initial zorch requires an *ad hoc* number that has significant effect on the marker-passing behavior of the system.

In the above parallel models, however, we believe that the role of zorch, and how the number is to be set, has a better explanation that reduces the *ad hoc* nature of this constant. In all of these models the marker-passer, running in parallel, continues to find paths for evaluation until the system is stopped. Marks propogate from several sources at once, and the paths are evaluated as found, without waiting for others. The factor controlling how long these marks propogate is no longer the initial zorch factor, but rather is based on the time the problem-solver takes to reach its goal. Thus, we believe that what we have called initial zorch can now be viewed, in essence, as a feedback mechanism allowing the system to control the passing of marks.

In each of the systems outlined in this chapter, the problem-solver and path evaluator are essentially racing with each other. If the path evaluator is able to find information before the planner, then the planner is able to avoid redundant work. If, on the other hand, the planner is ahead of the path evaluator, then the path evaluator can at best stop the planner or add information that will be used only later if the planner backs up for other reasons. When the systems are working in parallel, controlling this "race" becomes of crucial importance.

The path evaluator needs a mechanism by which it can cause the marker-passer to return less paths when it is falling behind. If, instead, the path evaluator is sitting idle, it can cause the marker-passer to go further, thus finding "deeper" paths for analysis. The zorch attenuation algorithm provides such a mechanism. Thus, in this situation, we believe that zorch can be best viewed as the mechanism that controls the race. If the path evaluator is falling behind, the zorch number is reduced, if the path evaluator is sitting idle, the zorch number is increased. Such a feedback mechanism is now being designed into the systems described above, which run on these various parallel processors.

CHAPTER 8

Cognitive Aspects

Sometimes a cigar is just a cigar
— attributed to Sigmund Freud *[ca. 1920]*

On a superficial level the behavior of SCRAPS appears to model human cognitive behavior: Marker-passing seems to resemble neurophysical models of activation, the paths found seem to resemble actual inferences, and the overall behavior of the system seems to resemble the behavior of some sort of "subconscious process" that screens information prior to conscious processing. It should be clear, however, that this is far from the truth of the matter: Neurons don't correspond to the frames in FRAIL, human inferences are far more complex than the simple assertions SCRAPS generates, the information passed in marks is too complex to be neurologically plausible, and there's no clear dividing line in my system that would let one distinguish between what is subconscious and what isn't. Why then a chapter entitled "cognitive aspects"?

One temptation for an AI researcher examining the cognitive relevance of a program is the tendency to add *ad hoc* features to "tune" the model to "perform as it should." These features are often added solely so that the program models existing data, not in order to improve performance or to handle problems formerly unsolved. Predictive power and theoretical elegance are lost.

On the other hand, undervaluing cognitive research is also a mistake, since this can make one disregard valid research that contributes to one's understanding of the process being examined — an understanding of human cognition can suggest research directions for our programs (Ringle, 1983).

In this chapter I attempt to walk the fine line between these errors. I discuss some ways in which SCRAPS relates to research in cognitive psychology and some ways in which it doesn't.

Instead of claiming SCRAPS as a psychological model, we show some psychological theories and results that correspond to features found in SCRAPS. Instead of adding features to SCRAPS for the sake of psychological validity, we discuss those features and show why they've been omitted from the present model.

We proceed in two ways. First we examine some of the extensive literature on spreading activation and discuss how it relates to our marker-passer. We then discuss the implications of using such a spreading activation model during planning.

1. Cognitive aspects — spreading-activation

The theoretical tradition in psychology that has given rise to the modern work in spreading activation is *associationism*. This tradition, which includes such diverse thinkers as Aristotle, the British associationist school, and the American behaviorists, holds that mental elements are associated in the mind via experience and stored in terms of some basic set of "simple" ideas. A set of rules is postulated to permit the combining of such ideas to allow for more complex associative structures. Parallelism entered associationism in the form of neural networks proposed in the 1940s as models of human cognitive processing (cf. Hebb, 1949). (A discussion of associationism and its history can be found in Anderson & Bower, 1979.)

The work of Quillian (particularly the TLC program discussed in Chapter 3, Section 2.1) is largely credited with causing a resurgence of interest in spreading activation.[1] Experiments were performed to investigate fact retrieval and priming effects in semantic memory. In this chapter we do not discuss all these results or even to enumerate the many conflicting models; instead, we review certain of these results that are suggestive in considering how the model embodied in SCRAPS might relate to certain cognitive processes.

The foci of most psychological research dealing with activation have been located in the fields of natural language comprehension and memory retrieval — not planning. This makes

---

[1] In fact, Quillian is credited with being the originator of the term.

it difficult to identify cognitive research of direct consequence to the SCRAPS program. SCRAPS' marker-passing scheme (as outlined in Chapter 6), however, does seem to correspond to some aspects of several models proposed in the psychological literature. We start, therefore, by examining the marker-passer in the light of these results and postpone discussion of the planner until the end of this chapter.

1.1. Roots

Although not designed as a cognitive model, the marker-passing system used in SCRAPS has its roots in two cognitive traditions: the spreading activation work of the early 1970s and the lexical access work that followed.

1.1.1. Spreading-activation as a memory model

In Chapter 2, Section 2.1, we described the memory program designed by Quillian in which spreading activation is a basic component. This work was designed as a computer model of human processing and sparked great interest in the psychological community. Collins and Quillian (cf. 1969; 1970) sought to expand this model and to take into account various experimental findings. This effort culminated in the model developed by Collins and Loftus (1975), which resembles our present marker-passer in several important ways.

The Collins and Loftus model was based on the same principle as the Quillian model. Activation was spread through the memory network leaving marks, nodes marked from multiple origins were detected, and paths through these nodes were reported. One defect of the Quillian model was ambiguity in the description of certain features, the new model sought to make explicit decisions based on experimental evidence.

Collins and Loftus described several features needed by an activation theory in order to take into account the experimental data they wished to model. These included:

(1) *Attenuation of marking.* As activation spread through the network, the strength of activation decreased. Activation was likened to "a signal from a source that is attenuated as it travels outward" (Collins & Loftus, 1975).

(2)   *Criterial links.* Quillian's model provided for links to have different "criterialities"; these were "numbers indicating how essential each link is to the meaning of the concept" (Collins & Loftus, 1975). Quillian's program did not make explicit use of these, but the model of Collins and Loftus did.

(3)   *Decaying links.* Activation of links decreased over time. No explicit mechanism was proposed for such a decay.

(4)   *Activation thresholds.* The assumption was made in the Collins and Loftus model that activation was a variable quality and had to reach a certain threshold before an intersection would cause a path to be reported.

Collins and Loftus also discuss some assumptions about the design of a semantic memory, the processing of memory structures, and the semantic matching process. Among these assumptions are:

(1)   *Network structure corresponds to semantic similarity.* The model assumed that the conceptual network was organized so that nodes with many properties in common would be "close" to each other — the more links between them, the closer they were.

(2)   *A network of lexical information.* It was assumed that a second network, a dictionary of lexical information, existed. This network was tied to the first by relating words to concepts. A further assumption was made that a person could control in which of the networks activation was to be spread. Thus a person could control, say, whether to prime the concepts that sound like a target word or to activate the concepts that correspond to the word's meaning.[2]

(3)   *Evaluation heuristics to determine if semantic concepts match.* The process of semantic matching is necessary for various cognitive tasks, among them "matching referents,

---

2– The model does not make it clear whether this is a "conscious" control process, although it implies that this is the case.

assigning cases, and answering questions" (Collins & Loftus, 1975). Several different rules for adding positive and negative weight to such matches were developed.

The theory as described accounted for several sets of experimental results having to do with categorization. These included experiments: testing the ability of subjects to produce instances of a category given certain conditions (Freedman & Loftus, 1973; Loftus, 1973), showing a relationship between reaction time and the number of categories a subject needed to consider (Juola & Atkinson, 1971), dealing with reaction times in an inheritance hierarchy (Conrad, 1972), and concerning typicality judgments and reaction time (Rips, Shoben & Smith, 1973; Rosch, 1973; Smith, Shoben, & Rips, 1974).[3]

1.1.2. Lexical access

The primary method used to explore the spreading of activation is the *priming* paradigm designed by Meyer and Schvaneveldt (Meyer, 1973; Meyer & Schvaneveldt, 1971; Schvaneveldt & Meyer, 1973). In this type of experiment a subject sees two strings of letters in sequential order and is asked to identify them as either words or random letters. In some cases the subject is shown two unrelated words ("nurse" followed by "butter"), in others the subject is shown related words ("bread" preceding "butter"). It is consistently found that the second word is identified more quickly in the latter case — the related concepts of the first word have apparently been "primed." These results implied an activation spreading model.

Much of the modern interest in natural language processing systems based on spreading activation (cf. Chapter 3, Section 2.3) stems from a variation of the priming methodology used in an experiment performed by Swinney (1979) to examine context effects on lexical access during sentence comprehension. Subjects heard a brief set of connected sentences while watching a display. At an appropriate time they were given a visual stimulus (a letter

---

3– See Collins & Loftus (1975) for a detailed account of these and a comparison to the contrasting semantic theory of Smith, Shoben, and Rips (1974).

string) and asked to identify it as a word or non-word. Some of these sentences set up a biasing context for the word to be seen, some did not. Further, Swinney also varied whether this context was ambiguous. The word displayed to the subjects was in one of three conditions: contextually related, contextually inappropriate, or unrelated. A sample of the experimental materials used by Swinney (1979) is shown in Inset 11.

The results obtained by Swinney show a significant effect of priming for the contextually related word in all four conditions. More interestingly, however, Swinney also found a significant priming effect for contextually inappropriate words in each of the ambiguous conditions — the strong contextual biasing did not negate this priming effect.

In a second experiment Swinney presented the same stimuli but with the visual word appearing three syllables (about 1.5 seconds) later than the Δ shown in the sample (Inset 11). In this case the ambiguous word was no longer primed. Lucas (1983) showed a facilitation still available after 100 milliseconds, while Tanenhaus, Leiman, and Seidenberg (1976) found the effect had disappeared within 200 milliseconds.[4] Thus activation appears to spread to all word senses but is followed by a rapid decay of those not contextually selected.

This result went counter to many AI models of word sense disambiguation. In these models contextual biasing had a strong interaction with lexical access — in a given context only appropriate senses were accessed. The experiments above clearly favor a model in which all word senses are activated, Other experiments (Lucas, 1983; Onifer & Swinney, 1981; Tanenhaus, Leiman, & Seidenberg, 1976) showed that similar effects occurred with other sources of ambiguity and modification with the exception of certain cases of noun-noun semantic priming (Seidenberg, Tanenhaus, Leiman, & Bienkowski, 1982). A discussion of these results can be found in (Hirst, 1983, Section

---

4– It should be noted that the materials in these two experiments were not the same. The timings are thus not strictly comparable; we cite them here to suggest a rapid decay and suggest an "order of magnitude" estimate for the result.

Δ represents the point at which the visual stimulus is presented:

AMBIGUOUS:

No context:
Rumor had it that, for years, the government building
had been plagued with problems. The man was not surprised
when he found several bugs$_\Delta$ in the corner of his
room.

Biasing context:
Rumor had it that, for years, the government building
had been plagued with problems. The man was not surprised
when he found several spiders, roaches and other
bugs$_\Delta$ in his room.

UNAMBIGUOUS:

No context:
Rumor had it that, for years, the government building
had been plagued with problems. The man was not surprised
when he found several insects$_\Delta$ in the corner of his
room.

Biasing context:
Rumor had it that, for years, the government building
had been plagued with problems. The man was not surprised
when he found several spiders, roaches and other
insects$_\Delta$ in his room.

VISUAL WORDS DISPLAYED AT Δ:
ANT (contextually related)
SPY (contextually inappropriate)
SEW (unrelated)

Inset 11: Sample of materials used by Swinney (1979).

4.3.4).

Charniak's marker-passing system (Charniak, 1983, as
discussed in Chapter 3, Section 2.3.1.) was motivated in part by
Swinney's results. In this system the marker-passer, running in

parallel with a syntactic mechanism, activates the various senses of a word as it is perceived, before the effects of context are taken into account. Paths between these senses are found and examined by a path-checking mechanism that can utilize the contextual information. The senses that provide the best fit with each other are preferred (see also Hirst, 1983). Such a model can account for Swinney's results. Another model taking into account Swinney's result is the connectionist word access model of Cottrell (1985).[5]

1.2. ACT*

Before continuing with our discussion of the cognitive aspects of SCRAPS, we need to consider a different approach to marker-passing: Anderson's ACT* model (Anderson, 1983). Whereas the work of Quillian, Collins and Loftus, and Swinney leads to models with similar properties to the marker-passer in SCRAPS, Anderson's program uses an alternative basis. Instead of viewing activation as a discrete flow of marks spreading outward from an origin, it is seen as an energy state of the nodes of a network; thus activation of a memory element corresponds to the level of energy on a node.

In this model the memory is seen as a set of weighted links between concepts. Nodes have an activation level based on the activation levels of their neighbors and the strengths of the connections between them. This level is mathematically determined via a set of equations that set the network to be in a stable state. The equations used correspond to a set of differential equations that includes factors such as activation level of nodes, strength of connectivity to the neighbors, time delays in transmission of information, rate of decay of activation, and the time factors involved in the equation. After the network is disturbed, a new state of equilibrium is reached, which represents a new set of activation strengths. (The interested reader should see Anderson, 1983).

The primary difference between this model and the other is that there is no longer anything corresponding to "intersections"

5– More discussion of Hirst's and Cottrell's models is covered in Chapter 9.

and "paths." When activation energy is added to the network a spreading effect does occur, but it no longer has the breadth-first behavior of the previous models. If energy is added at several points the whole network adjusts to reach a new stable state. One cannot tell which activations of a given node were caused by which specific inputs. The notion of intersection finding and path evaluation thus becomes meaningless.[6]

In Anderson's model activation roughly corresponds to the ease with which a node in memory can be accessed — the higher the energy, the easier to retrieve. The most activated nodes are considered to correspond to working memory, the others are viewed as long-term memory which can be accessed, but not as quickly. This is quite a different notion of memory from that used in the models discussed previously. While those models do consider the network to be the long-term memory, activation is viewed as a memory process disjoint from the issue of short-term or working memory. In this, the marker-passer in SCRAPS corresponds to the earlier models, not to ACT*.[7]

There are also several other interesting differences between the ACT* model and the earlier activation models in terms of the structure of the proposed memories. Anderson's system stores much information in the form of production rules that are brought to bear when the activation energies on the nodes corresponding to working memory elements reaches certain levels. While this has many cognitive implications, the issues relevant to viewing marker-passing as a cognitive process are those already described. The reader wishing to find out more about this model of cognitive processing should refer to Anderson (1983) and the work on the SOAR model of memory (Rosenbloom, Laird, Newell, & Orciuch, 1984).

6– Pearl (1985) has worked on finding.paths and intersections in such networks. While his networks don't directly correspond to Anderson's model, they are close enough to be suggestive.

7– It is interesting, however, to consider the marked nodes in SCRAPS using Anderson's view. Some speculation along these lines, and a brief proposal for some near-future research, are found in Section 3.5 of the Conclusion, Chapter 11.

1.3. Scraps as a spreading-activation model

The model of marker-passing used in SCRAPS has some similarities with the spreading activation models proposed by Collins and Loftus and others. In this section we discuss how the marker-passing algorithms discussed in Chapter 6 relate to the spreading activation theories described so far. But first, two short digressions.

1.3.1. Digression — neurophysiology

One of the primary differences between Anderson's model and the Collins and Loftus model (hereafter the C&L model)[8] is in how well they correspond to known neurophysiology. Neurons seem best modeled by networks of connecting cells with weights between them and energy spreading over them. Modern thinking holds that the stable states of such networks correspond to ideas and thought. The C&L model has no direct correspondence to this sort of structure, while Anderson's model is at least somewhat consistent with it.

It might seem, at first glance, that the SCRAPS model falls somewhere in between these two. The marker-passer appears to use the spreading model of C&L while being built out of massively parallel components that seem to resemble some sort of neurological elements. A closer look, however, shows that this is not the case.

The problem with viewing our form of marker-passing as a neurological model is that the nodes in our network do not correspond to neurons. To make this correspondence would require claiming that our frames correspond directly to neurons — a conjecture not consonant with present knowledge of neurophysiology. Further, the type of processors we need to perform the massively parallel marker-passing do not match the

---

8– In this section we ignore the differences between the various spreading-activation models and lump them all together under the Collins and Loftus name. See Lorch (1982) for a comparison of the models of Collins and Loftus and Anderson (1976), Hayes-Roth (1977), and Meyer and Schvaneveldt (1971). See also Granger, Eiselt and Holbrook (1984) for a discussion of a more recent spreading activation model.

functions presently attributed to neurons.[9] It seems fatuous to claim marker-passing, even in the most parallel form we've discussed, as a direct model of human neural processing. Why then consider it as a cognitive model at all?

One answer to this is to consider the possibility that something like marker-passing, and in fact the various symbolic levels of processing used in traditional AI work, are high-level descriptions of the cognitive processes taking place in the neurons of the brain. These descriptions, however, are inadequate for talking about the lower level processes that may be taking place. Further, as massive parallelism and connectionist models are developed, new metaphors for describing these lower level cognitive processes, perhaps even the actual neurological level processes themselves, are needed.

The marker-passing process we are examining still functions on the symbolic level descriptions we in AI have developed for modeling higher level functioning. The marker-passer itself, however, is a step down — it is a mechanism that uses the symbolic descriptions as "data" and finds paths through this data. The path evaluator, on the other hand, is a traditional symbolic mechanism. Thus, our work focuses on examining processes within the traditional framework, rather than on defining or examining the lower level. The best hope we can hold for such a model is that it corresponds to the higher-level processing built on top of the neural hardware.[10] In the rest of this chapter we assume that whatever resemblances may exist between the marker-passer and human spreading activation behavior are found at this higher level and not "in the hardware."

1.3.2. Digression 2 — automatic- *vs.* effortful-priming

Psychologists generally believe that there are two processes involved in the spreading of activation in memory. The first of these is an automatic spread of activation (ASA), which is done

---

9– These processors would be able to perform the "mark" and "report-to" function and to contain local memory in which the marking information was stored. Neurons don't seem to be built in a way to correspond with any of these.

10– One of the first steps in this regard is the work of Touretsky and Hinton (1985) towards modeling production systems in a distributed connectionist model.

without conscious control. The second is a conscious processing, often associated with an attention mechanism.[11] The automatic priming starts quickly and falls away. The conscious process starts prior to this "fall" and continues after the automatic effect stops.

If we are to use SCRAPS as a cognitive model, there is only one view of it that fits this time ordering: marking, path reporting, and path strength computation together form the "automatic" mechanism, and path evaluation is the conscious processing. Any effort to account for SCRAPS as a psychological model needs this distinction, so we assume it to hold in the rest of this chapter, even though the only model of SCRAPS presented so far which could account for such a decomposition is the massively parallel version presented in Chapter 7.

1.3 (continued) SCRAPS as a Spreading Activation Model

The marker-passer presented in Chapter 6 was not formulated to be a cognitive model. It does, however, bear close relation to some of the spreading activation models proposed in the cognitive literature (especially the C&L model). At this point we consider the implications of using this marker-passer as such a model. To do this we shall go through various of the marker-passing issues presented in the earlier chapter and see where our model corresponds to, falls short of, or has possible implications for the design of such cognitive models.

1.3.3. Weighted links

Various experiments have produced results indicating that priming effects and categorization judgments are facilitated when the objects coupled have high "typicality" relations with each other. As an example, Wilkins (1971) found a faster reaction time when judgments were made between objects that were more typical of the category (for instance "robin" and "bird") than those less

---

11- This idea was put forth by Neisser (1967) in regards to various cognitive processes and examined in regard to activation (cf. Posner, 1978; Posner & Snyder, 1975; Shiffrin & Snyder, 1977). It has also been discussed with respect to the development of expertise (Larkin, 1981).

typical ("goose" and "bird").[12] Other research (Becker, 1980; Fischler & Goodman, 1978; Lorch, 1982; Massaro, Jones, Lipscomb, & Scholz, 1978; Myers & Lorch, 1980; Ratcliff & McKoon, 1981; Rosch, 1975; Sanford, Garrod & Boyle, 1977) showed a similar effect in priming studies: Priming facilitation was greater when the prime and the probe were strongly associated.

Two general models have been offered to explain this kind of typicality effect. Anderson's model represents typicality directly in the links between nodes. In his model nodes may be connected via links of various weights. Thus "sparrow" can be connected to "bird" with a high weight and "goose" with a lower weight. When energy is added to a node the associated nodes are activated according to such weights.

The C&L model uses a notion of semantic similarity to correspond to weights. Instead of various types of links between nodes, the number of similar properties shared by two nodes determines how "far apart" they are in the memory. Closeness facilitates activation spreading in such a network. In this model "sparrow" would have more properties in common with the prototypical "bird" than would "goose," and thus "sparrow" would prime "bird" more than "goose" would.

In Chapter 6, Section 2.3.2 we discussed the issues involved in adding weighted links to a marker-passer and remarked that no such weights were presently used in our marker-passer. While this provides a "cleaner" model, since no *ad hoc* assignment of weights need be done, it is directly contradicted by the experimental evidence described here. Lack of such weights is a major shortcoming in our system in terms of its direct correlation to cognitive processing, and weights would have to be added before such a claim could begin to be made.

1.3.4. Attenuation

While all of the models of spreading activation proposed have some sort of attenuation limit, either explicit, as in C&L, or

---

12- This result was reproduced and generalized by Rips, Shoben & Smith, (1973), Rosch (1973) and Smith, Shoben, & Rips (1974).

implicit, as in Anderson, little research has been done to determine how this attenuation behaves or whether, in fact, it exists at all. Attenuation is necessary in a computational model of activation, but its cognitive effect has not really been studied.

One experiment to examine the range of activation spreading was performed by DeGroot (1983). As in most priming studies, subjects were shown paired words, except here the words used were sometimes unrelated except via intermediate nodes.[13] As an example, subjects might be sometimes be shown the word "milk" and tested with the word "bull" (since "milk" is highly associated with "cow," which in turn is highly associated with "bull"). At other times the words would be highly related ("cow" and "milk") or unrelated ("cow" and "sew"). Her results showed a significant effect of priming of highly associated items versus intermediately associated items and unrelated items, implying that little or no priming was occurring between these others. DeGroot concluded that only immediate neighbors were primed.

DeGroot's result is encouraging in that it does show an attenuation effect, but a little discouraging in that the attenuation occurs so quickly. Neither the C&L model or the Anderson model would appear to account for such attenuation.

A counter to this is to point out that the DeGroot experiment showed a significant effect only when the priming stimulus was applied with a stimulus onset asynchrony (SOA)[14] of 240ms or less.[15] Given this short SOA, the C&L model can be saved by saying that the activation may not yet have had time to reach the later nodes: the probe "bull," say, might be occurring before activation from "milk" has had a chance to reach "bull." This is particularly possible given the C&L assumption that the amount of activation at node ("cow") must reach a certain level before it is passed on. Thus, the short SOAs needed to get the result might be biasing the effect.

13– Paired association data was used to form the basis of relatedness judgments.

14– The time between stimulus and target.

15– When SOA is short, the subject is considered not to have time for "conscious" processing to occur. Thus, short SOA times are used to probe for differences between ASA and non-automatic effects.

If one uses the Anderson model, a different explanation would hold. In this case the short SOA corresponds to less energy being added to the network at the "milk" node. The effect of this on the network is therefore less and the amount of extra activation energy reaching the "bull" node is lessened.

In our marker-passer we would explain these experimental results in terms of our attenuation mechanism. The short SOA could be said to correspond to a small amount of zorch in the massively parallel model, where zorch is equal to the time (see Chapter 6, Section 3.4). In such a system a short SOA lessens the spread of activation. Thus, the lack of spreading found by DeGroot would be explained as a lack of zorch resulting from the short SOA.

Notice, however, that this explanation requires that our mechanism be a correlate to the attenuation process in the human cognitive system. For this to be the case we would need to make a strong claim: Each frame must have a unique representation and facts known about such frames must correspond to links between them. Essentially we need to claim that memory directly corresponds to the sort of associative network on which our zorch mechanism operates.

This claim, while not directly falsifiable, is stronger than that made in the literature for either the C&L model or the others. The C&L models represent frames as being interrelated via a "semantic relatedness" relationship — the more properties they have in common, the greater the semantic relatedness. Notice, however, that this claim does not say that these relationships are directly modeled as links in the system. Activation spreads between nodes as a result of the semantic relatedness, not based on the individual links. (For example, although fire engines are related to roses via the node for "red,"[16] activation would not

---

16- The C&L model was proposed at a time when the prototypical fire engine was red. In the decade since the paper was written fire companies have been increasingly using white, lime green, yellow, and other bright colors for their engines. *Sic transit gloria mundi.*

spread from one to the other due to their lack of relatedness.[17])

Thus, while not necessarily wrong, the SCRAPS model requires a strong assumption to be taken seriously in this regard.

1.3.5. Mark decay

Lexical access experiments have reliably shown a decay of priming strength over time. One particular result is that, although all senses of a word appear to be activated, those word senses that are not correct for either syntactic or semantic reasons show a rapid lessening of activation strength.[18] ASA appears to reach a high level quickly and then either decay rapidly or be actively supressed by the competing word senses. The preferred word senses gain activation from the non-automatic processes and therefore stay primed.

In the ACT* program this decay effect is modeled mathematically. Links lose activation exponentially over time, accounting for the decay in ASA. Selection of a node for processing returns activation to that node and this activation keeps it selected until the node is no longer used. At that point the decay function takes precedence and the node's activation decays.

The C&L model does not describe the decay process in detail — the model was developed before most of the work discussing such an effect. The authors do, however, state, "Activation decreases over time and/or intervening activity. This is a noncommital assumption that activation goes away gradually by some mechanism" (Collins & Loftus, 1975, p. 411). They thus take into account, however briefly, the notion of intervening activity — the non-automatic processes.

17– This might seem to be a direct explanation for DeGroot's effect. Though "milk" and "bull" both relate to "cow," they have few properties in common and are therefore of distant relatedness. I hesitate, however, to use this argument since it may not be true of the other materials used in the experiment. Also, DeGroot does show large priming effects between each of the paired words and the intermediary (i.e., between "cow-bull" and "cow-milk"). Therefore, we would conclude that these words were close to the central node. It is hard to design a model in which two entities can be close to a third while far from each other.

18– See Seidenberg (1985) for a comprehensive discussion of the time course of activation discovered in the lexical access studies.

In proposing SCRAPS as a model we cannot make this type of simplifying assumption. We pointed out in Section 3.2 that the only decomposition of SCRAPS fitting the time profile for ASA and non-automatic processing is to have path evaluation count as the "conscious" process. This means that the path evaluator is required to keep those nodes in successful paths activated. At present there is no mechanism such as this in the path evaluators used by either SCRAPS or Charniak's natural language system. This too would need to be added before we could propose that SCRAPS could be seen as a cognitive model.

1.3.6. Order effects

Freedman and Loftus (1971) performed an experiment in which subjects were asked to produce instances fitting a property and a category. The property was given as an adjective ("name a fruit which is red") or as a letter to start the instance with ("name a fruit beginning with the letter 'a'"). Subjects showed faster reaction times when the category was offered prior to the descriptor ("name a fruit which is red") than when the order was reversed ("name something red which is a fruit"). This effect was significant for both the adjectives and the initial letters. Can our model account for this result?

There are only two mechanisms in our system that might cause such a result: The path strength mechanism could assign different values to the paths found in the different directions, or one-way links could be involved causing marking to proceed faster in one direction than the other. Unfortunately, neither of these mechanism can be used to account for the determined effect.

The path strength heuristic has no feature that changes with order. Path strength relies only on the nodes marked, the strength of the marks at the intersection, and the branchout of the nodes on the path. Order does not affect any of these. A path from "X" to "Y" has the same strength as the path from "Y" to "X" traversing the same nodes.

The one-way links explanation is even worse: such links predict exactly the opposite behavior from the one observed. Consider the case in which we wish to find the connection between "fruit" and the adjective "sour." In our system a mark from "sour" reaches "lemon" via an assertion like (**Taste-of lemon sour**). Following this we would mark "fruit" via (**ISA lemon fruit**). Thus "sour" primes "fruit" via the path through "lemon." When the category is given, the mark is already there, the path is quickly computed, and the reaction time is small.

If, on the other hand, we are given "fruit" first, "lemon" is not marked since the path requires traversing an ISA link in the wrong direction. Instead, when "sour" was heard the marking would proceed as previously and only then would the path be found. Thus "sour – fruit" is predicted to be faster than "fruit – sour" — the opposite of the result found.

Our marker-passer simply cannot account for this result.

1.3.7. Activating links

Another feature of our model is the fact that only nodes are marked. Traversing a link does not correspond to marking a fact — we solely mark the frames involved, not the assertions relating them. This differs from one of the basic assumptions of the C&L model. Thus, in our model we do not provide for marks intersecting at an assertion, only at a node. For example, if two different rules implied that "Clyde is an elephant" our model would provide for paths meeting at CLYDE, or at ELEPHANT, but not at (ISA CLYDE ELEPHANT).

In Anderson's model each of the nodes in memory is linked to other nodes in what is called "production memory." This production memory is a set of "if-then" rules which are run when all of the "if" clauses are active. It is the firing of these rules that corresponds to observable behavior. If we activate various nodes in memory these cause the activation energy of various of the rules in production memory to increase. When the activation energy on one of these rules is high enough that production is run.

In this model there is nothing that corresponds one-to-one with our links between frames. Any node can be activating a whole set of productions that are unrelated to each other. When one fires we cannot say "this rule fired because of this node"; instead, we must take into account the state of the network. Thus, in Anderson's model the question "are links primed?" is meaningless.

In the C&L model marking proceeds as it did in Quillian: A node is marked, the links from this node are then marked, the nodes reached by these links are marked, and so on until either an intersection is found or a limit is reached. The reason for this is that in Quillian's system the links themselves count as concepts, ones which have a close semantic relatedness with the elements in each.

No experimental evidence is given by Quillian or C&L to justify this marking — it is simply offered as necessary to Quillian's model. In our system we do no such marking. The algorithm is more efficient without it, in terms of space and number of marking operations. Any serious attempt to use our marker-passer as a model of cognition would need to resolve this issue.

1.3.8. Zorch

Another paradigm for examining memory retrieval is the *fact retrieval paradigm* (cf. Anderson, 1974; Hayes-Roth, 1977; King & Anderson, 1976; Lewis & Anderson, 1976; Thorndyke & Bower, 1974). In these experiments subjects are asked to tell whether or not they recognize a fact that was either previously known or learned in the experiment. As an example, a subject was expected to recognize a fact like "Hank Aaron hit home runs" and reject a fact like "Hank Aaron came from India."

A consistent finding in these experiments is that the more facts presented about a topic, the slower is the recognition of any one of these facts (usually referred to as the "fan" effect). The C&L model does not account for this result; the ACT* program models it directly in the equations used for activation spread.

This effect can be explained by the marker-passer used in SCRAPS, and seems to fit well with our notion of zorch and our path strength computation. If more facts pertain to a frame, the zorch is divided by a greater branching factor. The path strength computation therefore yields a lower value corresponding (if we are using marker-passing as a cognitive model) to activation energy. The fewer facts presented about a subject the greater the path strength returned when one of the facts causes a path to be marked, and thus the shorter the time needed to find it.

1.4. Is our marker-passer a cognitive model?

In the previous sections we've shown that the marker-passer

(1) Doesn't correspond to a neurophysiological model.

(2) Doesn't account for the differences between ASA and non-automatic priming.

(3) Doesn't handle weighted links.

(4) Requires strong assumptions about the internal representation used in memory.

(5) Cannot account for the time course of activation experimentally determined.

(6) Cannot account for order effects between primes and probes.

(7) Doesn't mark links or facts, only frames in memory.

This offers pretty overwhelming evidence that the marker-passer used in SCRAPS is not very useful as a direct cognitive model. What then has been the value of this exercise?

Psychological results seem to indicate clearly the existence of weighted links and order effects. While we have not yet added these to our marker-passer, we are presently examining these to see how they would benefit our model. The marker-passer in SCRAPS doesn't seem to need them for the problem-solving behaviors we've examined, but they may be of use for some of the extensions to our system proposed in the future work section of the Conclusion (Chapter 11).

Our model does, however, seem to correspond, if not directly, with the cognitive models presented. Our spread of activation seems similar to that of the C&L model, and our zorch and path strength models seem to have some correspondence with Anderson's weighted links. Given such correspondences, even if they are not one-to-one, the models do indicate directions in which other researchers might look. For example, our attenuation and path-strength mechanisms offers a tentative explanation of the fan effect in a C&L-like model. While this explanation requires assumptions not currently found in such a model, it might indicate a direction in which to look for an interesting result.

More than this, the natural language work described in Chapter 3 and the planning research described in this book on planning offer some possible directions in examining the use of such an activation model. In the remainder of this chapter we examine whether the planning mechanism proposed might have psychological implications.

2. Cognitive aspects — planning

In the previous chapters we have presented a theory of planning that involves a spreading activation system as a major component. This component is important from a computational viewpoint; might it actually serve as a cognitive model? Assuming that we were to use a "cognitively correct" marker-passer, would the model in SCRAPS be testable?

Cognitive psychologists have done very little work exploring choice decisions during planning. Byrne (1977) examined protocols of people asked to plan elaborate meals. The results indicated that people made choices by selecting bindings for various variables in a meal schema. Choices involved figuring out if the current bindings were consistent with other bindings and with making choices between existing bindings.

Barsalou (1985, personal communication) has also performed protocol analyses of human planning behavior. Subjects were asked to plan vacations and their protocols were examined. Results show that people plan based on constraints imposed by their environment. Variables such as "where to go on vacation" are constrained by information such as "little money is available."

These results are consistent with the overall model proposed by SCRAPS, although not weighing heavily in its favor. In the rest of this chapter we propose some possible outlines for experiments that could be performed to examine planning based on a SCRAPS-like model.

2.1. Flags

The first component of SCRAPS not seen in other planning theories is the mutual interaction between the activation algorithm and the deductive processes. Other models include a marker-passer that provides information to a deductive mechanism, but none of these provide for the reverse. In SCRAPS this interaction occurs via the flag mechanism. A node in memory can be set up in such a way that it is noticed by the spreading activation mechanism — just as if it were activated by the marker-passer itself.

Among the set of flags proposed, PERCEPTUAL flags would be easiest to test experimentally. According to our theory, items in the percetual environment are activated in a way such that the spreading activation mechanism can take advantage of them. This would predict that they can cause priming effects. Retrieval time of facts and reaction time in word experiments should be shorter for items being encountered by the subject. Thus, for example, reaction time should be shorter to recognize the letter string "desk" by a subject sitting at a desk than by a subject sitting near a table.[19]

A second testable element is the existence of the long-term activation that is predicted by nonperceptual flags. In our model, facts such as "the air traffic controllers are on strike" must activate nodes in such a way that the marker-passer can find paths reaching them. Our model predicts that such activation not only differs from the normal time course, but lasts until explicit information removes the activation. The appropriate concepts in memory should show activation effects even after long time periods (SOAs of minutes or days rather than milliseconds). Such an effect should be testable in a laboratory setting.

2.1.1. Examining choices

Our model predicts that paths found via the marker-passer will be considered by the choice mechanism before those which are not examined. This means that we should see an observable difference in the choices made if different biasing clues are used. Further, in the presence of a biasing stimulus, paths other than the default path may be tried first. A testable experimental hypothesis is

---

19– Beiderman, Glass, and Stacy (1973) have done some work indirectly related to this. In these experiments elements of scenes are recognized differently depending on features having to do with how they relate to their normal positions. Items out of place are found more quickly than the same items in their usual positions. This work seems to indicate some type of relation between perceptual cues and the activation and/or attention mechanisms.

that activation energy at a frame will bias toward a choice that has a path using that node. This should occur even when that activation is placed by the automatic spreading activation mechanism. Thus, we should be able to bias planning via the ASA.

A simple experimental design would be to use the equivalent of short SOAs in a planning event. The basic idea would be to flash a biasing word (say "gun") at a speed where it could have a subliminal effect only. Spreading activation theory predicts that this would make the ASA cause at least a small amount of activation. If we now asked the subject to generate a plan, the one involving this node should be chosen ("suicide" planning should result in a "shoot self" plan being proposed). When we use an "unrelated" bias ("moose" should not bias a "suicide" planner), default plans would be used.

2.1.2. Debugging incorrect paths

Another prediction based on our theory is the existence of what we might call "garden-path" plans:[20] Situations in which a planner chooses an incorrect path when biased via extraneous information. This seems plausible enough from anecdotal evidence. A person who has just lost his or her wallet might well, when hungry, think "Gee, I can't go to a restaurant" — even if she or he had no previous intention of doing so. The problematic path seems to be preferred. In fact, one often sees people debugging incorrect plans, rather than backing up and using a more correct one (deciding to borrow money instead of using an alternative means to satisfy hunger).

This sort of behavior should be observable in a controlled setting. One can set up a situation that forms a negative bias ("the air traffic controllers are on strike") and ask subjects to plan an event that interacts with it ("take a trip"). The hypothesis is that subjects will consider the incorrect path rather than the path

---

20– Here we use the term as natural language researchers do for "garden-path" sentences: those in which the reader must back up in the processing after making an erroneous parse. An example would be: "I saw the Statue of Liberty entering the harbor."

that might normally be used.[21]

3. Conclusion

While the marker-passer in SCRAPS is not a psychologically valid model, we hold out more hope for the theoretical principles involved in SCRAPS. Our model offers yet another rationale for the existence of spreading activation — to improve the choice mechanism used in planning situations. However, this said, it must be noted that the details of our mechanism are motivated by computational considerations, not cognitive modeling. I believe that our model might suggest an approach to psychologists interested in planning and in uses of activation. I certainly do not propose it as the definitive psychological model.

21– Before I am accused of psychological naivete, let me point out that such a situation would be difficult to set up without careful work. The existence of the negative information, if not carefully controlled, might allow an alternate hypothesis like "subjects want to use the information they've been told." I leave the design of such an experiment as an exercise for the psychologically inclined reader.

CHAPTER 9

On Marker-passing and connectionism

Nonsense and beauty have close connections.
— Edward M. Forster, *The Longest Journey [1907]*

One obvious question about this work is how it is related to the field of connectionism — some have accused it of having a connectionist air, others have disdained it for being purely symbolic. In this chapter we compare this work to several connectionist models in an effort to help answer that question.

One difficulty in writing a chapter such as this is that *connectionism* has become a very broad and poorly defined term. In its inclusive form connectionism includes work in neurophysiology, operations research and engineering, parallel computer architectures, cognitive science, and mathematical network models. This chapter does not attempt to provide any sort of comprehensive overview of the field.[1] Instead, we identify some common features of connectionist models and examine how our model compares. We also examine some specific examples of connectionist systems aimed at solving problems similar to those SCRAPS faces.

1. Themes

In searching for a working definition of connectionist models five main themes can be found: neurophysiological plausibility, learning, activation energy spreading over a network of excitation and inhibition arcs, local computations designed for massively parallel architectures, and distributed representations. Most models branded as connectionist show more than one of these

---

[1] We highly recommend Rumelhart & McClelland, 1986 to the reader looking for a more definitive reference.

themes, although few, if any, show all of them. It is these themes we use in examining how the marker-passing model of SCRAPS compares with connectionist models.

1.1. Neurophysiological plausibility

Connectionist models are often based on an attempt to have the computer model match, on an architectural level, a neurologically plausible model of the human brain. Some component of the model is identified as being a lot like the cortical tissue (cf. Colvin, Tromp, & Eeckman, 1986) while some other is, perhaps, compared to a "pyramidal cell" (Parker, 1986) or other component of the brain. This work is motivated to a large degree by comparisons in which it is shown that the architecture of the human brain is significantly different than that of a sequential digital computer. (An oft-cited work describing these differences is Crick, 1979).

We really don't have much to say on this issue. We have previously shown that the marker-passer in SCRAPS appears not to have any significance as a plausible neuron level model (Chapter 8, Section 1.3.1). Further, we have little to say on whether connectionist models do any better. This is still very much a live research topic, and the interested reader is directed to the large body of work discussing this issue (including, but not limited to, the aforementioned Rumelhart and McClelland (1986) and Crick (1979) and the work of Feldman and Ballard (1982)).

1.2. Learning

We also have very little to say on the matter of the theme of learning. Our model of marker-passing has been formulated with no thought to the process of acquisition of the knowledge in memory. Connectionist models, on the other hand, have often used learning as a primary motivation. This has included the design of theoretical machines (for example, the Boltzmann machine; Fahlman, Hinton, & Sejnowski, 1983) and learning algorithms (for example, back propogation; cf. Rumelhart, Hinton,& Williams, 1986) as well as the development of systems that have performed fairly complex learning tasks (for example, the NETtalk system of Sejnowski and Rosenberg, 1986, which has been trained to do a fairly good job of producing speech from text[2]). The interested reader is directed to the works cited above.

1.3. Excitatory and inhibitory links

One theme that can be found in many connectionist models is that of passing some type of activation over a set of arcs, and examining the activation of the nodes connected by these arcs. By examining the behavior of such networks, and finding out how various inputs relate to various node activations, it is possible to create computer models performing memory-retrieval type tasks. This notion of a discrete spreading appears primarily in local connectionist models, although weighted arcs are also of crucial importance to distributed connectionist systems (as we discuss in Section 1.5). Here we discuss this notion and show how it is used in several connectionist systems.

Local connectionist models generally assume that each node in memory corresponds to a specific concept — we could have a single node for CLYDE, a single node for ELEPHANT, etc. (Distributed connectionist models represent these concepts as patterns of activation over sets of nodes, as discussed below.) These nodes are connected to each other via links that cause either inhibition or excitation between the connected nodes. In most of these models the links encode purely numerical information about the relationship, rather than about semantic relations between the concepts (although, as we'll see when we discuss the work of Shastri in Section 1.4.1.1, this is not necessarily the case). Thus, a typical local connectionist network might look like that shown in Figure 29, which represents the relations between the letters A, C, H, and T and the words CAT and HAT. We see from this network that A and T reinforce both words, C reinforces CAT but inhibits HAT, and H does the reverse.

One key feature of these networks is the manner in which inhibition and reinforcement work. Some systems use a simple binary scheme in which nodes are either on or off, while other systems use a numerical weighting system to represent the amount

---

2– We discuss this system in more detail later in this chapter.

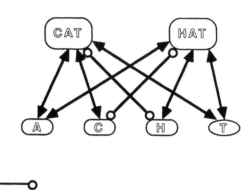

INHIBITORY

EXCITORY

Figure 29: A simple "local connectionist" network.

of inhibition and excitation energy to spread.

McClelland and Rumelhart (1981) proposed a model of word recognition based on letter orthography using a complex network similar to that of Figure 29. Figure 30 shows a section of the network they used. The nodes in this system represented components of letters, letters, and words. Unlike the ACT* model (described in Chapter 8), their model didn't simulate the spreading of activation via a set of differential equations, but rather had the activation spread over time. Thus, if a node was activated at time N, it's neighbors were activated at time $N+1$, their neighbors at time $N+2$, and so on. Similarly, those links representing inhibition caused a weakening of their neighbors at time $N+1$, and so on. The activation of a given node at time $N+i$ was thus based on the activation strengths of its neighbors at time $N+(i-1)$, where those neighbors with inhibitory connections were treated as negative weights. Over time, some node, or set of nodes, became the most highly activated. This node was "the winner," the node representing the correct word composed of these letters.

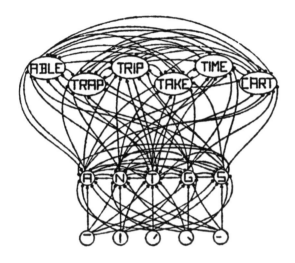

Figure 30: An example of a more complex connectionist network.
From (McClelland and Rumelhart, 1981).

The approach of using weighted arcs is similar but activation spread becomes proportional to arc strength. Thus, in Figure 31 we see the network of Figure 29 with some numeric weights thrown in. If we now activate the letters C, A, and T, then the word CAT is activated with a strength of 1, while HAT is activated with a strength of .1 (two positive weights of .3 added to one negative weight of .5). The initial setting of these weights, the rules for combination (addition, multiplication, various formulae), the directionality of the links (are they symmetric or not), and the connectivity of the network (is everything connected or only some items), as well as the initial set of nodes, are some of the main features differentiating the various models.

One example of the many systems that use a spread of activation over numerically weighted nodes is the BACAS system of Sharkey, Sutcliffe, and Wobcke (1986). which is designed to act

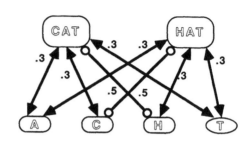

Figure 31: Adding numeric information to a connectionist system.

as a memory for a natural language processing system. The system, which is composed of several different network layers and various types of time-outs, performs a script recognition type task, picking the appropriate context based on a set of inputs representing events. Thus, this system might see a representation of "Sam waited in line, paid some money, and bought some popcorn" and conclude that the GOING-TO-THE-MOVIES frame is active.

The BACAS system is composed of two primary layers, the *micro-layer*, that consists of a set of units which correspond to individual events, and a *macro-layer*, corresponding to the frames being recognized. The various units are connected via weighted arcs, both positive and negative. Thus, GOING-TO-THE-MOVIES might be negatively linked to RESTUARANT so that if one frame is active the other is supressed. One interesting feature of the BACAS model is that different types of links have different types of activation spreading behavior. The micro-layer uses a continuous activation spreading, like that of the McClelland and Rumelhart model, while the macro-level uses thresholded binary outputs: As soon as a particular unit in the macro-level reaches some threshold activation, it changes its behavior, primarily by doing more active suppression of its neighbors.

The systems described above work by finding highly activated nodes and recognizing them as somehow special — an idea which seems similar to our notion of marker-passing in SCRAPS, The details, however, are clearly very different. We have already discussed the lack of weighted links in SCRAPS (Chapter 8). Our marker-passer treats all links the same, with the exception of the "one way" links. Thus, this is already one major difference between our system and that of Sharkey and the like.

Another, and probably more important, difference between the model in SCRAPS and the local connectionist models described above, and in fact most local connectionist models, is the lack of inhibitory links in our system. Nowhere in SCRAPS is there a notion corresponding to a node inhibiting another — marking a node never prevents another node from being marked. Could the inhibitory behaviors needed to create "winner take all" networks be simulated without explicit inhibitory links?

Reggia (1986) proposes a model of competitive activation that does produce such a virtual lateral inhibition. In his system the spread of activation from a node varies according to the amount of activation already occuring on the neighbors it activates. Thus, when a node passes activation to previously unactivated nodes it activates them according solely to the weights on the links to these nodes. If, on the other hand, the nodes are already activated, the amount of new activation is a function based on the weights of the links and the amount of previous activation — the more activation already on a neighbor, the more it gets.[3] This scheme has been shown to produce the same behaviors as having explicit inhibitory links: stable

---

3– The exact form of these functions is still being worked out by Reggia and his students. Reggia, Milheim and Freeman (1986) present a comparitive study of various different additive and multiplicative functions for computing the activation of the neighbors.

coalitions, winner take all networks, and context effects. Thus, Reggia produces inhibitory effects without explicit inhibition effects. How does this relate to the model in SCRAPS?

Clearly, this type of model is still not like the marker-passer in SCRAPS — there is no direct correspondence between them. Yet, it appears that there is some similarity between the goals of Reggia's system, producing stronger and weaker activation based on neighboring nodes, and our notion of path strength. Our goal is to have some paths, rather than some nodes, be chosen for earlier examination than others. If we postulate a "race condition" between the problem solver and the path evaluator (where those paths evaluated before a choice correspond to the winners of the race), then a higher path zorch means a better chance of winning.

At the moment, however, the use of a mechanism more like Reggia's is still far from what we have implemented in SCRAPS. Again, weighted links and value-passing activation are a different approach than the one we've chosen. Further, the mechanism in SCRAPS is based on the notion of finding paths, rather than individual nodes. The local connectionist models focus on the finding of individual network elements, rather than paths through the network. If we activate BUYING and CLEAVER our model returns a path that includes the inference rule causing the problem (the WEAPONS and WEAPONS-CHECK rule) whereas a connectionist model might activate only a single node. If that node is the inference rule we seek, then we would be okay, but if not (say the node BUYING wins out), then we would have gained little.

We are, however, looking into the creation of a model partially combining the ideas of Reggia with ours. If a network such as his could somehow activate all and only the nodes corresponding to a path having a high path zorch, then possibly we could create a different form of path evaluator, or even a smart marker-passer, which could check such "paths." For now, however, this idea is fairly speculative. Thus, at least for the near future, we must say that in relation to the theme of passing values over weighted arcs SCRAPS is clearly different than these local connectionist models.

1.4. Massive parallelism

One of the driving motivations of many connectionist models is the exploitation of massive parallelism. Connectionist models take parallelism as a given, and "use it to guide the search for interesting solutions in the space of possible solutions" (Shastri, 1985). This assumption is made for efficiency considerations and/or cognitive reasons — massive parallelism appears to be a good model for many cognitive functions. This involves designs of systems for specific theoretical machines (for example, Feldman & Ballard, 1982), and for actual systems such as the Connection Machine.

In Chapter 6 we presented the psuedocode for a local computation algorithm for marker-passing, in Chapter 7 we presented the outline of a design for running the marker-passer on the massively parallel connection machine. Does this then mean our system is, at least in this dimension, like the connectionists?

The answer appears to us to be "yes and no." On the plus side we clearly do care about efficiency considerations and about massively parallel systems, but on the "no" side is the fact that we view only one part of our system, the marker-passer, as being the massively parallel component. The true connectionist tries to put more, and usually *all*, of the functionality into the networks. What serial processing there is is used, at best, for providing switching and/or gating and control of a network's processing.

It may be, however, that as in the previous section, a future version of SCRAPS could be designed to put far more functionality into the massively-parallel component. We take this opportunity to present some current systems relating directly to our model, and examine some of the differences.

1.4.1. Some Massively Parallel Models of Relevance to SCRAPS

In this section we consider whether more than just the marker-passer of SCRAPS could be moved into a massively parallel system. We present several systems that are of relevance to ours and discuss implications for potential future versions of SCRAPS. In particular, we examine three systems: an evidential reasoning model (Shastri, 1985) and a natural language processing program

(Cottrell, 1985) both designed at the University of Rocheter, and a planning model (Blelloch, 1986) designed for a connection machine.

1.4.1.1. Two works from Rochester.

The Rochester Computer Science Department has done research in using connectionist models for vision, motor control, natural language, knowledge representation and inference, and simulation.[4] We discuss two of these that both give an example of the approach used and also relate to issues described elsewhere in this book. These models include a knowledge representation system designed by Lokendra Shastri (1985) and a word-sense disambiguation program done by Garrison Cottrell (1985).

Both of these systems use a model in which the network, or memory, is made up of a large number of simple computing elements called *units*. Each unit is connected to many others by way of input and output connections. The communication between units is done by passing values to other elements, with each unit passing a single value to all of its neighbors, those nodes connected via output links. This output value reflects the amount of activation received from the neighbors connected via input arcs. All inputs are weighted and combined in a manner specified by a set of three functions that define the values of a unit's potential (or level of activation), state, and output (where the output is based on the potential and state). For details of this model see Feldman and Ballard (1982). Of key importance to this idea is that each unit corresponds to a base concept — it is a local connectionist scheme like those described above.

Shastri's work centers on the development of a formal representation scheme, and associated inferential model, implementable using the Rochester connectionist framework. We do not discuss the details of this model (see the aforementioned Shastri, 1985, for that), but rather some of the implications. In particular, Shastri's work implies that some fairly complex reasoning, of the type we leave for our path evaluator, can be

---

4– A complete list of Rochester Connectionist Papers from 1979–1984 can be found in Feldman, Ballard, Brown, and Small (1984).

done by direct use of local algorithms for massively parallel computing.

Shastri's work addresses the making of inferences based on evidential reasoning in such a network. His system is similar in intent to NETL, except it is not subject to some of NETL's limitations. In particular, the model Shastri has developed handles multiple inheritance and exception-handling without being susceptible to the "race conditions" which cause problems for Fahlman's marker-passing scheme. Let's examine what might happen if Shastri's system was set up to perform the context recognition problem of the "suicide/hang" example that motivated much of our work. As you'll recall given the sentences

John wanted to commit suicide. He picked up a rope.

the goal was to find the context, or frame, which best described the events occuring. In Shastri's system, assuming the appropriate knowledge, it can be shown that one particular unit, that pertaining to the equivalent of HANG, would be mostly highly activated.

This differs from what might happen in a system like NETL, where the node of intersection might be HANG, KILL, or NOOSE, depending on the results of various race conditions. This limitation of NETL, however, was one of the things causing Charniak (1982) to favor a dumb marker-passer, returning paths instead of nodes, over the Fahlman type of approach.

A further motivation of our marker-passing scheme was the need to check various properties of what was found in the paths. Our dumb marker-passer can't take into account unification information or make inferences during marker-passing. Our model makes this the job of a traditional AI mechanism: the path evaluator. Shastri, however, demonstrates that various classes of inferences can be made directly by a massively-parallel algorithm.[5] Further, the evidential reasoning inferences made by Shastri's model are similar to some used by Charniak in his WIMP system

---

5– Again, we ignore the details of these inference classes here. They are fully described, however, and formally demonstrated, in the cited material.

(cf. Chapter 2).[6] Can connectionist models, using weighted links and continuous values rather than the discrete links of the marker-passing schemes, possibly replace our approach, rather than augmenting it (as we had proposed in Section 1.3)?

A concrete example of the comparison of such models can be found by contrasting the marker-passing word sense disambiguation system of Hirst (1983; cf. Chapter 2) with a system proposed by Cottrell (1985), which uses a massively parallel, connectionist model, to perform the same task. Hirst's model approaches ambiguity by setting up a set of frames that put word senses in one to one correspondence with semantic meanings. Each sense of a given word "competes" for recognition based on two criteria: the syntactic information available and the connectedness of the words to each other. This connectedness was found via an early version of the marker-passer used in SCRAPS.

As an example of his use of marker-passing, consider how Hirst's system would handle the word "ball" in the phrases

(1) The rubber ball
(2) The formal ball

The dictionary entry for BALL would contain two word senses, one corresponding to the frame SPHERE and one corresponding to DANCE; let us call these BALL-SPHERE and BALL-DANCE. When phrase 1 was encountered the system would pass markers between RUBBER and BALL and a path such as

RUBBER → MATERIAL → PHYSOBJ
→ BALL-SPHERE → BALL

would be found. This would cause the preference of BALL-SPHERE over BALL-DANCE. If, on the other hand, phrase 2 was found, a path like

FORMAL → DRESS-STYLE → SOCIAL-GATHERING
→ DANCE → BALL-DANCE → BALL

would be found and the BALL-DANCE meaning used. When paths were found to more than one meaning of a word, Hirst's

---

6– Charniak (personal commuication, 1986) is presently examining replacing much of his marker-passing system with an evidence-based inferencer using probabilities instead of weighted links. Shastri's approach would then be a possible contender for a massively parallel implementation of Charniak's.

system used a path strength heuristic (based mainly on the number of intermediate nodes) to determine which meaning to prefer.

Cottrell, on the other hand, uses a massively parallel activation spreading algorithm as more than a single part of a word sense disambiguation system. His model uses a local connectionist network to take into account not only the effects Hirst handles, but also, at the same time, to perform case-slot assignment. As an example, Cottrell's system would use the network of Figure 32 (weights on the arcs are omitted) to handle the disambiguation of THREW in the sentence

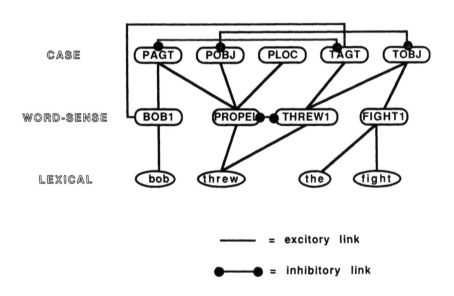

Figure 32: Using a connectionist network for word sense disambiguation.
Based on (Cottrell, 1985).

Bob threw the fight.

The correct interpretation of the sentence would be found at the end of activation spreading by examining the nodes remaining activated in the stable configuration. (In the above example these would be BOB1 as TAGT, THREW1, and FIGHT1 as TOBJ.)

From the above examples we see that what Hirst accomplishes with marker-passing is a subset of what Cottrell achieves with the network. On the other hand, Hirst's system ties into a traditional AI syntactic parser, which Cottrell's system can't do. Thus, for Cottrell to produce a syntactic parse to provide information to the disambiguator (as is done in Hirst's system) would require Cottrell to design a syntactic parsing scheme within the massively parallel framework.[7]

The moral we draw from this comparison is that our approach to marker-passing dovetails with present AI technology, the *symbolic* approach, while the more strongly connectionist models require moving more and more of that technology into the connectionist framework, what is sometimes called the *subsymbolic* approach. We expect, over time, more and more of the path evaluation function will be moved directly into the marker-passer, following Shastri's approach, but we are not yet ready to move the planner itself into a connectionist framework. In fact, one of the weaknesses of the connectionist framework is the inability, at present, to perform tasks requiring hypothetical reasoning, as in planning. In the next section we present a model designed to implement a planner on a connection machine and discuss some of the differences of this model and our own.

1.4.1.2. A connection machine planning system

Blelloch (1986) describes a programming language/knowledge representation system for massively parallel computers, in particular the connection machine. He discusses how such a language can be used to perform various knowledge-intensive processes, including parts of natural language processing and vision, a production rule system, and a planner. We discuss the

---

7– Cottrell (1985b) discusses some steps in exactly such a direction.

latter in this section.

Blelloch's system is directed at designing a NOAH-like planner for the connection machine, using a language he has designed called AFL-1. The planner, AFPLAN, produces an ordered list of operators to solve a problem. This list is designed to take into account preconditions and add- and delete-list like information to produce a correct plan. There are some serious limitation on AFPLAN's capabilities, but we shall ignore these for a bit and present the basics of the system's operation.

AFPLAN works by compiling a set of planning "programs" into a set of plausible plan steps. It then links these plan steps into a network with excitory and inhibitory links (based on the preconditions and add and delete information). The system works by performing a loop (on the Lisp Machine driving the connection machine) which finds all possible operators for a given time, chooses one, and asserts it as completed. This loop continues until the goal state is asserted as completed. Via the inhibitory information, the system only chooses operators that can satisfy a goal proposition and won't delete a proposition needed to achieve another goal. The network form of an operator is shown in Figure 33.

The most important feature of this work, when viewed from the point of view of SCRAPS, is how Blelloch chooses a rule when multiple possibilities are present. His choice mechanism is very simple: AFPLAN finds the operator that will satisfy the most goals if applied. This operator is easily found because each goal an operator can satisy adds activation to that operator. The "best operator" is therefore the one with the most activation. In the event of a tie, a "cost" field, associated with each operator, is used, and the operator with the lowest cost is chosen. These costs are assigned *a priori* and cannot be changed within the running of the system (say via context).

It is clear that this choice mechanism is quite limited. It does not take into account context effects (such as our FLAGS) nor can costs change based on situation. Interesting, however, is the fact that the activation energy on an operator is related to the potential use of that operator later in the planning situation. Further, a minor addition to Blelloch's scheme would allow

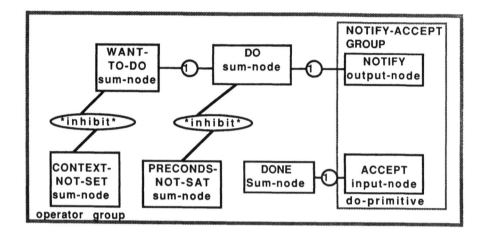

Figure 33: An operator in a Connection Machine planning system."
Based on (Blelloch, 1986).

operators to receive less activation if they might later cause a precondition not to fire. Thus, Blelloch's system could be able to choose SHOOT if holding a gun and not to choose RESTAURANT if no money is available. These pieces of information, however, would have to be compiled in. The system cannot dynamically change precondition satisfaction based on external knowledge (as SCRAPS does when a new assertion concerning, for example, a STRIKE is added or deleted).

The intriguing possibility here, in our jaundiced opinion as proponents of SCRAPS, is the ability of the choice mechanism to take into account some information, however limited, as to the later effects of using an operator. This is exactly what our marker-passer does. If, as suggested previously, we could move more of our path evaluation into the marker-passer, then perhaps we could integrate this information to feed back as activation (or inhibition) to a given goal. Thus RULE-IN and RULE-OUT assertions could be factored directly into the memory of the planner.

Unfortunately, for now this must remain an intriguing possibility (or, in fact an active research topic) due to many limitations still inherent in such systems. A primary limitation of Blelloch's system, for example, is that the knowledge is precompiled into the network. Given a plan for "MOVING X TO Y," his system must build special network components for each possible move that could be made. The range of X and Y must be predefined and the system can only plan on those. For example, given N blocks we generate the $2\sigma(N\text{-}1)^8$ plans for MOVE-A-TO-B, MOVE-B-TO-A, MOVE-A-TO-C, etc. These are then the only operators usable, and new blocks cannot be added without changing the system. The resulting planner, therefore, is not as general purpose as a planner like NOAH or NASL, which can generate plans for any objects fitting the conditions of the operators.

The Blelloch scheme also relies heavily on the availability of the symbolic machine to generate the instructions to the massively parallel machine. The loop driving AFPLAN, telling it when to plan, when to choose, and when to assert, is not implemented within the massively parallel architecture. Thus, like the system we designed in Chapter 7, AFPLAN is a hybrid, with the planner living on a Lisp Machine and the memory implemented on an attached connection machine. Still, Blelloch's design uses the massively parallel machine for more than we propose, an interesting possibility for future generations of planners.

1.5. Distributed Representations

So far we have only compared SCRAPS with local connectionist models. Connectionism, however, comes in two forms: local and *distributed*. In this section we discuss the relationship between SCRAPS and the latter.

An examination of distributed connectionist systems reveals three relatively distinct types of systems. These include what we

---

8– Where $\sigma(N)$ is $1 + 2 + ... + N$.

shall call weighted networks, distributed memory, and micro-feature based representations. In the rest of this section we describe these three approaches, contrasting to SCRAPS as we go.

1.5.1. Weighted Networks

This class of distributed connectionist models focuses on networks of nodes with weighted connections, where the networks have an input layer, an output layer, and one or more layers in between. These differ from those presented earlier, however, in that the intermediate levels have no direct correspondence to semantic categories. The system is trained by being fed the correspondences between sets of inputs and outputs. The system, over time, "learns" these correspondences via algorithms that change the weights of the internal nodes. Thus, when the system is fully trained, the information is stored via the weights in the links, with no external information available as to what link or links correspond to various internal memory structures.

An example of this is the NETtalk system (Sejnowski & Rosenberg, 1986). NETtalk is a network that learns to translate English letters into phonemes and their associated stresses (i.e., it is trained to pronounce words from the associated text). The system works by connecting input units to a layer of "hidden" units, and thence to a layer of output units corresponding to the phonemes and stresses.

Figure 34 shows an example of the network in NETtalk. The input units are given an encoding of five letters of the text to be learned. The output is shown an encoding of the correct pronounciation of the central letter of the five. A learning algorithm, in this case back-propogation, is used to change the weights of the many connections.[9] After many learning trials,(typically numbering in the thousands) on about one thousand dictionary words, NETtalk produces correct output about 90–95% of the time (Sejnowski, personal communication).

9– Each input unit is connected to each hidden unit, and each of the hidden units is connected to the 26 output units. Thus, in a typical network configuration, NETtalk would have 5 sets of 29 input units, each of these connected to 60 hidden units and each of these connected to 26 output units for a total of 231 units with 10,260 connections.

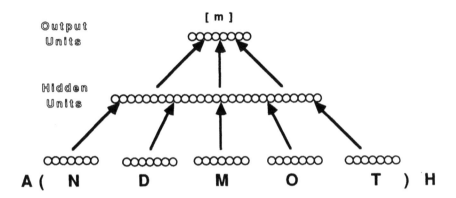

Figure 34: A distributed connectionist network.
A schematic of the operation of NETtalk. The input layer is an encoding of a window of letters (from the word "grand-mother") and the output is an encoding of an output phoneme.

For NETtalk to learn the pronounciations of a thousand words, and thus significantly more than a thousand sets of 5-letter combinations, with only 231 units, shows clearly that the encoding cannot be one to one. There is clearly a distributed representation of this complex knowledge.

SCRAPS has nothing that remotely compares with a system like this. The concept memory is composed solely of this large number of connecion weights, and there is no clear correspondence between any particular area of memory and any given concept. One weakness of such systems, at present, is the inability to create a symbolic structure or inference scheme for such networks, thus, there is at present no way the marker-passer could even be implemented on such a system.

1.5.2 Distributed memory

A very different view of distributed memory is represented by the work of Touretzky and Hinton (1985). This work describes a very limited production rule recognizer designed for a theoretical massively parallel machine (the Boltzman machine; Fahlman, Hinton, & Sejnowski, 1983). In this model, triples of letters were represented as sets of memory units in a larger memory. Each of these memory units was made up of 18 elements; 3 columns of 6 randomly assigned letters (see Table 1.) A unit received activation if it matched some component of a triple. For example, the unit represented in Table 1 would get some activation from the triplet (a l l) since it matches the "a" in the first column. The more matches, the more activation. Thus, the unit in Table 1 would be fully activated for (a r x) since both the unit and the pattern have an "a" in the first column, an "r" in the second column, and an "x" in the third.

Using this scheme we see that each memory unit corresponds to many different possible triplets (in this case, $6^3 = 216$). However, in a large memory (say 2000 units), with each unit randomly assigned, the chances of any two units activating all the same elements is exceedingly small. Thus, the pattern of activation of the whole memory corresponds to the concept for a

a	q	z
s	w	x
d	e	c
f	r	v
g	t	b
h	y	n

Table 1: A distributed memory element *a la* Touretzky.

single triple. By appropriately gating memory activations in various ways, such distribution patterns can be used to fire a very limited class of production-rule like entities.[10]

This type of distributed memory, using a small set of memory items (2000) to represent a larger number of entities (26^3 = 17,576), is another approach that we cannot use directly in SCRAPS. While it is encouraging that discrete patterns (in this case the triples) can be represented in a compact form and used, via gating and the like, for symbolic computation, a working version that could be used for the type of planning and inferencing done by SCRAPS is still a long way off.

1.5.3. Microfeatures

The third type of distributed memory uses what are often called microfeatures: representing our traditional symbolic units as sets of nodes, rather than as single entities. Unlike the Touretzky scheme, however, each of these smaller nodes codes for some specific feature, rather than for some large set of features. As an example, instead of discretely coding a human face, we could divide into sets of smaller features and code according to those. Thus, given, say, a thousand faces, we might be able to uniquely characterize them based on 10 types of left eyes, 10 types of right eyes, 5 types of noses, and 12 types of mouths. By simply finding four pieces of information for a face (which type of right eye, left eye, nose, and mouth) we can identify which, if any, of the thousand faces is being seen.[11]

One major advantage of such a scheme is that there is no longer one single piece of information representing a given face — its representation is now divided into four different places. If we are given a face with three of these features that match some

---

10– Primarily, the system can match rules like:
(A B C)
(D E F)
-->
(G H I)
(meaning if the triples (A B C) and (D E F) are presently activated in memory then activate the triple (G H I)).

11– This example was pointed out to me by Jordan Pollack.

particular face, but one which doesn't, we can say that the one we are viewing most closely resembles that particular face — no single feature defines a given node. Further, the more microfeatures used, the more useful this property becomes. If we use an encoding of 50 or 60 parts for a set of faces, then given a different face we could tell which one it most resembled by finding the original face with the most features in common. Thus, a "noisy" picture of a face (say with an obscured left eyebrow) might be recognizable, despite the lack of a complete match.

We believe that the use of microfeatures is an important step in knowledge representation, and one that a system like SCRAPS must be able to take advantage of. To see this, consider our CLEAVER example, changed slightly to:

You are on a business trip. You want to buy a long, sharp, pointed object.

The present SCRAPS will not be able to avoid buying this object since none of the discrete properties (long, sharp, or pointed) are necessarily connected to weapon (consider a gun). Still, the "ensemble" of these three properties is a strong indicator of weapon. A future version of SCRAPS should be able to handle such a situation. This is presently an active area of our research, we wish to expand SCRAPS to handle such cases using a micro-feature based model.[12]

1.0 THEMES (Continued)

We now turn once again to the issue of whether SCRAPS is actually a connectionist model. The scorecard, as we see it, appears in Table 2.

12– See also Chapter 11, Section 3.6.

Scraps' Connectionist Scorecard	
Learning	No
Neurophysiological plausibility	No
Weighted Arcs	some intriguing possibilities, but No
Massive parallelism	Yes
Distributed Representations	possibilities for microfeatures, but No

Table 2: Is SCRAPS a connectionist model?

So, is SCRAPS connectionist? We leave that decision in the hands of the reader.

CHAPTER 10

SCRAPS In Action

Few things are harder to put up with than the annoyance of a good example.
— Mark Twain, *Pudd'nhead Wilson [1894]*

In this chapter we examine the output of the SCRAPS program as it solves the problems presented in Chapter 4. We use examples to: contrast SCRAPS to the NASL problem solver, which uses no marker-passer, show that SCRAPS works as described previously, and contrast SCRAPS to the concurrent program C-SCRAPS.

1. NASL *vs.* SCRAPS

Here we show how NASL and SCRAPS differ in solving the problem

A person on a business trip, *me*, tries to plan the buying of a cleaver, *cleaver-1*.

The system knows two ways to "get-to" a place: taking the bus and flying. It also contains an assertion ruling out taking a bus when it is on such a trip.

1.1. NASL buys a cleaver

We start by showing the output of the NASL program — no marker passing is used. Comments are included in *italics*

;start the program
(b t1)
I have the top level task T1
;nasl start working on the task names T1

The initial conditions are:
(INST T1 BUYING)
(:= '(BUYER T1) ME)
(:= '(BOUGHT T1) CLEAVER-1))
;the initial situation is ME BUYING CLEAVER-1.

The next task to work on is
T1
Task can be reduced through its sub-acts:
((:= '(RETURN-STEP T1) GET-TO176)
(INST GET-TO176 GET-TO)
(:= '(GOER GET-TO176) ME)
(:= '(GOPLACE GET-TO176) BROWN-UNIVERSITY)
(:= '(TAKING GET-TO176) CLEAVER-1))
((:= '(TRANSACTION-SCENE T1) DICKERING85)
(INST DICKERING85 DICKERING)
(:= '(D-AGENT DICKERING85) (SELLER T1))
(:= '(D-PATIENT DICKERING85) ME))
((:= '(ENTER-STEP T1) GO-PLACE236)
(INST GO-PLACE236 GO-PLACE)
(:= '(AGENT GO-PLACE236) ME)
(:= '(PT-PATIENT GO-PLACE236) ME))
;The task is decomposed into subtasks. These include entering
;the store, doing the price and payment step (we leave it simply
;as "dickering" here so as to save showing unnecessary work),
;and returning the item to my home (in this case this means
;taking CLEAVER-1 to BROWN-UNIVERSITY).

**** Sub-act of T1 is GET-TO176
**** DICKERING85 comes before GET-TO176
**** Sub-act of T1 is DICKERING85
**** GO-PLACE236 comes before DICKERING85
**** Sub-act of T1 is GO-PLACE236
;We also check the ordering statements on this task. We discover
;the order described above.

The next task to work on is
GO-PLACE236

;We start by going to the place of the transaction

It is a model manipulation so I am
asserting
(:= '(LOCATION-OF ME) (PT-LOCATION GO-PLACE236))
;model-manipulation is NASL's term for what we have referred to
;as a "primitive task." Primitives change states of the world:
;in this case we set my location to the location of the buying.

The next task to work on is
DICKERING85
Task can be reduced through its sub-acts:
((:= '(GIVE-OK-STEP DICKERING85) COMMUNICATE257)
(INST COMMUNICATE257 COMMUNICATE)
(:= '(AGENT COMMUNICATE257) ME)
(:= '(TO COMMUNICATE257) (SELLER T1)))
((:= '(TELL-STEP DICKERING85) COMMUNICATE258)
(INST COMMUNICATE258 COMMUNICATE)
(:= '(AGENT COMMUNICATE258) (SELLER T1))
(:= '(TO COMMUNICATE258) ME))
((:= '(ASK-STEP DICKERING85) COMMUNICATE259)
(INST COMMUNICATE259 COMMUNICATE)
(:= '(AGENT COMMUNICATE259) ME)
(:= '(TO COMMUNICATE259) (SELLER T1)))
**** Sub-act of DICKERING85 is COMMUNICATE257
**** COMMUNICATE258 comes before COMMUNICATE257
**** Sub-act of DICKERING85 is COMMUNICATE258
**** COMMUNICATE259 comes before COMMUNICATE258
**** Sub-act of DICKERING85 is COMMUNICATE259
;Dickering also involves subtasks which are now expanded

;I ask the price...
The next task to work on is
COMMUNICATE259
It is a model manipulation.

;I'm told the price...
The next task to work on is
COMMUNICATE258
It is a model manipulation.

;I agree to buy...
The next task to work on is
COMMUNICATE257

It is a model manipulation.

The next task to work on is
GET-TO176
;At this point the GET-TO task is found. We have no subtasks to
;divide it into. Instead, we find the alternative ways to perform
;the action and set up a choice task:

I am setting up a choice task
CHOOSE22 to decide among these options:
(BUSING (? BUSING451)
(PASSENGER ME)
(TO-PLACE BROWN-UNIVERSITY)
(B-BAGGAGE CLEAVER-1))
(FLYING (? FLYING681)
(PASSENGER ME)
(TO-PLACE BROWN-UNIVERSITY)
(F-BAGGAGE CLEAVER-1))
;these are the alternative for Get-to: busing and flying

**** Sub-act of GET-TO176 is CHOOSE22
The next task to work on is
CHOOSE22
CHOOSE is primitive so I am just doing it
;we perform the choice.

After ruling out we are left with
(FLYING (? FLYING6811)
(PASSENGER ME)
(TO-PLACE BROWN-UNIVERSITY)
(F-BAGGAGE CLEAVER-1))
;We have ruled-out the bus option because of the business trip.

So I choose
(FLYING (? FLYING6811)
(PASSENGER ME)
(TO-PLACE BROWN-UNIVERSITY)
(F-BAGGAGE CLEAVER-1))
; Since this is a unique choice we need not check for rule-in rules
; We simply perform the action:

**** Sub-act of GET-TO176 is FLYING69
The next task to work on is
FLYING69

Task can be reduced through its sub-acts:
((:= '(PLANE-FLIGHT-SCENE FLYING69) PLANING116)
(INST PLANING116 PLANING)
(:= '(AGENT PLANING116) ME))
((:= '(GAIN-TAKE-OFF-CLEARANCE-SCENE FLYING69) CLEARANCING69)
(INST CLEARANCING69 CLEARANCING)
(:= '(PILOT CLEARANCING69) (PILOT FLYING69))
(:= '(C-ATC CLEARANCING69) (F-ATC FLYING69)))
((:= '(BOARD-PLANE-STEP FLYING69) GO-TO-GATE10)
(INST GO-TO-GATE10 GO-TO-GATE)
(:= '(AGENT GO-TO-GATE10) ME)
(:= '(GATE GO-TO-GATE10) (GATE-OF FLYING69))
(:= '(PLANE-OF GO-TO-GATE10) (FLIGHT FLYING69)))
((:= '(WEAPONS-CHECK-SCENE FLYING69) WEAPONS-CHECKING69)
(INST WEAPONS-CHECKING69 WEAPONS-CHECKING)
(:= '(CHECKER WEAPONS-CHECKING69) (GUARD FLYING69))
(:= '(CHECKEE WEAPONS-CHECKING69) ME)
(:= '(WC-BAGGAGE WEAPONS-CHECKING69) CLEAVER-1))
((:= '(CHECK-IN-SCENE FLYING69) AIRPORT-CHECK-IN68)
(INST AIRPORT-CHECK-IN68 AIRPORT-CHECK-IN)
(:= '(CHECKEE AIRPORT-CHECK-IN68) ME)
(:= '(CHECKER AIRPORT-CHECK-IN68) (AIR-AGENT FLYING69))
(:= '(BOUGHT AIRPORT-CHECK-IN68) FLYING69))
((:= '(GO-AIRPORT-STEP FLYING69) GO-PLACE237)
(INST GO-PLACE237 GO-PLACE)
(:= '(AGENT GO-PLACE237) ME)
(:= '(PT-LOCATION GO-PLACE237) (FROM-PLACE FLYING69)))
**** Sub-act of FLYING69 is PLANING116
**** CLEARANCING69 comes before PLANING116
**** Sub-act of FLYING69 is CLEARANCING69
**** GO-TO-GATE10 comes before CLEARANCING69
**** Sub-act of FLYING69 is GO-TO-GATE10
**** WEAPONS-CHECKING69 comes before GO-TO-GATE10
**** Sub-act of FLYING69 is WEAPONS-CHECKING69
**** AIRPORT-CHECK-IN68 comes before WEAPONS-CHECKING69
**** Sub-act of FLYING69 is AIRPORT-CHECK-IN68
**** GO-PLACE237 comes before AIRPORT-CHECK-IN68
**** Sub-act of FLYING69 is GO-PLACE237
; NASL's information about taking a plane includes Go to the
; airport, check in, go through the weapons detector, go to the
; gate, the pilot asks for clearance, and the plane takes off
; and flies

The next task to work on is

GO-PLACE237
It is a model manipulation so I am
asserting
(:= '(LOCATION-OF ME) (FROM-PLACE FLYING69)))
;I am at the airport

The next task to work on is
AIRPORT-CHECK-IN68
It is a model manipulation so I am
asserting
((HAS ME TICKET))
; *I get my ticket*

The next task to work on is
WEAPONS-CHECKING69
It is a model manipulation so I am
asserting
(IS-ARRESTED ME)
; *This has occured due of a forward chaining rule saying that*
; *if one goes through a weapons-check with a weapon s/he gets*
; *arrested (and cleaver-1 can be considered a weapon)*

(RULE-OUT (? ACT3) (GO-PLACE (? GO-PLACE2271) (AGENT ME)))
; *We also have a forward chaining rule that says if an agent is*
; *arrested s/he cannot go anywhere.*

he next task to work on is
GO-TO-GATE10
Task can be reduced through its sub-acts:
((:= '(GET-ON-PLANE-STEP GO-TO-GATE10) GO-PLACE238)
(INST GO-PLACE238 GO-PLACE)
(:= '(AGENT GO-PLACE238) ME)
(:= '(PT-LOCATION GO-PLACE238) (FLIGHT FLYING69)))
((:= '(WALK-TO-GATE-STEP GO-TO-GATE10) GO-PLACE239)
(INST GO-PLACE239 GO-PLACE)
(:= '(AGENT GO-PLACE239) ME)
(:= '(PT-LOCATION GO-PLACE239) (GATE-OF GO-TO-GATE10)))
**** Sub-act of GO-TO-GATE10 is GO-PLACE238
**** Sub-act of GO-TO-GATE10 is GO-PLACE239
; *the next step in this task would be to go to the gate, so NASL*
; *attempts it*

The next task to work on is
GO-PLACE239

This requires a ruled-out task: GO-PLACE239
; *GO-PLACE was ruled-out by the arrest!*

Stopping Work:
PLAN FAILURE (boy, I wish I could back-up)
; *As mentioned previously, NASL does not back up in a failure*
; *situation. Instead, as in this case, it reports a plan failure*

1.2. SCRAPS buys a cleaver

Notice how much work NASL needed to perform prior to reaching the point of the error — it planned several of the steps of the flight home before encountering an error. We now see how SCRAPS attacks this same problem.

```
; Using the formula described in Chapter 6 we compute the starting
; zorch factor. We use an average path length of 7.  Note:  path
; length refers to the number of NODES in the path.
(compute-zorch 7)
Average branchout is: 5.7913604
Path length average desired is: 7
Initial zorch is being set to 194

(cl t1)
I have the top level task T1
It is of type: BUYING
The initial conditions are
((:= '(BUYER T1) ME) (:= '(BOUGHT T1) CLEAVER-1))
INITIAL TASK = T1
; We start SCRAPS going on the same problem as we did for NASL

PASSING MARKERS ON: (BUYING CLEAVER-1 ME)
; The first thing SCRAPS does is to pass markers on the constants
; involved in the initial conditions

Marker-passer returns 6 paths for examination
; and examines the paths returned
```

```
CHECKING PATH
(CLEAVER-1
(INST CLEAVER-1 CLEAVER)
CLEAVER
(FUNCTION-OF (CLEAVER (? CL))
(WEAPON (? W)))
WEAPON
(<- (HAS (CHECKEE (WEAPONS-CHECKING (? WC)))
(WEAPON (? WEAPON)))
(IS-ARRESTED (CHECKEE (WEAPONS-CHECKING (? WC)))))
WEAPONS-CHECKING
(RESTRICTION (WEAPONS-CHECK-SCENE (FLYING (? F)))
(WEAPONS-CHECKING
(? WEAPONS-CHECKING6)
(CHECKER (GUARD (FLYING (? F))))
(CHECKEE (PASSENGER (FLYING (? F))))
(WC-BAGGAGE (F-BAGGAGE (FLYING (? F))))))
FLYING
(TO-DO (GET-TO (? GET-TO18)
(GOER (? G))
(GOPLACE (? P))
(TAKING (? T)))
(FLYING (? FLYING6)
(PASSENGER (? G))
(TO-PLACE (? P))
(F-BAGGAGE (? T))))
GET-TO
(RESTRICTION (RETURN-STEP (BUYING (? B)))
(GET-TO (? GET-TO17)
(GOER (BUYER (BUYING (? B))))
(GOPLACE (HOME-OF (BUYER (BUYING (? B)))))
(TAKING (BOUGHT (BUYING (? B)))))))
BUYING)
```
; *The first path examined is the one which we described. If you*
; *buy the cleaver and fly home you will be arrested.*

```
PATH RESULTS IN NEGATIVE CONSEQUENCES:
ASSERTING: (<- (RULE-OUT (? TASK) (WEAPONS-CHECKING (? TASK)))
(TOP-LEVEL-TASK T1))
```
; *IS-ARRESTED is considered a bad thing. We therefore rule-out*
; *doing the task which causes it.*

```
ASSERTING: (<- (RULE-OUT (? TASK) (FLYING (? TASK)))
(TOP-LEVEL-TASK T1))
```

; *We check the path and find WEAPONS-CHECKING is proceeded by,*
; *and is a sub-task of, FLYING so that is ruled out also*

CHECKING PATH
(CLEAVER-1
(INST CLEAVER-1 CLEAVER)
CLEAVER
(ISA CLEAVER THING)
THING
(RESTRICTION (BOUGHT (BUYING (? B))) (THING (? THING71)))
BUYING)
NO ACTION TAKEN FOR THIS PATH
; *This path doesn't match any of the heuristics. No action is*
; *taken.*

CHECKING PATH
(CLEAVER-1
(INST CLEAVER-1 CLEAVER)
CLEAVER
(FUNCTION-OF (CLEAVER (? CL)) (WEAPON (? W)))
WEAPON
(ISA WEAPON THING)
THING
(RESTRICTION (BOUGHT (BUYING (? B))) (THING (? THING71)))
BUYING)
NO ACTION TAKEN FOR THIS PATH
; *This path also matches none of the patterns the heuristics check*
; *for*

CHECKING PATH
(ME
(:= '(PET-OF ME) BRUCE)
BRUCE
(INST BRUCE RAT)
RAT
(ISA RAT ANIMAL)
ANIMAL
(ISA ANIMAL THING)
THING
(ISA CLEAVER THING)
CLEAVER
(INST CLEAVER-1 CLEAVER)
CLEAVER-1)
; *This is a path found between some information about ME*
; *(I own a pet rat) and CLEAVER-1. It has a path strength*
; *of 1, just barely making it (not shown). If the node "thing"*
; *had higher outbranching, as it would in a larger data-base, the*
; *path would not be reported.*

Rejecting path due to ISA plateau.
; *This path is an ISA-plateau so it is rejected prior to being*
; *examined*

CHECKING PATH
(ME
(:= '(CAR-OF ME) HONDA)
HONDA
(ISA HONDA CAR)
CAR
(ISA CAR VEHICLE)
VEHICLE
(ISA VEHICLE THING)
THING
(ISA CLEAVER THING)
CLEAVER
(INST CLEAVER-1 CLEAVER)
CLEAVER-1)
Rejecting path due to ISA plateau.
; similar to the above

> CHECKING PATH
> (ME
> (:= '(JOB-OF ME) STUDENT)
> STUDENT
> (ISA STUDENT OCCUPATION)
> OCCUPATION
> (ISA OCCUPATION THING)
> THING
> (ISA CLEAVER THING)
> CLEAVER
> (INST CLEAVER-1 CLEAVER)
> CLEAVER-1)
> Rejecting path due to ISA plateau.
> ; also similar

INVOKING NASL
; All the paths were examined, so we now invoke NASL.

The next task to work on is
T1
Task can be reduced through its sub-acts:
((:= '(RETURN-STEP T1) GET-TO20)
...
((:= '(TRANSACTION-SCENE T1) DICKERING8)
...
((:= '(ENTER-STEP T1) GO-PLACE56)
...
; The enter-step and transaction-scene (go-place and dickering)
; are exactly the same as in the NASL example

●●●

The next task to work on is
GET-TO20
; now we get to the step where we take the cleaver home.

I am setting up a choice task
CHOOSE2 to decide among these options:
(BUSING (? BUSING61)
(PASSENGER ME)
(TO-PLACE BROWN-UNIVERSITY)
(B-BAGGAGE CLEAVER-1))
(FLYING (? FLYING61)

(PASSENGER ME)
(TO-PLACE BROWN-UNIVERSITY)
(F-BAGGAGE CLEAVER-1))
; we once again examine the alternative ways of getting home.

**** Sub-act of GET-TO20 is CHOOSE2
The next task to work on is
CHOOSE2
CHOOSE is primitive so I am just doing it
After ruling out we are left with:
NOTHING!!
; This time however BOTH of our plans have been ruled out: Bus because
; of the business trip and FLYING from the rule-out asserted by the
; path evaluator.

PLAN FAILURE (boy, I wish I could back-up)
; we fail earlier, we have not done the redundant work required
; in the NASL example.

2. SCRAPS alone

In this section we examine the behavior of SCRAPS on two more
of the examples given in Chapter 4: committing suicide while
holding a gun and getting a newspaper on a rainy day.

2.1. SCRAPS commits suicide

SCRAPS is asked to plan a suicide event for the agent *me*. We
also assert (HAS ME GUN).

(compute-zorch 7)
Average branchout is
Path length average desired is: 7
Initial is being set to 194
; Again we start by setting the initial zorch.

(ASSERT '(HAS ME GUN))
; we assert the possession of the gun

SETTING FLAG OF TYPE PERCEPTUAL ON NODE GUN
; a forward chaining rule causes a flag to be set on gun
; (as described in Chapter 4).

(su t1)
I have the top level task T1
It is of type: SUICIDE
The initial conditions are
((:= '(AGENT T1) ME))
INITIAL TASK = T1
; we start with the initial conditions that we wish to plan
; a suicide by agent "me."

PASSING MARKERS ON: (SUICIDE ME)
; pass marks on the initial conditions

Marker-passer returns 8 paths for examination
; and examine the paths returned

CHECKING PATH
(SUICIDE
(TO-DO (SUICIDE (? S))
(ACHIEVE (? ACHIEVE35)
(AGENT (AGENT (SUICIDE (? S))))
(STATE-OF (KILLING (? KILLING41)
(AGENT (AGENT (SUICIDE (? S))))
(PATIENT (AGENT (SUICIDE (? S)))))))))
KILLING
(CAUSES (SHOOT (? SHOOT11)
(AGENT (? X))
(PATIENT (? Y)))
(KILLING (? KILLING42)
(AGENT (? X))
(PATIENT (? Y))))
SHOOT
(RESTRICTION
(S-INSTR (SHOOT (? S))) (GUN (? GUN11)))
GUN
(HAS ME GUN)
FLAG7)
; This path ends in a PERCEPTUAL flag and the variables match

ASSERTING: (<- (RULE-IN (? TASK) (SHOOT (? TASK))) (HAS ME GUN))
; so SCRAPS rules-in the use of shooting conditionalized by
; the possession of the gun.

CHECKING PATH
(ME (:= '(PET-OF ME) BRUCE)
BRUCE
(INST BRUCE RAT)
RAT
(ISA RAT ANIMAL)
ANIMAL
(RESTRICTION (PET-OF (PERSON (? PERSON))) (ANIMAL (? ANIMAL11)))
PERSON
(RESTRICTION (AGENT (SUICIDE (? S))) (PERSON (? PERSON478)))
SUICIDE)
NO ACTION TAKEN FOR THIS PATH
; another low-strength path as in the previous section.

CHECKING PATH
(ME (:= '(CAR-OF ME) HONDA)
HONDA
(ISA HONDA CAR)
CAR
(ISA CAR VEHICLE)
VEHICLE
(RESTRICTION (CAR-OF (PERSON (? PERSON))) (VEHICLE (? VEHICLE11))
PERSON
(RESTRICTION (AGENT (SUICIDE (? S))) (PERSON (? PERSON478)))
SUICIDE)
NO ACTION TAKEN FOR THIS PATH
; ditto

CHECKING PATH
(ME (:= '(JOB-OF ME) STUDENT)
STUDENT
(ISA STUDENT OCCUPATION)
OCCUPATION
(RESTRICTION (JOB-OF (PERSON (? PERSON)))
            (OCCUPATION (? OCCUPATION11)))
PERSON
(RESTRICTION (AGENT (SUICIDE (? S)))
            (PERSON (? PERSON478)))
SUICIDE)
NO ACTION TAKEN FOR THIS PATH
; and again a low strength path.

CHECKING PATH
(ME (:= '(SPOUSE-OF ME) TERRY)
TERRY
(INST TERRY PERSON)
PERSON
(RESTRICTION (AGENT (SUICIDE (? S))) (PERSON (? PERSON478)))
SUICIDE)
Rejecting path: Node PERSONis promiscuous
; In this case the path meets at the node "person" which has a high
; branchout in proportion to the system. The path is rejected immediately
; Again, this was a low path-strength path.

CHECKING PATH
(ME
(HAS ME GUN)
GUN
(RESTRICTION (S-INSTR (SHOOT (? S))) (GUN (? GUN11)))
SHOOT
(CAUSES (SHOOT (? SHOOT11)
(AGENT (? X))
(PATIENT (? Y)))
(KILLING (? KILLING42)
(AGENT (? X))
(PATIENT (? Y))))
KILLING
(TO-DO (SUICIDE (? S))
(ACHIEVE (? ACHIEVE35)
(AGENT (AGENT (SUICIDE (? S))))
(STATE-OF
(KILLING (? KILLING41)
(AGENT (AGENT (SUICIDE (? S))))
(PATIENT (AGENT (SUICIDE (? S)))))))))
SUICIDE)
; This path is similar to the path found before, but notice that it
; starts at the node for ME, rather than the flagged node GUN.

NO ACTION TAKEN FOR THIS PATH
; None of our rules matched, so no action was taken.

CHECKING PATH
(ME
(INST ME PERSON)
PERSON
(RESTRICTION
(AGENT (SUICIDE (? S)))
(PERSON (? PERSON478)))
SUICIDE)
Rejecting path: Node PERSONis promiscuous
; the path meets at a promiscuous node so it is rejected.

CHECKING PATH
(ME
(HAS ME GUN)
GUN
(HAS ME GUN)
FLAG7)
; this path ends at a flagged node and, since there are no variables,
; it cannot be rejected due to variable mismatches
; the heuristics which detects perceptual flags (Heuristic 2 of
; Chapter 5) would rule in the interesting frames traversed on this
; path.

No Frames to RULE-IN
; However, since there are none, it does nothing.

INVOKING NASL
; *The NASL part of SCRAPS now takes over:*

The next task to work on is
T1
There is only one way to do the task:
((SUB-ACT T1 ACHIEVE36)
(INST ACHIEVE36 ACHIEVE)
(:= '(AGENT ACHIEVE36) ME)
(:= '(STATE-OF ACHIEVE36)
(KILLING (? KILLING411) (AGENT ME) (PATIENT ME))))
; *Suicide is represented by achieving a state in which*
; *death of the patient has occured via an action of the agent.*

**** Sub-act of T1 is ACHIEVE36
The next task to work on is
ACHIEVE36
I am setting up a choice task
CHOOSE5 to decide among these options:

(SHOOT (? SHOOT1111) (AGENT ME) (PATIENT ME))
(HANG (? HANG1111) (AGENT ME) (PATIENT ME))
(POISONING (? POISONING1111) (AGENT ME) (PATIENT ME))
; *NASL chooses among the ways it knows of committing suicide.*

**** Sub-act of ACHIEVE36 is CHOOSE5
The next task to work on is
CHOOSE5

CHOOSE is primitive so I am just doing it
; *We start by looking for frames which we can rule out*

After ruling out we are left with
(SHOOT (? SHOOT11111) (AGENT ME) (PATIENT ME))
(HANG (? HANG11111) (AGENT ME) (PATIENT ME))
(POISONING (? POISONING11111) (AGENT ME) (PATIENT ME))
(ASPHIXIATION (? ASPHIXIATION1111) (AGENT ME) (PATIENT ME))
(DEFENESTRATION (? DEFENESTRATION1111) (AGENT ME) (PATIENT M
; *but none are found, so we try to find rule-in rules.*

And then we rule-in...
(SHOOT (? SHOOT11111) (AGENT ME) (PATIENT ME))
; *This is chosen because SCRAPS ruled in the shoot event.*

So I choose
(SHOOT (? SHOOT11111) (AGENT ME) (PATIENT ME))
**** Sub-act of ACHIEVE36 is SHOOT12
The next task to work on is
SHOOT12

•••

; We skip showing how NASL decomposes the shoot event, suffice
; it to say that it expands and executes the subtasks of suicide
; and ends with:

PLAN IS COMPLETED SUCCESSFULLY
DONE

2.2 SCRAPS gets a newspaper

In this section we examine how SCRAPS solves the problem of getting a newspaper on a rainy day as discussed in Chapter 4, Section 2.1.4. This involved using the DEMON rule

```
(DEMON (AND (GO-PLACE (PERSON ?p)
                      (LOCATION OUTSIDE))
            (CLIMATE OUTSIDE RAINING))
       (ADD-REQ (AND (CARRY (AGENT ?p)
                            (PATIENT ?object))
                     (INST ?object UMBRELLA)))))
```

SCRAPS stores such demons as frames with slots for antecedent conditions and consequent actions. In the following example we use the actual definition as represented in FRAIL

```
(inst demon1 demon)
(/:= '(antecedent demon1)
     (AND (go-place (goer ?p)
                    (goplace OUTSIDE))
          (/:= '(CLIMATE OUTSIDE) RAINING)))
(/:= '(consequent demon1)
     (ADD-REQ (CARRY
               (AGENT ?P)
               (PATIENT (UMBRELLA ?U)))))
```

(compute-zorch 7)
Average branchout is: 5.7913604
Path length average desired is: 7
Initial zorch is being set to 194
; compute the starting zorch as before

(um t1)
SETTING FLAG OF TYPE PERCEPTUAL ON NODE OUTSIDE
; set the flag on raining -- part of the initial situation

I have the top level task T1
It is of type: GET-NEWSPAPER
The initial conditions are
((:= '(AGENT T1) ME) (:= '(GN-ITEM T1) NEWSP1))
INITIAL TASK = T1
; The task is for ME to get NEWSP1

PASSING MARKERS ON: (GET-NEWSPAPER NEWSP1 ME)
; we pass markers on the initial conditions

Marker-passer returns 18 paths for examination
; and examine the paths returned

CHECKING PATH
(GET-NEWSPAPER
(RESTRICTION
(GET-NP-STEP (GET-NEWSPAPER (? N)))
(GO-PLACE (? GO-PLACE328)
(AGENT (GN-AGENT (GET-NEWSPAPER (? N))))
(PT-PATIENT (GN-ITEM (GET-NEWSPAPER (? N))))
(PT-LOCATION (LOCATION-OF (GN-ITEM (GET-NEWSPAPER (? N)))))))))
GO-PLACE
(:= '(ANTECEDENT DEMON1)
(AND (GO-PLACE (? GO-PLACE329) (GOER (? P)) (GOPLACE OUTSIDE))
(:= '(CLIMATE OUTSIDE) RAINING)))
OUTSIDE
(CLIMATE OUTSIDE RAINING)
FLAG56)
; We find a path through the demon as expected

Demon - asserting:
the-frame: GET-NEWSPAPER
step-thing= ((DEMON-BUILT-STEP-23
(CARRY (? CARRY351)
(AGENT (? P25))
(PATIENT (UMBRELLA (? U25))))))
; and add a carry step to the get-newspaper frame.
; as described in Chapter 4.

CHECKING PATH
(NEWSP1
(ISA NEWSP1 NEWSPAPER)
NEWSPAPER
(RESTRICTION
(GN-ITEM (GET-NEWSPAPER (? N))) (NEWSPAPER (? NEWSPAPER32)))
GET-NEWSPAPER
(RESTRICTION
(GET-NP-STEP (GET-NEWSPAPER (? N)))
(GO-PLACE (? GO-PLACE328)
(AGENT (GN-AGENT (GET-NEWSPAPER (? N))))
(PT-PATIENT (GN-ITEM (GET-NEWSPAPER (? N))))
(PT-LOCATION (LOCATION-OF (GN-ITEM (GET-NEWSPAPER (? N)))))))))
GO-PLACE
(:= '(ANTECEDENT DEMON1)
(AND (GO-PLACE (? GO-PLACE329) (GOER (? P)) (GOPLACE OUTSIDE))
(:= '(CLIMATE OUTSIDE) RAINING)))
OUTSIDE
(CLIMATE OUTSIDE RAINING)
FLAG56)
; This path involves the demon, but it requires an unknown agent

Path rejected: No agent variable involved in the Demon
;we cannot, therefore, use it as a demon.

Variable mismatching -- cannot RULE-IN
; The path also ended at a Perceptual flag so that Heuristic 2 took
; a shot at it. Heuristic 2, however, requires that the item being
; flagged is involved in an action to rule-in. In this case the
; variables in the get-newspaper frame don't include anything bound
; directly to "outside," so this cannot be the case. Nothing is ruled
; in.

CHECKING PATH
(NEWSP1
(ISA NEWSP1 NEWSPAPER)
NEWSPAPER
(RESTRICTION
(GN-ITEM (GET-NEWSPAPER (? N)))
(NEWSPAPER (? NEWSPAPER32)))
GET-NEWSPAPER)
NO ACTION TAKEN FOR THIS PATH
; This matched none of the rules

CHECKING PATH
(NEWSP1
(:= '(LOCATION-OF NEWSP1) OUTSIDE)
OUTSIDE
(CLIMATE OUTSIDE RAINING)
FLAG56)
No Frames to RULE-IN
; We find a perceptual flag, but it adds no new information

```
CHECKING PATH
(NEWSP1
(:= '(LOCATION-OF NEWSP1) OUTSIDE)
OUTSIDE
(:= '(ANTECEDENT DEMON1)
(AND (GO-PLACE (? GO-PLACE329)
(GOER (? P))
(GOPLACE OUTSIDE))
(:= '(CLIMATE OUTSIDE) RAINING)))
GO-PLACE
(RESTRICTION (GET-NP-STEP (GET-NEWSPAPER (? N)))
(GO-PLACE (? GO-PLACE328)
(AGENT
(GN-AGENT (GET-NEWSPAPER (? N))))
(PT-PATIENT
(GN-ITEM (GET-NEWSPAPER (? N))))
(PT-LOCATION
(LOCATION-OF (GN-ITEM (GET-NEWSPAPER (? N)))))))))
GET-NEWSPAPER)
```

Path rejected: Demon not necessarily invoked
; In this case only one of the clauses of the demon was marked, not
; both. The first condition of the and is marked from go-place,
; but the second is not marked from raining. This is discovered
; during the variable checking step and causes the path to be
; rejected.

•••

; At this point we have ten paths of the low zorch type
; which are rejected as isa-plateaus. They are deleted here
; to spare the reader

```
CHECKING PATH
(ME
(HAS ME GUN)
GUN
(RESTRICTION
(S-INSTR (SHOOT (? S))) (GUN (? GUN32)))
SHOOT
(RESTRICTION
(S-GET-INSTR-STEP (SHOOT (? S)))
(GO-PLACE (? GO-PLACE325)
(AGENT (AGENT (SHOOT (? S))))
(PT-PATIENT (S-INSTR (SHOOT (? S))))))
GO-PLACE
(RESTRICTION
(GET-NP-STEP (GET-NEWSPAPER (? N)))
(GO-PLACE (? GO-PLACE328)
(AGENT (GN-AGENT (GET-NEWSPAPER (? N))))
(PT-PATIENT (GN-ITEM (GET-NEWSPAPER (? N))))
(PT-LOCATION
(LOCATION-OF (GN-ITEM (GET-NEWSPAPER (? N)))))))))
GET-NEWSPAPER
(RESTRICTION
(GN-ITEM (GET-NEWSPAPER (? N))) (NEWSPAPER (? NEWSPAPER32)))
NEWSPAPER
(ISA NEWSP1 NEWSPAPER)
NEWSP1)
```

; *This path contains what we call a "restriction" plateau.*
; *It occurs when two slots in different frames require the*
; *same sub-task. It is similar to the isa-plateau in that*
; *it offers no interesting information*

Rejecting path due to RESTRICTION plateau.
; *and like the isa-plateau it is quickly rejected*

CHECKING PATH
(ME
(HAS ME GUN)
GUN
(RESTRICTION (S-INSTR (SHOOT (? S))) (GUN (? GUN32)))
SHOOT
(RESTRICTION
(S-GET-INSTR-STEP (SHOOT (? S)))
(GO-PLACE (? GO-PLACE325)
(AGENT (AGENT (SHOOT (? S))))
(PT-PATIENT (S-INSTR (SHOOT (? S))))))
GO-PLACE
(RESTRICTION
(GET-NP-STEP (GET-NEWSPAPER (? N)))
(GO-PLACE (? GO-PLACE328)
(AGENT (GN-AGENT (GET-NEWSPAPER (? N))))
(PT-PATIENT (GN-ITEM (GET-NEWSPAPER (? N))))
(PT-LOCATION
(LOCATION-OF (GN-ITEM (GET-NEWSPAPER (? N))))))))
GET-NEWSPAPER)
Rejecting path due to RESTRICTION plateau.
; same as above

CHECKING PATH
(ME
(INST ME PERSON)
PERSON
(RESTRICTION
(GN-AGENT (GET-NEWSPAPER (? N)))
(PERSON (? PERSON1426)))
GET-NEWSPAPER)
Rejecting path: Node PERSONis promiscuous
; another path easily rejected

INVOKING NASL
; The planner is invoked

The next task to work on is
T1
Task can be reduced through its sub-acts:
((:= '(DEMON-BUILT-STEP-1 T1) CARRY36)
(INST CARRY36 CARRY)

```
(:= '(AGENT CARRY36) (? P251))
(:= '(PATIENT CARRY36) (UMBRELLA (? U251))))
```
; *This step has been added by SCRAPS. It is not part of the*
; *usual get-newspaper frame!*

```
((:= '(GET-NP-STEP T1) GO-PLACE331)
(INST GO-PLACE331 GO-PLACE)
(:= '(AGENT GO-PLACE331) (GN-AGENT T1))
(:= '(PT-PATIENT GO-PLACE331) NEWSP1)
(:= '(PT-LOCATION GO-PLACE331) OUTSIDE))
```
; *the Get-Newspaper frame involves only this one subtask. (It is*
; *enough to illustrate our point. A full frame would have more*
; *steps that would be irrelevant to our present example.)*

**** Sub-act of T1 is CARRY36
**** Sub-act of T1 is GO-PLACE331

**The next task to work on is
CARRY36
It is a model manipulation so I am
asserting**
```
((HAS ME (UMBRELLA (? UM3))))
```
; *NASL has done the carry operation (a primitive in this example)*
; *and asserts that I am carrying an umbrella.*

**The next task to work on is
GO-PLACE331
It is a model manipulation so I am
asserting**
```
((:= '(LOCATION-OF NEWSP1) OUTSIDE)
(:= '(LOCATION-OF (GN-AGENT T1)) OUTSIDE))
```
; *It now performs the go-place operation asserting that I am*
; *outside.*

**PLAN IS COMPLETED SUCCESSFULLY
DONE**
; *At this point we have completed all the steps of the*
; *get-newspaper plan.*

3. SCRAPS *vs.* C-SCRAPS

As a final example we show the behavior of the concurrent version
of the SCRAPS program. We compare the behavior of SCRAPS
and C-SCRAPS in the case where we wish to plan an airflight but
the Air Traffic Controllers are on strike.

3.1. SCRAPS and the air traffic controllers' strike

We start by showing how SCRAPS runs on a simple problem:
planning flying during the air traffic controllers' strike

```
(Compute-zorch 7)
Average branchout is: 5.7913604
Path length average desired is: 7
Initial is being set to 194
; as usual we start by computing the zorch

(assert '(on-strike (atc ?x)))
SETTING FLAG OF TYPE FAIL ON NODE ATCING
NIL
; we assert the information that ATCs are on strike.
; a forward chaining rule sets the fail flag on ATCing.

(atc t1)
I have the top level task T1
It is of type: FLYING
The initial conditions are
((:= '(PASSENGER T1) ME)
(:= '(FROM-PLACE T1) WASHINGTON-DC)
(:= '(TO-PLACE T1) BROWN-UNIVERSITY))
INITIAL TASK = T1
; We start planning the Flying frame

PASSING MARKERS ON: (FLYING BROWN-UNIVERSITY WASHINGTON-D
; and pass markers on the initial conditions

Marker-passer returns 1 path for examination
; only one path is returned.
; The database contains a large number of locations.  The paths
; between Brown-university and Washington-DC are not reported
```

```
CHECKING PATH
(FLYING
(RESTRICTION
(GAIN-TAKE-OFF-CLEARANCE-SCENE (FLYING (? F)))
(CLEARANCING (? CLEARANCING7)
(PILOT (PILOT (FLYING (? F))))
(C-ATC (F-ATC (FLYING (? F))))))
CLEARANCING
(RESTRICTION
(CHECK-STEP (CLEARANCING (? C)))
(ATCING (? ATCING7)
(AGENT (C-ATC (CLEARANCING (? C))))))
ATCING
(ON-STRIKE (ATC (? X2)))
FLAG1)
```
; the path found is the path between FLYING and ATCing involving the
; strike flag (as described in Chapter 4 Section 2.1.2)

```
ATCING:
ASSERTING: (<- (RULE-OUT (? TASK) (ATCING (? TASK)))
(ON-STRIKE (ATC (? X2))))
CLEARANCING:
ASSERTING: (<- (RULE-OUT (? TASK) (CLEARANCING (? TASK)))
(ON-STRIKE (ATC (? X2))))
FLYING:
ASSERTING: (<- (RULE-OUT (? TASK) (FLYING (? TASK)))
(ON-STRIKE (ATC (? X2))))
```
; we rule out ATCing, and the those items on the path it is a
; subtask of: Clearancing and Flying.

INVOKING NASL
The next task to work on is
T1
This requires a ruled-out task: T1 (FLYING)
; the only way to perform T1 is to use the flying frame
; but SCRAPS has ruled that out. The planner finds no
; way to complete this task

PLAN FAILURE (boy, I wish I could back-up)
; and fails.

3.2. C-SCRAPS and the air traffic controllers' strike

When C-SCRAPS runs on the ATC strike the situation is somewhat different. The problem-solver first tells the marker-passer which nodes to pass marks on and then continues — it starts planning the flying frame before the path evaluator has a chance to rule the frame out.

This situation is solved by using the technique described in Chapter 7. The path evaluator examines the frames already used by the planner and, if it rules out a frame already being pursued, puts that information into the memory. The problem-solver periodically checks to see if this information is there. If it is, PLAN FAILURE is recognized and the problem solver quits.

Some notes about the output:

(1)   C-SCRAPS is implemented using the concurrent processes available on a Lisp Machine. These machines have a single processor and use the scheduler to simulate concurrency. This means that each process is swapped in for short time periods. No two events can happen at precisely the same time.

(2)   When run, C-SCRAPS invokes three separate windows, one for each process. The output here is made by diverting each window to a file and then merging the three files. This merging is done by having the millisecond timer tag each message printed by the processes. Items are then put into chronological order.

(3)   Each line of output is tagged by which process produced it. The marker-passer is tagged as "MP," the path evaluator as "PE" and the problem-solver as "PS." Each second the time is printed out as a separate line in the file.

Here, then, is the output for C-SCRAPS. Once again, comments appear in *italics*

5390000
; time stamp. One is printed out each second.

MP: (perpetual-marker-passer)
MP: Marker-passer is WAITING: 5390467
; we start the marker-passer in a loop waiting for input

PE: (perpetual-path-evaluator)
5391000
PE: PATH EVALUATOR is WAITING: 5391308
; we start the path evaluator in a loop waiting for input

5392000
PS: (assert '(on-strike (atc ?x)))
PS: SETTING FLAG OF TYPE FAIL ON NODE ATCING: 5392093
; we assert that air traffic controllers are on strike.
; The flag is set on ATCing as previously.

PS: (c-atc t1)
PS: I have the top level task T1: 5392103
PS: The initial conditions are
PS: ((INST T1 FLYING)
PS: (:= '(PASSENGER T1) ME)
PS: (:= '(FROM-PLACE T1) WASHINGTON-DC)
PS: (:= '(TO-PLACE T1) BROWN-UNIVERSITY)): 5392116
; The planner is invoked with the same initial conditions as before

PS: NASL: Setting up nodes for marker passer: 5392122
PS: Adding WASHINGTON-DC to marker queue: 5392124
PS: Adding ME to marker queue: 5392125
PS: adding BROWN-UNIVERSITY to marker queue: 5392127
; The problem solver places the initial conditions on a queue
; which the marker-passer will examine

PS: The next task to work on is
PS: T1: 5392167
; The problem solver starts the task

MP: Adding FLYING to marker queue: 5392126
MP: PASSING-MARKERS ON: FLYING: 5392286
MP: found path at: ATCING, strength = 53: 5392308
; The marker passer starts spreading activation from the original
; nodes and a path is found

PS: Task can be reduced through its sub-acts:: 5392401
; *Meanwhile, the problem solver continues working on the*
; *flying task.*

PE: CHECKING PATH:
PE: (FLYING
PE: (RESTRICTION
PE: (GAIN-TAKE-OFF-CLEARANCE-SCENE (FLYING (? F)))
PE: (CLEARANCING (? CLEARANCING14)
PE: (PILOT (PILOT (FLYING (? F))))
PE: (C-ATC (F-ATC (FLYING (? F))))))))
PE: CLEARANCING
PE: (RESTRICTION
PE: (CHECK-STEP (CLEARANCING (? C)))
PE: (ATCING (? ATCING9)
PE: (AGENT (C-ATC (CLEARANCING (? C))))))))
PE: ATCING
PE: (ON-STRIKE (ATC (? X14)))
PE: FLAG7): 5392426
; *and the Path Evaluator starts examining the returned path*

PE: ASSERTING: (RULE-OUT (? TASK) (ATCING (? TASK))): 5392430
PE: ASSERTING: (RULE-OUT (? TASK) (CLEARANCING (? TASK))): 5392433
PE: ASSERTING: (RULE-OUT (? TASK) (FLYING (? TASK))): 5392437
; *and asserts the appropriate rule-outs (as in SCRAPS)*

PE: PLACING INFORMATION TO STOP PROBLEM SOLVER
; *The PE has ruled out a frame already being expanded*
; *by the planner. It places this information in the memory*

PE: PATH EVALUATOR is WAITING (after 1 paths): 5392441
; *and goes back to waiting for more paths*

PS: ((:= '(PLANE-FLIGHT-SCENE T1)
PS: PLANING23)
; *The problem solver, meanwhile is expanding the flying plan*
; *this involves all the following:*

PS: (INST PLANING23 PLANING)
PS: (:= '(AGENT PLANING23) ME)): 5392554
PS: ((:= '(GAIN-TAKE-OFF-CLEARANCE-SCENE
PS: T1) CLEARANCING15)
PS: (INST CLEARANCING15 CLEARANCING)

PS: (:= '(PILOT CLEARANCING15)
PS: (PILOT T1))
PS: (:= '(C-ATC CLEARANCING15)
PS: (F-ATC T1))): 5392582
PS: ((:= '(BOARD-PLANE-STEP T1)
PS: GO-TO-GATE15)
PS: (INST GO-TO-GATE15 GO-TO-GATE)
PS: (:= '(AGENT GO-TO-GATE15) ME)
PS: (:= '(GATE GO-TO-GATE15)
PS: (GATE-OF T1))
PS: (:= '(PLANE-OF GO-TO-GATE15)
PS: (FLIGHT T1))): 5392863
PS: ((:= '(WEAPONS-CHECK-SCENE T1)
PS: WEAPONS-CHECKING15)   •
PS: (INST WEAPONS-CHECKING15
PS: WEAPONS-CHECKING)
PS: (:= '(CHECKER WEAPONS-CHECKING15)
PS: (GUARD T1))
PS: (:= '(CHECKEE WEAPONS-CHECKING15)
PS: ME)
PS: (:=
PS: '(WC-BAGGAGE WEAPONS-CHECKING15)
PS: (F-BAGGAGE T1))): 5392902
PS: ((:= '(CHECK-IN-SCENE T1)
PS: AIRPORT-CHECK-IN15)
PS: (INST AIRPORT-CHECK-IN15
PS: AIRPORT-CHECK-IN)
PS: (:= '(CHECKEE AIRPORT-CHECK-IN15)
PS: ME)
PS: (:= '(CHECKER AIRPORT-CHECK-IN15)
PS: (AIR-AGENT T1))
PS: (:= '(BOUGHT AIRPORT-CHECK-IN15)
PS: T1)): 5392938
PS: ((:= '(GO-AIRPORT-STEP T1)
PS: GO-PLACE97)
PS: (INST GO-PLACE97 GO-PLACE)
PS: (:= '(AGENT GO-PLACE97) ME)
PS: (:= '(PT-LOCATION GO-PLACE97)
PS: WASHINGTON-DC)): 5392964
5393000
PS: **** Sub-act of T1 is PLANING23: 5393154
PS: **** CLEARANCING15 comes before PLANING23: 5393304
PS: **** Sub-act of T1 is CLEARANCING15: 5393337
PS: **** GO-TO-GATE15 comes before CLEARANCING15: 5393608

PS: **** Sub-act of T1 is GO-TO-GATE15: 5393619
PS: **** WEAPONS-CHECKING15 comes before GO-TO-GATE15: 5393642
PS: **** Sub-act of T1 is WEAPONS-CHECKING15: 5393779
PS: **** AIRPORT-CHECK-IN15 comes before WEAPONS-CHECKING15: 5393
PS: **** Sub-act of T1 is AIRPORT-CHECK-IN15: 5393814
PS: **** GO-PLACE97 comes before AIRPORT-CHECK-IN15: 5393962
PS: **** Sub-act of T1 is GO-PLACE97: 5393983
; At this point the problem solver has decomposed the flying task
; into an ordered set of subtasks.   Before continuing,
; it checks to see if the path evaluator has added anything of import
; to the memory.

5394000
PS: Stopping Work: Error reported by Path Evaluator:: 5394003
; the information is found...

PS: -- Problem solver is already working on FLYING: 5394004
PS: -- Which has just been RULED-OUT: 5394005
; reported...

PS: PLAN FAILURE (boy, I wish I could back-up): 5394006
; and acted upon. In this case a failure is caused. The problem
; solver reports failure...

MP: STOPPING ON SIGNAL FROM Problem solver: 5394051
PE: STOPPING IN SIGNAL FROM Problem solver: 5394108
; and signals the other processes to stop

3.3. C-SCRAPS commits suicide

As a final example we see a longer example of C-SCRAPS as it
handles the suicide planning task

PE: (perpetual-path-evaluator)
PE: PATH EVALUATOR is WAITING: 8284968
MP: (perpetual-marker-passer)
MP: Marker-passer is WAITING: 8285420
;we start the processes

PS: (ASSERT '(HAS ME GUN))
PS: SETTING FLAG OF TYPE PERCEPTUAL ON NODE GUN: 8287193
; chaining rule sets the flag

PS: (c-su t1)
; The planner is invoked

8289000

PS: I have the top level task T1: 8289095
PS: The initial conditions are
PS: ((INST T1 SUICIDE) (:= '(AGENT T1) ME)): 8289100
PS: NASL: Setting up nodes for marker passer: 8289103
PS: Adding ME to marker queue: 8289105
PS: Adding SUICIDE to marker queue: 8289106
; The initial conditions are sent to the marker-passer

PS: The next task to work on is
PS: T1: 8289115
; and the task decomposition in started

MP: PASSING-MARKERS ON: SUICIDE: 8289155
MP: PASSING-MARKERS ON: ME: 8289156
; the marker-passer starts work on the given nodes.

MP: found path at: GUN, strength = 1881: 8289159
MP: sent to path evaluator: 8289160
MP: found path at: PERSON, strength = 1: 8289163
MP: sent to path evaluator: 8289164
MP: found path at: SHOOT, strength = 14: 8289179
MP: sent to path evaluator: 8289180
MP: found path at: PERSON, strength = 1: 8289183
MP: sent to path evaluator: 8289184
MP: found path at: OCCUPATION, strength = 1: 8289186
MP: sent to path evaluator: 8289187
MP: found path at: GUN, strength = 14: 8289193
MP: sent to path evaluator: 8289194

MP: found path at: GUN, strength = 149: 8289196
MP: sent to path evaluator: 8289197
MP: found path at: VEHICLE, strength = 1: 8289203
MP: sent to path evaluator: 8289204
MP: found path at: ANIMAL, strength = 1: 8289206
MP: sent to path evaluator: 8289207
; and reports the paths as they're found

PE: CHECKING PATH
PE: (ME
PE: (:= '(PET-OF ME) BRUCE)
PE: BRUCE
PE: (INST BRUCE RAT)
PE: RAT
PE: (ISA RAT ANIMAL)
PE: ANIMAL
PE: (RESTRICTION
PE: (PET-OF (PERSON (? PERSON)))
PE: (ANIMAL (? ANIMAL20)))
PE: PERSON
PE: (RESTRICTION
PE: (AGENT (SUICIDE (? S)))
PE: (PERSON (? PERSON854)))
PE: SUICIDE): 8289237
PE: NO ACTION TAKEN FOR THIS PATH
; The first path found is a low strength path, it does nothing

PE: : 8289255
PE: PATH EVALUATOR is WAITING (after 1 paths): 8289256
; and the path evaluator waits for the next path

PS: There is only one way to do the task:
PS: ((SUB-ACT T1 ACHIEVE63)
PS: (INST ACHIEVE63 ACHIEVE)
PS: (:= '(AGENT ACHIEVE63) ME)
PS: (:= '(STATE-OF ACHIEVE63)
PS: (KILLING (? KILLING731)
PS: (AGENT ME)
PS: (PATIENT ME))))): 8289286
PS: **** Sub-act of T1 is ACHIEVE63: 8289292
PS: The next task to work on is
PS: ACHIEVE63: 8289303
PS: I am setting up a choice task
; The problem solver continues planning the suicide event

; by finding the methods of achieving the killing

MP: found path at: ME, strength = 14: 8289341
MP: Already reported -- not sent: 8289342
MP: found path at: PERSON, strength = 1: 8289344
MP: sent to path evaluator: 8289344
MP: found path at: PERSON, strength = 1: 8289346
MP: sent to path evaluator: 8289347
MP: Marker-passer is WAITING: 8289349
; and the marker-passer continues marking and reporting paths

PE: CHECKING PATH
PE: (ME
PE: (:= '(CAR-OF ME) HONDA)
PE: HONDA
PE: (ISA HONDA CAR)
PE: CAR
PE: (ISA CAR VEHICLE)
PE: VEHICLE
PE: (RESTRICTION
PE: (CAR-OF (PERSON (? PERSON)))
PE: (VEHICLE (? VEHICLE20)))
PE: PERSON
PE: (RESTRICTION
PE: (AGENT (SUICIDE (? S)))
PE: (PERSON (? PERSON854)))
PE: SUICIDE): 8289404
PE: NO ACTION TAKEN FOR THIS PATH
PE: : 8289418
PE: PATH EVALUATOR is WAITING (after 2 paths): 8289419
; which the path evaluator continues to examine

PE: CHECKING PATH
PE: (ME
PE: (:= '(PET-OF ME) BRUCE)
PE: BRUCE
PE: (INST BRUCE RAT)
PE: RAT
PE: (ISA RAT ANIMAL)
PE: ANIMAL
PE: (RESTRICTION
PE: (PET-OF (PERSON (? PERSON)))
PE: (ANIMAL (? ANIMAL20)))
PE: PERSON

PE: (RESTRICTION
PE: (AGENT (SUICIDE (? S)))
PE: (PERSON (? PERSON854)))
PE: SUICIDE): 8289442
PE: REJECTED: PATH ALREADY EXAMINED: 8289443
; because the path evaluator examines paths as they come, it
; is occasionally the case that a path is found by the marker-
; passer for a second time after the PE has already checked
; it. When this happens the path is quickly rejected by
; Heuristic 0 (Chapter 5, Section 2.1)

PE: PATH EVALUATOR is WAITING (after 3 paths): 8289444

PS: CHOOSE7 to decide among these options:: 8289502
PS: (SHOOT (? SHOOT2311)
PS: (AGENT ME)
PS: (PATIENT ME)): 8289509
PS: (HANG (? HANG1911)
PS: (AGENT ME)
PS: (PATIENT ME)): 8289515
PS: (POISONING (? POISONING1911)
PS: (AGENT ME)
PS: (PATIENT ME)): 8289522
; The problem solver is setting up the choice points

PE: CHECKING PATH
PE: (ME
PE: (:= '(CAR-OF ME) HONDA)
PE: HONDA
PE: (ISA HONDA CAR)
PE: CAR
PE: (ISA CAR VEHICLE)
PE: VEHICLE
PE: (RESTRICTION
PE: (CAR-OF (PERSON (? PERSON)))
PE: (VEHICLE (? VEHICLE20)))
PE: PERSON
PE: (RESTRICTION
PE: (AGENT (SUICIDE (? S)))
PE: (PERSON (? PERSON854)))
PE: SUICIDE): 8289592
PE: REJECTED: PATH ALREADY EXAMINED: 8289593
PE: PATH EVALUATOR is WAITING (after 4 paths): 8289594
; while the path evaluator continues

PS: **** Sub-act of ACHIEVE63 is CHOOSE7: 8289661
PS: The next task to work on is
PS: CHOOSE7: 8289666
PS: CHOOSE is primitive so I am just doing it: 8289675
; we try ruling out the bad options:

PS: After ruling out we are left with: 8289688
PS:
PS: (SHOOT (? SHOOT23111)
PS: (AGENT ME)
PS: (PATIENT ME)): 8289695
PS:
PS: (HANG (? HANG19111)
PS: (AGENT ME)
PS: (PATIENT ME)): 8289702
PS:
PS: (POISONING (? POISONING19111)
PS: (AGENT ME)
PS: (PATIENT ME)): 8289709
; but cannot rule any out.

PE: CHECKING PATH
PE: (SUICIDE
PE: (TO-DO (SUICIDE (? S))
PE: (ACHIEVE (? ACHIEVE62)
PE: (AGENT (AGENT (SUICIDE (? S))))
PE: (STATE-OF (KILLING (? KILLING73)
PE: (AGENT (AGENT (SUICIDE (? S))))
PE: (PATIENT (AGENT (SUICIDE (? S))))))))))
PE: KILLING
PE: (CAUSES (SHOOT (? SHOOT23)
PE: (AGENT (? X))
PE: (PATIENT (? Y)))
PE: (KILLING (? KILLING74)
PE: (AGENT (? X))
PE: (PATIENT (? Y))))
PE: SHOOT
PE: (RESTRICTION
PE: (S-INSTR (SHOOT (? S))) (GUN (? GUN19)))
PE: GUN
PE: (HAS ME GUN)
PE: FLAG17): 8289645

; The Path Evaluator finds the important path.

PE: ASSERTING: (<- (RULE-IN (? TASK) (SHOOT (? TASK)))
                    (HAS ME GUN)): 8289874
; and makes the appropriate rule-in (Just in the nick of time!)

PE: PATH EVALUATOR is WAITING (after 5 paths): 8289875

PS: And then we rule-in...: 8289898
; the PS looks for rule-in statements and finds the one just added
; by the Path Evaluator. If the rule-in has not yet been asserted
; the PS would not be able to make a choice. In C-SCRAPS it will
; go into a loop waiting until either a rule-in appears (is
; asserted by the PE) or the PE signals that it is out of paths
; to evaluate. In the latter case we would get a PLAN FAILURE

PS: (SHOOT (? SHOOT23111)
PS: (AGENT ME)
PS: (PATIENT ME)): 8289910
PS: So I choose
PS: (SHOOT (? SHOOT23111)
PS: (AGENT ME)
PS: (PATIENT ME)): 8289923
PS: **** Sub-act of ACHIEVE63 is SHOOT24: 8289929
PS: The next task to work on is
PS: SHOOT24: 8289948
; The planner continues to work on. It decomposes the shoot
; event and plans the subtasks (omitted)

●●●

PE: CHECKING PATH
PE: (SUICIDE
PE: (TO-DO (SUICIDE (? S))
PE: (ACHIEVE (? ACHIEVE62)
PE: (AGENT (AGENT (SUICIDE (? S))))
PE: (STATE-OF (KILLING (? KILLING73)
PE: (AGENT (AGENT (SUICIDE (? S))))
PE: (PATIENT (AGENT (SUICIDE (? S)))))))))
PE: KILLING
PE: (CAUSES (SHOOT (? SHOOT23)
PE: (AGENT (? X))
PE: (PATIENT (? Y)))

```
PE:   (KILLING (? KILLING74)
PE:        (AGENT (? X))
PE:        (PATIENT (? Y))))
PE: SHOOT
PE: (RESTRICTION
PE:   (S-INSTR (SHOOT (? S))) (GUN (? GUN19)))
PE: GUN
PE: (HAS ME GUN)
PE: ME): 8290113
PE: REJECTED: PATH ALREADY EXAMINED: 8290142
PE: PATH EVALUATOR is WAITING (after 6 paths): 8290144
; Meanwhile the PE continues examining paths.
```

•••

```
PS: PLAN IS COMPLETED SUCCESSFULLY
; The planner eventually completes successfully.

PE: STOPPING ON SIGNAL FROM Problem Solver: 8290446
MP: STOPPING ON SIGNAL FROM Problem Solver: 8290498
; which stops the other processes
```

CHAPTER 11

Conclusion

... Implementing Version I, whose shortcomings are all too obvious, was exhausting; it made him feel grubby for nothing. (Not at all like the TECO macros he took time out for along the way!) He feels as if he's paid his dues; now he can join the theoreticians. What's more, he *should*. Implementation details will make his thesis dull. The people want *epistemology*.

... The final report usually pleases most people (more people than it should), impressing them but leaving them a little hungover. They are likely to be taken with [the technique], especially if a theorem about it is proved, but the overall approach to the real problem lacks definition. Performance and promise run together like the colors of a sunset. The happy feeling is kindled that indefinite progress has already started ... the document fails to stimulate or challenge; it merely feeds the addict's desire for reassurance that AI is not standing still, and it raises his tolerance a little.

— Drew McDermott, *Artificial Intelligence Meets Natural Stupidity [1981]*

In this chapter we attempt to summarize the work presented in this book. We examine its strengths and weaknesses, and discuss directions for future research that it suggests.

1. A brief summary

SCRAPS attacks the problem of choice in planning, a subset of the general "relevance" problem. It does this by using a marker-passer: a nondeductive, activation-spreading program that can be realized as a massively parallel algorithm. (The system is presently implemented on a serial machine using queues to simulate breadth-first parallel behavior — algorithms for several parallel versions are described.) This marker-passing technique has previously been shown to be useful in the context of natural language processing systems and cognitive modeling.

The marker-passer is used to generate a set of paths which are then evaluated by a path evaluator. This evaluator checks the paths for various types of information. If this information is found, the path evaluator can cause the planner to accept, reject, or modify those plans being used.

An implementation of such a system has been described. It adds a dumb marker-passer and a path evaluator to the NASL planner. (NASL is a "plan interpreter" as opposed to a "plan compiler.") This plan evaluator is a set of cascaded heuristics that check paths for certain patterns. If these are found, variable bindings are then checked to see whether following the path can add information in the present planning context. If so, the path evaluator adds statements in the memory that the planner can take advantage of. The marker-passing and plan evaluation stages can be done in parallel with the actual planning. A program demonstrating this, C-SCRAPS, has also been implemented.

An important feature of the SCRAPS program is the ability of other processes to leave information in memory that the marker-passer can use. (This information can be added by a deductive component or by a perceptual system.)

There are, however, some weaknesses in the present model. These are discussed below, along with research directions suggested by this work.

1.1. A brief summary (annotated and containing back pointers)

SCRAPS attacks the problem of choice in planning, a subset of the general "relevance" problem.

> This is the problem of making sure that information already contained in the knowledge base can be brought to bear at appropriate times. SCRAPS addresses the issue of making choices during planning in the presence of such information — what we have called the "early decision / late information" problem.
> *Chapter 4, Section 2.1.1*
>
> Previous approaches to this problem have included using preconditions
> *Chapter 4, Section 2.1.1.1*
> and logical analysis.
> *Chapter 4, Section 2.1.1.2*

It does this by using a marker-passer: a nondeductive, activation-spreading program

> A description of the issues involved in creating such systems was presented.
> *Chapter 6*

that can be realized as a massively parallel algorithm.

> Massive Parallelism is also one of the primary themes of connectionist systems. A comparison of SCRAPS to connectionist models was presented. Various connectionist systems were compared to SCRAPS and we examined both whether SCRAPS itself might be considered a connectionist system and if not, how it might benefit from the connectionist approach.
> *Chapter 9*

(The system is presently implemented on a serial machine using queues to simulate breadth-first parallel behavior —

algorithms for several parallel versions are described.)

Parallelism is an important part of getting a marker-passer to operate efficiently. We described "local algorithms" for the placing of marks and the reporting of paths assuming a SIMD, massively parallel machine. A psuedocode level description of these local algorithms was given.
Chapter 6, Section 3.3.1
We also showed how parallel versions of SCRAPS could be designed for three existing parallel architectures: the MCMOB processor of the University of Maryland
Chapter 7, Section 1.3.1
the BBN Butterfly using "futures"
Chapter 7, Section 1.3.2
and the TMC Connection Machine.
Chapter 7, Section 1.3.3
We also pointed out an interesting fact about parallel formulations of SCRAPS: Zorch can be seen as a feedback mechanism between the problem-solver and the marker-passing components of the system.
Chapter 7, Section 1.4

This marker-passing technique has previously been shown to be useful in the context of natural language processing systems

A review of past marker-passing systems and the recent work in natural language is found in
Chapter 3

and cognitive modeling.

The marker-passer used in SCRAPS resembles the cognitive spreading activation mechanisms proposed in the past. It has severe shortcomings, however, when considered as a cognitive model in its own right.
Chapter 8, Section 1
The book does, however, suggest some possible avenues of exploration to cognitive scientists seeking to study

planning behavior. In particular, it suggests the use of a spreading activation mechanism in the planning process.
Chapter 8, Section 2

The marker-passer is used to generate a set of paths that are then evaluated by a path evaluator. This evaluator checks the paths for various types of information. If this information is found the path evaluator can cause the planner to

This flow of control is essential to the SCRAPS model.
Chapter 4, Section 1

accept,

The path evaluator will suggest a plan be used when one of the objects used in that plan can already be found in the "perceptual environment" of the planner.
Chapter 5, Section 2.3
This is seen in the "commit suicide while holding a gun" example.
Chapter 4, Section 2.1.3
Chapter 10, Sections 2.1 and 3.3

reject,

The path evaluator suggests that plans should not be used if they lead to an inherent problem,
Chapter 5, Section 2.5
as in the "buy a cleaver on a business trip" example,
Chapter 4, Section 2.1.5
Chapter 10, Sections 1.2
or if they involve agents or objects that are known to be "failing,"
Chapter 5, Section 2.4
as in the "air traffic controllers' strike."
Chapter 4, Section 2.1.2
Chapter 10, Sections 3.1 and 3.2

or modify those plans being used.

> Modification occurs when "demons" are found in the paths
> (and are found to be applicable given the initial conditions
> of the plan and the variables in the paths).
> *Chapter 5, Section 2.2*
> This allows the demons to be activated at an earlier stage
> in the processing. This, in turn, allows plans to be
> modified before they are processed. An example of this is
> seen in the "getting a newspaper on a rainy day" problem,
> where the SCRAPS system was able to add a step to the
> GET-NEWSPAPER frame so that carrying an umbrella
> was included as a step prior to going outside.
> *Chapter 4, Section 2.1.4*
> *Chapter 10, Section 2.2*

An implementation of such a system has been described. It adds a dumb marker-passer

> The marker-passer used by SCRAPS finds sets of paths in
> a fast but "dumb" manner — very little checking for
> correctness is done until the evaluation stage. It uses an
> attenuation scheme and checks to avoid reporting
> redundant paths. The design of this system is presented in
> detail.
> *Chapter 6*

and a path evaluator
> *Chapter 5*

to the NASL planner. (NASL is a "plan interpreter" as opposed to a "plan compiler.")

> The planner that SCRAPS uses generates plans a step at a
> time and doesn't back up. When an error is encountered it
> either plans around it, or fails. Our version of NASL is
> based on the original version designed by McDermott
> (1977).
> *Chapter 1, Section 3.1*

As previously mentioned, SCRAPS addresses the issues arising from making choices during planning. Past work in planning has taken other approaches.
Chapter 2

This plan evaluator is a set of cascaded heuristics that check paths for certain patterns.

These patterns match the conditions mentioned previously.
Chapter 5

If these are found, variable bindings are then checked to see whether following the path can add information in the present planning context.

The mechanism used by SCRAPS to do this is quite heuristic. The heuristics are motivated, however, by formal principles developed by Eugene Charniak.
Chapter 5, Section 3

If so, the path evaluator adds statements in the memory which the planner can take advantage of.

These statements are in the form of rules that the FRAIL knowledge representation language can handle and which the NASL problem-solver can take advantage of: rule-in and rule-out statements and assertions that add steps to plans.
Chapter 1, Section 3.1

The marker-passing and plan evaluation stages can be done in parallel with the actual planning.

This requires a limited communication ability between the components. In particular, the path evaluator must be able to ascertain the plans already in use by the planner, since it must be able to stop the planner when it rules out a plan already in effect.
Chapter 7, Section 1.2

Chapter 10, Section 3.2

A program demonstrating this, C-SCRAPS, has also been implemented.
Chapter 7

An important feature of the SCRAPS program is the ability of other processes to leave information in memory that the marker-passer can use.

> This information is in the form of flags that can be seen by the marker-passer but are placed in memory and removed by other processes.
> *Chapter 4, Section 2.2*

(This information can be added by a deductive component

> Such as forward chaining rules in the knowledge base.
> *Chapter 4, Section 2.2.2*

or by a perceptual system.)

> SCRAPS has no access to an actual perceptual system. These flags must be placed in memory directly.
> *Chapter 4, Section 2.2.2*

There are, however, some weaknesses in the present model. These are discussed below along with research directions suggested by this work.
Read on...

2. Shortcomings

In making a complex AI program work one must sometimes sacrifice elegance for results. Further, to get the model to work one must either solve all the previously unsolved problems it encounters, or else provide patches providing for ignoring these problems until a later date. Finally, there is usually a set of known problems in a model that never quite seem to get fixed.

Instead of leaving the task of finding these weak spots as a guessing game for the reader, I'd like to suggest a few places to look.

2.1. Weaknesses

When I started this project I knew that I would not come up with a model that would be saluted as a pinnacle of formality. I did, however, hope I could tie up the loose ends. While I did manage to handle many of them, several still elude me.

2.1.1. Initial zorch

One of the more interesting features of this work is the attenuation mechanism in the marker-passer — the zorch function. This simple idea, associating a number with each mark and using branching factors to limit propagation, provides a single mechanism to handle attenuation, path strength, and the removal of links. What could be more elegant?

Unfortunately, this elegance is in a large part predicated on being able to come up with a formally justifiable initial value of zorch. Much thought has gone into coming up with a theory that would explain what number to start with. We have made some progress.

First, we were able to formulate the relative ranking of paths so that it did not depend on the value of the initial setting. Further, we've reduced the problem of setting the initial zorch to that of deciding on the average maximum length of paths to be returned by the system. Thus, in a serial implementation, path length, and thus initial zorch, must be an empirically derived constant until further notice.

In a parallel implementation, particularly on a massively parallel machine as proposed in Chapters 6 and 7, we feel somewhat better about zorch. The number is no longer a constant set at some point and remaining throughout the system, but rather is viewed as a feedback mechanism allowing the path evaluator to control the marker-passer as discussed in Chapter 7.

2.1.2. The set of path evaluators

A second source of "scruffiness" in the system is in the working of the path evaluator. In Chapter 5, Section 3, I described Charniak's formal basis for path evaluation. I even went so far as to claim that the path evaluator in SCRAPS was based on this model. What does that mean?

In honesty, I must admit that it does not mean as much as I'd like. The rules that reject bad paths are heuristic approximations to behavior that the formal system would have. The same is true of the steps in each of the heuristics which check variable bindings. When a path slips through unexpectedly, or is rejected without cause, I can check the results against his model. This is quite comforting.

Unfortunately, that's about as far as I can go. The rules that extract information about the paths are based on no model except necessity. I have no reason to believe that these heuristics are a sufficient set to cover all planning problems or the necessary set to cover the situations handled. Further, the path evaluation heuristics are dependent on the set of flags used in the system. I have presented a set that handles a large class of cases but may not be a sufficient set for all possible planning behaviors.

Our work has demonstrated that path evaluation can be done in the planning domain, but, like most experiments, many issues have been left only partially resolved. Clearly, more work is needed in this area.

2.1.3. Secondary marking

Finally, I am still stymied in an attempt to explain the exact points in the planning process at which the marker-passer must be called. The earliest versions of the SCRAPS program had to be told by the user exactly what nodes to pass marks on. These nodes were always a subset of the initial conditions given to the planner, and were limited to this subset so as to keep the set of returns small.

Extensive analysis of what was occurring during marker-passing showed why more paths were found than expected. This analysis led to the development of one-way links, the zorch mechanism, and the path strength computation. These in turn kept the number of total paths down to a managable size — we were able to invoke the marker-passer with the full set of initial conditions and have things work. This solved the problem of what nodes to pass marks to at the start of planning, but what about later in the process? All of the examples I've given need none of this secondary marking.

If we had a magical zorch oracle, or a truly smart marker-passer, the set of paths from the initial conditions would include, and perhaps even be limited to, all those paths which could add information in the current planning situation. The search space for the marker-passer is the set of plans reachable from this one and the set of objects involved in the plan.[1] Our magical zorch mechanism would make sure our search was successful. Unfortunately, such a mechanism would need to be as powerful as the planner itself, and thus creating such a mechanism defeats our purpose of keeping marker-passing an efficient, underlying, heuristic mechanism.

Unfortunately, our present zorch mechanism occasionally keeps us from getting all the paths we need just from the initial conditions. We may have enough zorch to reach "weapons-checking" from "flying" but not from "buying." In a truly comprehensive system we would need to pass markers again later in the process just to make sure.

This secondary marking doesn't work in our present system. As the problem-solver operates, it creates new frames and objects. Each of these is linked into the original knowledge base. When we pass secondary markers, the number of paths found explodes exponentially — any path previously reported will be reported again.

To see this, consider once again planning to commit suicide while holding a gun. The problem-solver generates a specific task, say TASK-25, which represents the top-level problem being solved. Variables are then assigned to the slots of this task. As subacts

---

1- The bindings of those variables for which specific values are important are stated in the initial conditions.

are needed, new task definitions are created. Thus, by the end of the planning session our knowledge base contains information like

(INST TASK-25 SUICIDE)
(:= (AGENT TASK-25) *ME*)

(TO-DO TASK-25 TASK-37)

(INST TASK-26 HANG)
(:= (AGENT TASK-26) *ME*)
(:= (HANG-INSTRUMENT TASK-26) NOOSE-27)
(:= (GET-HANG-INSTRUMENT-STEP TASK-26)
    TASK-27)

...
(MATERIAL-OF NOOSE-27 ROPE-1)

If we pass markers on ROPE during the problem-solving process, we would find the connection to SUICIDE not only via HANG but via TASK-25 as well. We find two (or more) paths for each one we would have found before.

The obvious solution is to keep this information separate. We could create datapools for planning information, or tag those nodes created by the problem-solver in a way that tells the marker-passer to ignore them. We make these nodes into "second-class" data. This works well if the problem-solver is viewed as an entity unto itself. Unfortunately, as mentioned in the Introduction, the problem-solver must share its knowledge base with other systems (primarily the story comprehender). When we go to solve a later problem, or wish to read a story involving previously generated plans, these formerly temporary nodes now are the very nodes over which the marker-passer wishes to spread activation. Again, consider the example: Having finished solving the suicide task, we might later read about "the hanging." We now wish to allow markers to reach TASK-26, the specific information about this hanging. Whereas previously we avoided marking TASK-26, we now must mark it.

This problem doesn't seem insurmountable. One could design yet another mechanism to determine when to change temporary nodes into permanent nodes. This would require a mechanism that takes into account the contexts in which planning and comprehension take place.

Unfortunately, the set of mechanisms we have outlined brings up many new issues for investigation. What seems to be a simple problem, when to do secondary marking, proves quite difficult in practice. The solution, although important, is as yet unclear. This is another area for future investigation.

2.2. A kludge

Getting the examples in Chapter 10 to work required one piece of legerdemain not yet discussed. The attenuation and path strength mechanisms in the marker-passer require promiscuous nodes to limit the flow of markers. Consider the case of the node "person." The PERSON frame serves as a slot restriction in virtually every action frame. The agent of a suicide is a person. So is the waitress in a restaurant, the salesperson we buy a cleaver from, the guard who checks for weapons, etc. In a large knowledge base, such a node has a very large branchout and paths between two such nodes are not found — zorch and path strength see to that.

Unfortunately, our formula for computing initial zorch was motivated by principles concerning average behavior. Our formula depends crucially on the average branchout of nodes in our system. In our small knowledge base a few "promiscuous" nodes (in this case "person," "thing," and "action") can heavily bias our average.

One way I attempted to handle this problem was to manipulate this average statistically so as to remove the bias. The initial zorch constant was computed by taking the log of the branchouts, averaging these, and taking the anti-log of the result to the power (length-1)/2. The number computed in this way, however, turned out to be too small in the present system. Too many of the nodes had little or no branchout and instead of the promiscuous nodes causing a high biasing, these nodes caused a bias in the other direction.

The solution I finally used in the examples shown was to enlarge the knowledge base with a relatively large number (1000) of randomly generated frames. These frames were all actions involving one or more persons and one or more objects. The initial zorch generated by the "compute-zorch" program in Chapter 10 takes these nodes into account. This accounts for both the lack of paths through promiscuous nodes seen in the examples, and also for the occasional "low-strength" path through personal data about the node "me."

One of my top research priorities for the future is to avoid this problem in the obvious way — I wish to try SCRAPS in a large knowledge base. We must show that the claims will hold up, and I believe they will, in a database not created with SCRAPS in mind.[2]

2.3. Limitations

SCRAPS is based on the NASL planner and the FRAIL knowledge representation language. This means that the program is restricted in what can be represented. It also means the planner cannot back up when it fails. Neither of these has been a serious problem in the implementation of SCRAPS.

The FRAIL representation language has proven adequate for exploring the issues raised in this work. I was able to represent the actions and objects I wished to, with one exception: FRAIL, like many other knowledge representation systems, has no means for bridging the gap between specific objects and "generics." If, for example, we had a restaurant frame where one ordered a hamburger, we could order HAMBURGER-23 (in which case the waitress is forced to bring us the exact one we ordered) or we can order (HAMBURGER ?x) (in which case no specific instance of a hamburger is created[3]).

SCRAPS ran into this problem when trying to add "getting an umbrella" to the get-newspaper frame. It was no trouble, as shown, to have the information added that an umbrella should be gotten, but there was no means to assert "now go to the place where that umbrella is" in a way that the planner could actually

---

2– We are presently examining integrating a marker-passer into a large knowledge base of medical facts currently being used the diagnosis of neurological disorders.

3– Wong (1981) points out that the technical meaning of a formula such as (HAMBURGER ?x) is the set of all things that are hamburgers. Not only do we end up not ordering a specific hamburger, we instead order every hamburger in the world.

go to a specific location. Instead, it must go to (location-of (umbrella ?u)) — an unspecified location. Thus, if we wished John to get an umbrella belonging to himself, and if we knew that all of John's umbrellas were in the hall closet, we would not be able to pass marks to the HALL-CLOSET-123 node. If we knew of a demon (occult, not a production rule) living in that closet, we could not decide to rule out this step: The marker-passer would not find it.

The second problem, lack of backtracking, has not affected our ability to examine the choice mechanism. Backtracking occurs after the failure is reached — our goal is to avoid the failure or, at least, reach it sooner. It would be nice, however, for SCRAPS to do some backtracking instead of asserting "PLAN FAILURE" when all the options were ruled out.

3. Research directions

As a final section, I'd like to suggest some possible future research directions growing out of the present work. These range through a spectrum from "doable" to "you're joking."

3.1. "Applied" SCRAPS

In this day and age of applied AI, I am intrigued by the notion of using SCRAPS in a "real-world" system. SCRAPS is designed to run in a large knowledge base and it would be ideal to try it on a system that was not designed with marker-passing in mind. Also attractive is the idea of running the marker-passer in a knowledge base that contains probabilistic information. In such a domain we could use the probabilities as weights to examine the behavior of an extended zorch mechanism.

SCRAPS addresses the issue of making choices. One type of choice mechanism that I have not examined, however, is that of conflict resolution in a production rule system. Supposing our system has a catastrophic failure state if certain conditions hold (not an unrealistic expectation given the present level of military AI spending). We would like to avoid these conditions at all costs. Is there some way a marker-passing type of mechanism could recognize these future possibilities in the same manner that SCRAPS recognizes demon rules?

3.2. Planning meets story comprehension

Early AI research viewed planning and story comprehension as totally separate endeavors. Later research suggested that they shared a common knowledge base (see Charniak, 1975; Allen, 1979; Wong, 1981; and Wilensky, 1983). SCRAPS was motivated by a belief that not only was the knowledge base shared, but that processes in the knowledge base were used by both. Charniak's system and mine can share not only the marker-passer but large portions of the path evaluator. Could it be that we could go even further?

Wilensky's (1978) PAM system understands stories based on plans. When told

John needed money. He got a gun. He walked into a liquor store.

PAM figures out what is happening. But PAM doesn't project the plans into the future: It never says "He could rob a liquor store" when told that John needs money.

SCRAPS, on the other hand, if told to solve "get money" while a flag is set on "(Has me gun)," will probably consider robbing a liquor store even before pulling out its wallet and checking. It could provide the predictive component that is missing from most story comprehension systems. We can even envision how such a system could be designed: Using a system such as Charniak's WIMP to do story comprehension would cause marker-passing to occur. Some of the paths found would match the patterns looked for in the path evaluation heuristics used for planning. These rules would cause planning behavior to occur in the guise of expectations for the story comprehender. We could add information like

I'd rule-in shooting, so John might try that.
I wouldn't take a plane today, maybe he'd better not.
He's going to get wet if he doesn't carry an umbrella.
I wonder how he plans to get that cleaver home?

3.3. Replanning

When I originally decided not to buy a cleaver while on a business trip, my primary reason was "I don't want to check my luggage." SCRAPS has no way to do anything like this. It notices the problem with carrying a cleaver on an airplane, but it cannot get around it: It simply says, "Don't fly home." How could we do better?

One of the difficulties in debugging plans is knowing where to look for the fix. How do we notice that getting arrested depends crucially on the checking of our luggage that occurred several branches ago in the planning tree? SCRAPS offers a mechanism for addressing this problem.

Consider that when SCRAPS rules out frames it is looking backwards through a short list — the path that contained the problem. We know where the problem occurs (somewhere between "flying" and "weapons checking"). Can we not search the space in-between these two with a specific goal in mind ("avoid **(Has me cleaver-1)**")? Certainly this search space would be reasonably well confined.

3.4. Complex planning

Present-day problem-solvers usually can only pursue a small number (usually one) of goals at a time. Most of them can only have one agent pursuing these goals. If we allow multiple goals and multiple agents, a whole can of worms has been opened. We must worry about goal subsumption, goal competition, and all those other issues that were discussed in Chapter 2, Section 2.2. These situations are not only hard to plan around, they are hard to detect! Consider the following example (based on Wilensky, 1978):

John wanted to get the treasure. A dragon was watching it.

You see the obvious problem; will your system?

SCRAPS is quite good at identifying situations where these interactions between agents occur — remember the case where Bill loses his wallet while John is hungry? Yet, we have to go to great lengths to avoid such paths. Can we not take advantage of SCRAPS' abilities to recognize such interactions?

Another interesting aspect of SCRAPS' behavior appears when we consider a planner with a large number of active goals (for example, that lunar rover we've described earlier). When a new event is observed, it must be compared with all possible active goals, a prohibitively large search space. Thus, the planner can miss a serendipitous chance of solving one goal while pursuing another (our rover misses out on the chance to use FOLLOW-MOON-MAN-23 and instead completes DRILL-YET-ANOTHER-CORE-SAMPLE-92651).   Marker-passers   discover   such connections even when we wish them not to.

As an example of this, consider one of the "useless" paths found in the cleaver buying example. We would find the path

(2) BUYING → TAKE-TRIP → PLANE → MEAL →
COOKING → CLEAVER → CLEAVER-1
(that is, a meal is served on the plane and cleavers can be used in the preparation of meals)

The path evaluator then had to spend time recognizing that this path added no information that the planner could take advantage of. A major design task for SCRAPS was developing a path evaluation heuristic that could quickly eliminate such paths. The result of our development yielded a system that did quickly reject such paths, but could not avoid finding them in the first place.

Analysis of the paths that were causing us trouble has led us to the realization that this seeming "bug" is really a feature. Many of what we assumed were bad paths in SCRAPS are turning out to be beneficial paths when we examine a system that tries to plan simultaneous goals. To understand this better, consider once again path 2. This path can be read as saying "If you carry a cleaver on an airplane you could use it for cooking the meal which is served." Instead of a path that adds no information, this path, in fact, explicates an interaction between plans. In this particular case it is not a useful one, but in other cases it often is.

Consider the following example (based on an example from Wilensky, 1983):

**You need to buy butter and you need to buy meat.
You live one mile from a butcher shop.
In the other direction, 1 mile, is a dairy.
1.5 miles away is a large grocery store.**

The elegant solution is to go to the large grocery rather than to make two separate trips. If, however, we use the traditional approach of solving each of the goals in turn, we will fail to recognize this interaction — two trips will be made.

A marker-passing planner might solve this problem using the following information

Butter is available in a dairy.
Meat is available in a butcher shop.
Butter is available in a large grocery store.
Meat is available in a large grocery store.
Dairies, butcher shops, and large grocery stores
are all stores.
Shopping occurs in a store.

When the system was asked to solve two shopping tasks, one with butter as the object to be bought, one with meat, it would pass markers from SHOPPING, BUTTER, and MEAT, as in SCRAPS, and find the following paths

(3) BUTTER → DAIRY → STORE → SHOPPING
(4) BUTTER → GROCERY → STORE → SHOPPING
(5) MEAT → BUTCHER → STORE → SHOPPING
(6) MEAT → GROCERY → STORE → SHOPPING
(7) MEAT → GROCERY → BUTTER

Paths 3–6 are exactly the sorts of paths which SCRAPS likes. They suggest the various plans that could be used to achieve the individual goals. It is Path 7, however, which used to annoy us, but now can prove useful.

Path 7 suggests that a connection can be found between BUTTER and MEAT — they can both be found in the GROCERY. The system could now examine the set of paths found and discover that GROCERY is also suggested as a plan that solves the subgoals. The path evaluator therefore would suggest to the planner that GROCERY will serve to join the two plans. The planner then can use the grocery trip, since the total distance is less. Thus, in a multiple goal planner the marker-passer can help us recognize a beneficial interaction among the goals it starts with.

Our proposed multiple-goal "MG-SCRAPS" could also be used to discover problematic interactions between goals. Consider the example of Bill, a student who wishes to buy some books and also to buy some dinner. Assuming that the combined cost is more than Bill has available, what would happen? If we used the traditional approach, Bill would first buy the books and then plan the restaurant trip. At this point a good planner (such as

SCRAPS) would recognize that the restaurant trip was impossible. Bill would end up with food for thought, but not for dinner.

Again, the solution is to recognize the interaction and then plan a solution. In this case the MG-SCRAPS marker-passer would find the path

(8) BUY (books) → PAY → PAY BILL → RESTAURANT

The path evaluation heuristics would recognize that it points out a potential conflict between the two goals. A conflict resolution mechanism might then be invoked to decide on the best plan. MG-SCRAPS can look at the priorities associated with the two goals and satisfy that goal specified as most important.

Another use of a marker-passing mechanism for a planner would be in a dynamically changing domain. Consider the case where the planner was, once again, on our hypothetical lunar rover. As items enter and leave the perceptual field of the moving rover, they might be marked via the robot's sensory system as having PERCEPTUAL flags. If current plans require use of an object that is so flagged, the robot is able to use such an object. Once the object left the perceptual field, it would no longer be flagged, and thus the robot wouldn't find these paths. Thus, in a constantly changing domain the marker-passing planner is able to take notice of items that are currently available.

3.5. Marker-passing as a context mechanism

The ACT* model, discussed in Chapter 8, used spreading activation to determine that one region of memory could be more readily accessed than another. Could the marker-passer used by SCRAPS do the same?

SCRAPS is formulated to report paths only when intersections are found. There is nothing inherently interesting about a node that has been marked once — it is the second vibrating of the same hockey puck that brings it to our notice. Could we try the other approach?

Perhaps the zorch mechanism can be viewed as more than an adjunct to be used by the marker-passer. Why not say that the region of nodes that is marked defines the active memory? Facts found in this region could be accessed faster (only? with greater certainty?). Perhaps marker-passing will solve more of the relevance problem than we've examined so far.

3.6. Mechanisms II

The final research direction we point out is that marker-passing is a mechanism that runs at a level "below" our normal symbolic computations. It is, in effect, the computational equivalent of a "subconscious" process. The planner in SCRAPS never looks at the marker-passer's paths; it only needs to see what is left for it by the path evaluator. What other mechanisms of this sort might exist?

Consider, once again, "getting the newspaper on a rainy day." We used a demon that said "If you go OUTSIDE and it is raining OUTSIDE then carry an umbrella." We could not assert "IF you go SOMEWHERE and it is raining AT THAT PLACE then carry an umbrella." The marker-passer matches constants, not variables. Could a mechanism be designed to perform a fast, minimal matching on variables during a marker-passing-like phase?

An even more complex mechanism might match whole patterns. If we had such a process, we might be able to solve what I've taken to calling the "meta-cleaver" problem. My first thought upon going to buy the cleaver was "I cannot buy this cleaver, I don't want to check my luggage on the flight home." (This has been what we've called the "cleaver problem.") The meta-cleaver problem is based on my second thought: "Wow, that's an example of the kind of problem I need in which to demonstrate that marker-passing is useful during planning."

Bilbliography

Pigmies placed on the shoulders of giants see more than the giants themselves.
— Lucan, *The Civil War, bk. I, [circa 50 A.D.]*

Abelson, R.P. Concepts for representing mundane reality in plans *Representation and Understanding,* (ed.) Bobrow, D.G and Collins, A.M, Academic Press, New York, 1975.

Abelson, R.P Constraint, construal, and cognitive science *Proceedings of the Third Annual Conference of the Cognitive Science Society,* 1981, *1-9.*

Allen, J.F. *A Plan-Based Approach to Speech Act Recognition,* Doctoral Dissertation, Department of Computer Science, University of Toronto, 1979.

Allen, J.F. and Koomen, J.A. Planning using a temporal world model *Proceedings of the Eighth International Joint Conference on Artificial Intelligence,* 1983, *741-747.*

Alterman, R. Adaptive planning: Refitting old plans to new situations *Proceedings of the Seventh Annual Conference of the Cognitive Science Society,* 1985, *222-226.*

Alterman,R. A dictionary based on concept coherence *Artificial Intelligence,* 25(*2*), 1985, *153-186.*

Anderson, J.R. *The Architecture of Cognition,* Harvard University Press, Massachusetts, 1983.

Anderson, J.R. and Bower, G.H. *Human Associative Memory,* Lawrence Erlbaum Associates, New Jersey, 1979.

Anderson, J.R. Retrieval of propositional information from long-term memory *Cognitive Psychology,* 6, 1974, *451-474.*

Baker, H. and Hewitt, C. The Incremental Garbage Collection of Processes, *Conference Record of the Conference on AI and Programming Languages,* August, 1977. *55-59.*

Becker, C.A. Semantic context effects in visual word recognition: an analysis of semantic strategies *Memory and Cognition,* 8, 1980, *493-512.*

Berlin, D.L.S. Integrating problem-solving tactics *Proceedings of the Ninth International Joint Conference on Artificial Intelligence,* 1985, *1047-1051.*

Beiderman, I., Glass, A.L., and Stacy, E.W. Searching for aspects in real world scenes *Journal of Experimental Psychology,* 97, 1973, *22-27.*

285

Blelloch, G.E. *AFL-1: A programming language for massively concurrent computers* MIT AI Laboratory, Technical Report AI-TR 918 (forthcoming, 1986).

Brachman, R. I Lied About the Trees *The AI Magazine*, VI(*3*), 1985, *80-93*.

Byrne, R. Planning meals: Problem-solving on a real-world database *Cognition*, 5, 1977, *287-332*.

Carbonell, J.G. *Subjective Understanding: Computer Models of Belief Systems* Doctoral Dissertation, Department of Computer Science, Yale University, (available as Research Report #150), 1979.

Carbonell, J.G. Learning by analogy: formulating and generalizing plans from past experience *Machine Learning: An Artificial Intelligence Approach*, (ed.) Mitchell, M.C., Tioga Press, California, 1983.

Chapman, D. Nonlinear planning: A rigorous reconstruction *Proceedings of the Ninth International Joint Conference on Artificial Intelligence*, 1985, *1022-1024*.

Charniak, E. *Toward a Model of Children's Story Comprehension*, Doctoral Dissertation, Massachusetts Institute of Technology, (Available as AI Laboratory Technical Report #266), 1972.

Charniak, E. A partial taxonomy of knowledge about actions *Proceedings of the Fourth International Joint Conference on Artificial Intelligence*, *91-97*.

Charniak, E. A common representation for problem-solving and language-comprehension information *Artificial Intelligence*, 16(*3*), 1975, *46-55*.

Charniak, E. The case-slot identity theory *Cognitive Science*, 5(*3*), 1981, *285-291*.

Charniak, E. Context recognition in language comprehension *Strategies for natural language processing*, (ed.) Lehnert, W.G. and Ringle, M.H., Lawrence Erlbaum Associates, 1982, *435-454*.

Charniak, E. Passing markers: A theory of contextual influence in language comprehension *Cognitive Science*, 7(*3*), 1983, *171-190*.

Charniak, E. *Knowledge Representation and the Plan-Recognition-as-Planning[-1] Theory*, Computer Science Department, Brown University, Technical Report CS-85-01, 1985.

Charniak, E. Motivation analysis, abductive unification, and non-monotonic equality, to be published in *Artificial Intelligence*, 1986.

Charniak, E. *A Single-Semantic-Process Theory of Parsing*, (forthcoming).

Charniak, E. *A Neat Theory of Marker-Passing*, (forthcoming-b).

Charniak, E., Gavin, M.K. and Hendler, J.A. *The FRAIL/NASL reference manual*, Computer Science Department, Brown University, Technical Report CS-83-06, 1983.

Charniak, E. and McDermott, D.V. *Introduction to Artificial Intelligence*, Addison-Wesley, Massachusetts, 1985.

Collins. A.M. and Loftus, E.F. A spreading-activation theory of semantic processing *Psychological Review*, 6, 1972, *407-428*.

Collins, A.M. and Quillian, M.R. Retrieval time from semantic memory *Journal of Verbal Learning and Verbal Behavior*, 8, 1969, *240-247*.

Collins, A.M. and Quillian, M.R. Facilitating Retrieval from Semantic Memory: The effect of repeating part of an inference *Acta Psychologica*, 33, 1970, *304-314*.

Collins, A.M. and Quillian, M.R. Does category size effect categorization time? *Journal of Verbal Learning and Verbal Behavior*, 9, 1970, *432-438*.

Colvin, M.E., Tromp, J.W. and Eeckman, F.H. *A model for Cortical Function*, Presented at "Neural Networks for Computing," Snowbird, Utah, April, 1986.

Conrad, C. Cognitive economy in semantic memory *Journal of Experimental Psychology*, 92, 1972, *149-154*.

Cottrell, G.W. *A Connectionist Approach to Word Sense Disambiguation* Doctoral Dissertation, Computer Science Department, University of Rochester, May, 1985.

Cottrell, G.W Connectionist parsing *Proceedings of the Seventh Annual Conference of the Cognitive Science Society*, 1985, *201-211*.

Crick, F. Thinking about the brain, *Scientific American*, Sept., 1979.

Cullingford, R.E. *Script Application: Computer understanding of newspaper stories*, Doctoral Dissertation, Computer Science Department, Yale University, (available as Research Report #116), 1978.

Davis, R. *Applications of Meta Level Knowledge to the Construction, Maintenance, and Use of Large Knowledge Bases*, AI Laboratory, Stanford University, Memo AIM-283, 1976.

Dean, T.L. *Temporal imagery: An approach to reasoning about time for planning and problem solving*, Doctoral Dissertation, Computer Science Department, Yale University, 1986.

DeGroot, A.M.B The range of automatic spreading activation in word priming *Journal of Verbal Learning and Verbal Behavior*, 22, 1983, *417-436*.

Doyle, J. *Truth Maintenance Systems for Problem Solving*, AI Laboratory, Massachusetts Institute of Technology, Working Paper #108, 1977.

Drummond, M.E. Refining and extending the procedural net *Proceedings of the Ninth International Joint Conference on Artificial Intelligence*, 1985, *1010-1012*.

Duck-Lewis, R.M. Workshop on the psychological reality of Lisp *AISB quarterly*, #40-41, 1981, *19-20*.

Ernst, G.W. and Newell, A. *GPS: A Case Study in Generality and Problem-Solving*, Academic Press, New York, 1969.

Fahlman, S.E. *NETL: A System for Representing and Using Real World Knowledge*, MIT Press, Massachusetts, 1979.

Fahlman, S.E. Representing implicit knowledge *Parallel Models in Associative Memory*, (ed.) Hinton, G.E and Anderson, J.A., Lawrence Erlbaum Associates, New Jersey, 1981.

Fahlman, S.E., Hinton, G.E. and Sejnowski, T.J. Massively parallel architectures for AI: NETL, Thistle, and Boltzmann machines *Proceedings of the National Conference on Artificial Intelligence*, 1983, *109-113*.

Feldman, J.A. and Ballard, D.H. Connectionist models and their properties *Cognitive Science*, 6, 1982. *205-254*.

Feldman, J.A., Ballard, D.H., Brown, C.M. and Small, C.L. *Rochester Connectionist Papers: 1979-1984* Computer Science Department, University of Rochester, Technical Report TR-124 Revised, June, 1984.

Fikes, R. and Nilsson, N.J. STRIPS: A new approach to the application of theorem proving to problem solving *Proceedings of the Second International Joint Conference on Artificial Intelligence,*, 1971, *189-208*.

Fischler, I. and Goodman, G.O. Latency of associative activation in memory *Journal of Experimental Psychology: Human Perception and Performance*, 4, 1978, *455-470*.

Freedman, J.L. and Loftus, E.F. Retrieval of words from long-term memory *Journal of Verbal Learning and Verbal Behavior*, I10), 1973 *107-115*.

Fodor, J.A. Tom Swift and his procedural grandmother *Cognition*, 6(*3*), 1978, *229-247*.

Georgeoff, M.P. Strategies in heuristic search *Artificial Intelligence*, 20, 1983, *393-425*.

Granger, R.H. , Eiselt, K.P. and Holbrook, J.K. *Parsing with Parallelism: A Spreading-Activation Model of Inference Processing During Text Understanding* Artificial Intelligence Project, University of California, Irvine Technical Report #228, Sept. 1984.

Granger. R.H. and Holbrook, J.K. *Perseverers, Recencies, and Deferrers: New Experimental Evidence for Multiple Inference Strategies in Understanding* Artificial Intelligence Project, University of California, Irvine Technical Report #195, May, 1983.

Hayes, P.J. On semantic nets, frames, and associations *Proceedings of the Fifth International Joint Conference on Artificial Intelligence*, 1977, *99-107*.

Hayes-Roth, B. and Hayes-Roth, F. A cognitive model of planning, *Cognitive Science*, 3, 1979, *559-565*.

Hayes-Roth, B. Evolution of cognitive structure and processes *Psychological Review*,84, 1977, *260-278*.

Hebb, D.O. *The Organization of Behavior*, Wiley, New York, 1949.

Hendler, J.A Integrating Marker-Passing and Problem Solving *Proceedings of the Seventh Annual Conference of the Cognitive Science Society*, 1985, *130-139*.

Hendler, J.A. *Integrating Marker-passing and problem-solving: A spreading activation approach to improved choice in planning* Doctoral Dissertation, Brown University, January, 1986.

Hendler, J.A. and Phillips, B. *A Flexible Control Structure for the Conceptual*

Analysis of Natural Language Using Message-Passing, Computer Research Laboratory, Texas Instruments Incorporated, Technical Report TR-08-81-03, 1981.

Hendler, J.A. and Sanborn, J. *Towards Dynamic Planning*, Computer Science Department, University of Maryland, Technical Report TR-1785, March, 1987.

Hewitt, C. *Description and Theoretical Analysis (Using Schemata) of PLANNER: A language for proving theorems and manipulating models in a robot* AI Laboratory, Massachusetts Institute of Technology, Technical Report TR-258, 1972.

Hillis, W.D *The Connection Machine*, MIT Press, Massachusetts, 1985.

Hinton, G.E. and Anderson, J.A. *Parallel Models of Associative Memory*, Lawrence Erlbaum Associates, New Jersey, 1981.

Hirst, G.J. *Semantic Interpretation Against Ambiguity* Doctoral Dissertation, Department of Computer Science, Brown University, (available as Technical Report CS-83-25), 1983.

Hirst, G.J. *Semantic Interpretation and the Resolution of Ambiguity* Cambridge University Press, Cambridge, England, 1986.

Hirst, G.J. and Charniak, E. Word sense and case slot disambiguation *Proceedings of the National Conference on Artificial Intelligence*, 1982, *95-98*.

Juola, J.F. and Atkinson, R.C. Memory scanning for words versus categories *Journal of Verbal Learning and Verbal Behavior*, 10, 1971, *522-527*.

King, D.R.W. and Anderson, J.R. Long-term memory search: an intersecting activation process *Journal of Verbal Learning and Verbal Behavior*, 15, 1976, *587-606*.

Kolodner, J.L. Reconstructive memory: A computer model *Cognitive Science*, 7, 1983, *281-328*.

Kolodner, J.L. and Simpson, R.L. Experience and problem solving: a framework *Proceedings of the Sixth Annual Conference of the Cognitive Science Society*, 1984.

Larkin, J.H. Enriching formal knowledge: a model for learning to solve textbook problems *Cognitive Skills and Their Acquisition*, (ed.) Anderson, J.R., Lawrence Erlbaum Associates, 1981.

Lewis, C.H. and Anderson, J.R. Interference with real world knowledge *Cognitive Psychology*, 8, 1976, *311-355*.

Loftus, E.F. Activation of semantic memory *American Journal of Psychology*, 86, 1973, *331-337*.

Loftus, E.F. Category dominance, instance dominance, and categorization time *Journal of Experimental Psychology*, 97, 1973, *70-74*.

Lorch, R.F. Jr. Priming and Search Processes in Semantic Memory: A test of three models of spreading activation *Journal of Verbal Learning and Verbal Behavior*, 21, 1982, *468-492*.

Lucas, M. Lexical access during sentence comprehension *Proceedings of the Fifth Annual Conference of the Cognitive Science Society*, 1983, *[unpaginated]*.

Manna, Z. and Waldinger, R. *Knowledge and Reasoning in Program Synthesis*, Stanford Research Institute, Technical Note 98, 1974.

Martin, N., Friedland, P., King, J. and Stefik, M. Knowledge base management for experiment planning *Proceedings of the Fifth International Joint Conference on Artificial Intelligence*, 1977, *882-887*.

Massaro, D.W., Jones, R.D., Lipscomb, C., and Scholz, R. Role of prior knowledge on naming and lexical decisions with good and poor stimulus information *Journal of Experimental Psychology: Human Learning and Memory*, 4, 1978, *498-512*.

McClelland, J.L. and Rumelhart, D.E. An interactive activation model of the effect of context in perception: Part I, An account of basic findings *Psychological Review*, 88, 1981.

McDermott, D.V. *Flexibility and Efficiency in a Computer Program for Designing Circuits*, AI Laboratory, Massachusetts Institute of Technology, Technical Report AI-TR-402, 1977.

Mcdermott, D.V. Planning and Acting *Cognitive Science*, 2(*2*), 1978, *71-109*.

McDermott, D.V. *The NISP Manual*, Department of Computer Science, Yale University, Research Report #274, 1983.

McDermott, D.V. Artificial intelligence meets natural stupidity, *Mind Design*,(ed.) Haugeland, J., Bradford Books, Publishers Inc., Montgomery, Vermont, 1981, *143-160*.

McKoon, G. and Ratcliff, R. Priming in item recognition: The organization of propositions in memory for text *Journal of Verbal Learning and Verbal Behavior*, 19, 1980, *369-386*.

Meehan, J. *The Metanovel: Writing stories by computer*, Doctoral Dissertation, Computer Science Department, Yale University, (available as Research Report #74), 1976.

Meyer, D.E. Correleated operations in searching stored semantic categories *Journal of Experimental Psychology*, 99, 1973, *124-133*.

Meyer, D.E. and Schvaneveldt, R.W. Facilitation in recognizing pairs of words: Evidence of a dependence between retrieval operations *Journal of Experimental Psychology*, 90, 1971, *227-234*.

Moore, R.C. *Reasoning From Incomplete Knowledge in a Procedural Deductive System*, AI Laboratory, Massachusetts Institute of Technology, Technical Report, TR-347, 1975.

Myers, J.L. and Lorch, R.F. Jr. Interference and facilitation effects of primes upon verification processes *Memory and Cognition*, 8, 1980, *405-414*.

Neisser, U. *Cognitive Psychology*, Appleton, New York, 1967.

Newell, A. Production systems: models of control structures *Visual Information*

Processing, (ed.) Chase, W.G., Academic Press, New York, 1973.

Newell,A. Shaw, J.C. and Simon, H.A. A variety of intelligent learning in a general problems solver *Self Organizing Systems*, (ed.) Yovits, W.C. and Cameron, S., Pergamon Press, New York, 1960, *153-189*.

Newell, A. (ed.) *IPL-V Programmer's Reference Manual*, The RAND Corporation, Memorandum RM-3739-RC, 1963.

Nevins, A. A human oriented logic for automatic theorem-proving *Journal of the ACM*, 21(*4*), 1974, *606*.

Nilsson, N.J. *Problem-Solving Methods in Artificial Intelligence*, McGraw-Hill, New York, 1971.

Norvig, P. *Unified Theory of Inference for Text Understanding*, Doctoral Dissertation, Computer Science Department, University of California at Berkeley, 1986 (available as: Report No. UCB/CSD 87/339, Department of Computer Science, University of California—Berkeley, Jan., 1987)

Onifer, W. and Swinney, D.A. Accessing lexical ambiguities during sentence comprehension: Effects of frequency of meaning and contextual bias *Memory and Cognition*, 9(*3*), 1981, *225-236*.

Parker, J. presentation at CMU Connectionist Models Summer School, Pittsburgh, Pa., June, 1986.

Pearl, J. Bayesian networks: A model of self-activated memory for evidential reasoning *Proceedings of the Seventh Annual Conference of the Cognitive Science Society*, 1985, *329-334*.

Posner, M.I. *Chronometric Explorations of Mind*, Lawrence Erlbaum Associates, New Jersey, 1978.

Posner, M.I. and Snyder, C.R.R. Attention and cognitive control *Information Processing and Cognition*, (ed.) Solso, R.L., Lawrence Erlbaum Associates, New Jersey, 1975.

Phillips, B. *Topic Analysis*, Doctoral Dissertation, Department of Computer Science, State University of New York at Buffalo, 1975.

Phillips, B. An object-oriented parser *Computational Models of Natural Language Processing*, (ed.) Bara, B.G. and Guida, G., Elsevier, North-Holland, 1984.

Phillips, B. and Hendler, J.A. A message-passing control structure for text understanding *Proceedings of the Ninth International Conference on Computational Linguistics*, 1982, *307-312*.

Pollack, J.B. and Waltz, D.L Natural Language Processing using spreading activation and lateral inhibition *Proceedings of the Fourth International Conference of the Cognitive Science Society*, 1982, *50-53*.

Quillian, M.R. *Semantic Memory*, Doctoral Dissertation, Carnegie Institute of Technology (Carnegie-Mellon University), 1966. Published as Report 2, Project 8668, Bolt, Baranek, and Newman Inc., 1966.

Quillian, M.R. The Teachable Language Comprehender: A simulation program and theory of language *Communications of the ACM*, 12, 1969, *459-476*.

Ratcliff, R. and McKoon, G. Does activation really spread? *Psychological Review*, 88, *454-457*.

Reggia, J. Virtual inhibition in parallel activation models of associative memory *Proceedings of the 9th International Joint Conference on Artificial Intelligence*, 1986, *244-148*.

Reggia, J., Milheim, S. and Freeman, A. Competition-based conectionist models of associative memory *Proceeding of the 1986 IEEE International Conference on Systems, Man, and Cybernetics*, 1986, *17-21*.

Rieger, C. An organization of knowledge for problem solving and language comprehension *Articial Intelligence*, 7(*2*), 1976.

Riesbeck, C.K. and Martin, C.E. *Direct Memory Access Parsing*, Computer Science Department, Yale University, Research Report #354, 1985.

Ringle, M.H. Psychological studies and artificial intelligence *The AI Magazine*, 4(*1*), 1983, *37-43*.

Rips, L.J., Shoben, E.J. and Smith, E.E. Semantic distance and the verification of semantic relations *Journal of Verbal Learning and Verbal Behavior*, 12, 1973 *410-430*.

Robinson, J.A. A machine-oriented logic based on the resolution principle *Journal of the ACM*, 12, 1965.

Rosch, E. On the internal structure of perceptual and semantic categories *Cognitive Development and Acquisition of Language*, (ed.) Moore, T.E., Academic Press, New York, 1973.

Rosch, E. Cognitive representations of semantic categories *Journal of Experimental Psychology: General*, 104, *192-233*.

Rosenbloom, P., Laird, J.E., Newell, A. and Orciuch, E. R1-Soar an experiment in knowledge-intensive programming in a problem-solving architecture *IEEE Workshop on Principles of Knowledge-Based Systems*, 1984.

Rulifson, J.F., Derkson, J.A., and Waldinger,R.J. *QA4: A Procedural Calculus for Intuitive Reasoning*, Stanford Research Institute, Technical Note 73, 1972.

Rumelhart, D.E., McClelland, J.L. and the PDP Research Group *Parallel Distributed Computing, (Volume 1 and Volume 2)* MIT Press, Cambridge, Ma., 1986.

Rumelhart, D.E., Hinton, G.E., and Williams, R.J. Learning internal representations by error propogation *Parallel Distributed Computing—Volume 1*, Rumelhart, D.E. and McClelland, J.L., MIT Press, Cambridge, Ma. 1986.

Rychener, M.D. *The Student Production System: A study of encoding knowledge in production rules*, Computer Science Department, Carnegie-Mellon University, 1975.

Sacerdoti, E.D. Planning in a hierarchy of abstraction spaces *Artificial Intelligence*, 5(*2*), 1974, *115-135*.

Sacerdoti, E.D. *A Structure for Plans and Behavior*, Elsevier, North-Holland, 1977.

Sanford, A.J, Garrod, S., and Boyle, J.M. An independence of mechanism in the origin of reading and classification-related semantic distance effects *Memory and Cognition*, 5, 1977, *214-220*.

Schank, R.C. Conceptual dependency: A theory of natural language understanding *Cognitive Psychology*, 3, 1972, *552-631*.

Schank, R.C. and Abelson, R.P. *Scripts, Plans, Goals, and Understanding: An enquiry into human knowledge structures*, Lawrence Erlbaum Associates, New Jersey, 1977.

Schmidt,C., Sridharan, N. and Goodson, J. The plan recognition problem *Artificial Intelligence*, 11(*1,2*), 1978, *45-83*.

Schvaneveldt, R.W. and Meyer, D.E. Retrieval and comparison processes in semantic memory *Attention and Performance IV*, (ed.) Kornblum, S., Academic Press, New York, 1973.

Scott, C.A. (ed.) *Butterfly LISP Reference Manual* BBN Labs, Apri, 1986.

Selman, B. and Hirst, G.J. A rule-based connectionist parsing system *Proceedings of the Seventh Annual Conference of the Cognitive Science Society*, 1985, *212-219*.

Seidenberg, M.S. The time course of information activation and utilization in visual word recognition *Reading Research: Advances in Theory and Practice, Vol. 5* (ed.) Bosner, Waller, and MacKinnon, Academic Press, New York, 1985, *199-252*.

Seidenberg, M.S., Tanenhaus, M.K., Lieman, J.M. and Bienkowski, M.A. Automatic access of the meaning of ambiguous words in context: Some limitations of knowledge-based processing *Cognitive Psychology*, 14(*4*), 1982, *489-537*.

Sejnowski, T. J. and Rosenberg, C. R. (1986). *NETtalk: A parallel network that learns to read aloud* Johns Hopkins University Electrical Engineering and Computer Science Technical Report JHU/EECS-86/01, 1986.

Sharkey, N.E., Sutcliffe, R.F.E., and Wobcke, W.R. Mixing binary and continuous connection schemes for knowledge access *Proceedings of the Fifth National COnference on Artificial Intelligence*, 1986.

Shastri, L. *Evidential Reasoning in Semantic Networks: A formal theory and its parallel implementation* Doctoral Dissertation, Computer Science Department, University of Rochester, Sept., 1985.

Shiffrin,R.M. and Schneider, W. Controlled and automatic human information processing. II. Perceptual learning, automatic attending, and a general theory *Psychological Review*, 84, 1977, *127-190*.

Simon, H.A. *The Sciences of the Artificial*, MIT Press, Massachusetts, 1969.

Small, S., Cottrell, G.W., and Shastri,L. Toward connectionist parsing

Proceedings of the National Conference on Artificial Intelligence, 1982, *247-250*.

Smith, E.E., Shoben, E.J. and Rips, L.J. Comparison processes in semantic memory *Psychological Review*, 81, 1974, *214-241*.

Smolensky, P. Schema selection and and stochastic inference in modular environments *Proceedings of the National Conference on Artificial Intelligence*, 1983, *378-382*.

Sobek, R.P. A robot planning structure using production rules *Proceedings of the Ninth International Joint Conference on Artificial Intelligence*, 1985, *1103-1115*.

Steele, G.L., Woods, D.R., Finkel, R.A., Crispin, M.R., Stallman, R.M., Goodfellow, G.S. *The Hacker's Dictionary*, Harper and Row, New York, 1983.

Stefik, M. Planning with constraints (MOLGEN: Part 1) *Artificial Intelligence*, 14(*2*), 1980, *111-140*.

Stefik, M. Planning and met-planning (MOLGEN: Part 2) *Artificial Intelligence*, 14(*2*), 1980, *141-170*.

Stuart, C. An implementation of a multi-agent plan synchronizer *Proceedings of the Ninth International Joint Conference on Artificial Intelligence*, 1985, *1031-1033*.

Sussman, G.J. *A Computer Model of Skill Acquisition*, Elsevier, New York, 1975.

Sussman, G.J. and McDermott, D.V. From PLANNER to CONNIVER — A genetic approach *Proceedings of the Fall Joint Computer Conference*, 1972, *1171*.

Sussman, G.J., Winograd, T., and Charniak, E. *Micro-PLANNER Reference Manual*, Project MAC, Massachusetts Institute of Technology, AI Memo 203, 1970.

Swinney, D.A. Lexical access during sentence comprehension: (Re)Consideration of context effects *Journal of Verbal Learning and Verbal Behavior*, 18, 1979, *645-659*.

Tanenhaus, M.K., Leiman, J.M., Seidenberg, M.S. Evidence for multiple stages in the processing of ambiguous words in syntactic contexts *Journal of Verbal Learning and Varbal Behavior*, 18(*4*), 1976, *681-689*.

Tate, A. *INTERPLAN: A plan generation system which can deal with interactions between goals*, Machine Intelligence Research Unit, University of Edinburgh, Memorandum MIP-R-109, 1974.

Tate, A. Interacting goals and their use *Proceedings Fourth International Joint Conference on Artificial Intelligence*, 1975.

Tate, A. Generating Project Networks *Proceedings of the Fifth International Joint Conferecne on Artificial Intelligence*, 1977, *888-893*.

Thorndyke, P.W. and Bower, G.H. Storage and retrieval processes in sentence memory *Cognitive Psychology*, 6, 1974, *515-543*.

Touretsky, D.S. *The Mathematics of Inheritance Systems*, Doctoral Dissertation, Computer Science Department, Carnegie-Mellon University, 1984.

Touretsky, D.S. and Hinton, G.E. Symbols among the neurons: Details of a connectionist inference architecture *Proceedings of the Ninth International Joint Conference on Artificial Intelligence*, 1985, *238-243*.

Vere, S.A. Planning in time: Windows and durations for activities and goals *IEEE Transactions on Pattern Analysis and Machine Intelligence*, PAMI-5(*3*), 1983, *246-247*.

Vere, S.A. Splicing plans to achieve misordered goals *Proceedings of the Ninth International Joint Conference on Artificial Intelligence*, 1985, *1016-1021*.

Vere, S.A. Temporal Scope of assertions and window cutoff *Proceedings of the Ninth International Joint Conference on Artificial Intelligence*, 1985, *1055-1059*.

Waltz, D.L. On the interdependence of language and perception *Proceedings of the Second Interdisciplinary Workshop on Theoretical Issues in Natural Language Processing*, 1978, *149-156*.

Warren, D.H.D. *WARPLAN: A system for generating plans*, Department of Computational Logic, University of Edinburgh, Memo #76, 1974.

Warren, R.E. Time and the spread of activation in memory *Journal of Experimental Psychology*, 102, 1974, *151-158*.

Weinreb, D. and Moon, D. *Lisp Machine Manual*, Massachusetts Institute of Technology, 1978.

Weiser, M., Kogge, S., McElvany, M., Pierson, R., Post, R.,and Thareja, A. Status and Performance of the Zmob Parallel Processing System *Proceeding of the IEEE CompCon Conference*, February, 1985.

Wilensky, R. *Understanding Goal-Based Stories* Yale University Computer Science Research Report No. 140, Sept. 1978

Wilensky, R. *Planning and Understanding* Addison-Wesley, 1983.

Wilkins, A.J. Conjoint frequency, category size, and categorization time *Journal of Verbal Learning and Verbal Behavior*, 10, 1971, 382-385.

Wilkins, D.E. Domain-independent planning: Representation and plan generation *Artificial Inteligence*, 22(*3*), 1984, *269-302*.

Wilks, Y.A. An artificial intelligence approach to machine translation *Computer Models of Thought and Language*, (ed.) Schank, R.C. and Colby, K.M., W.H. Freeman and Company, San Francisco, 1973.

Wong, D. *On the unification of language comprehension with problem solving*, Doctoral Dissertation, Brown University, (available as Technical Report CS-78), 1981.

Author Index

Page numbers by n indicate footnotes; page numbers in *italics* denote pages with complete bibliographic information.

A

Abelson, R. P., 49, *285, 293*
Allen, J. F., 9n, 53, 279, *285*
Alterman, R., 53, 68, 112, *285*
Anderson, J. R., 32, 71, 182, 188, 189, 190n, *285, 289*
Atkinson, R. C., 185, *289*

B

Baker, H., 174, *285*
Ballard, D. H., 206, 214, 214n, *288*
Becker, C. A., 193, *285*
Beiderman, I., 202n, *285*
Berlin, D. L. S., 47, *285*
Bienkowski, M. A., 186, *293*
Blelloch, G. E., 218, 220, *286*
Bower, G. H., 182, 199, *285, 294*
Boyle, J. M., 193, *293*
Brachman, R., 63n, *286*
Brown, C. M., 214n, *288*
Byrne, R., 201, *286*

C

Carbonell, J. G., 50, 53, *286*
Chapman, D., 47, *286*
Charniak, E., 9, 23, 25, 33n, 48, 49, 53, 55, 64, 67, 89, 118, 121n, 130, 144, 177, 187, 279, *286, 289, 294*
Collins, A. M., 183, 184–185, 185n, 190n, 196, *286, 287*
Colvin, M. E., 206, *287*
Conrad, C., 185, *287*
Cottrell, G. W., 70, 188, 214, 216, 217, 218n, *287, 293*
Crick, F., 206, *287*
Crispin, M. R., 58n, *294*
Cullingford, R. E., 29n, *287*

D

Davis, R., *287*
Dean, T. L., 53, *287*
DeGroot, A. M. B., 194, *287*
Derkson, J. A., 47, *292*
Doyle, J., *287*

Drummond, M. E., 47, *287*
Duck-Lewis, R. M., *287*

E

Eeckman, F. H., 206, *287*
Eiselt, K. P., 68, 69, 190n, *288*
Ernst, G. W., 39, *287*

F

Fahlman, S. E., 22, 32, 34, 60–64, 206, 224,
    287, 288
Feldman, J. A., 206, 214, 214n, *288*
Fikes, R., 29n, 39, *288*
Finkel, R. A., 58n, *294*
Fischler, I., 193, *288*
Fodor, J. A., 38n, *288*
Freedman, J. L., 185, 197, *288*
Freeman, A., 211n, *292*
Friedland, P., 45, *290*

G

Garrod, S., 193, *293*
Gavin, M. K., 23, 48, *286*
Georgeoff, M. P., 47, *288*
Glass, A. L., 202n, *285*
Goodfellow, G. S., 58n, *294*
Goodman, G. O., 193, *288*
Goodson, J., 50, *293*
Granger, R. H., 68, 69, 190n, *288*

H

Hayes, P. J., *288*
Hayes-Roth, B., 46n, 190n, 199, *288*
Hayes-Roth, F., 46n, *288*
Hebb, D. O., 182, *288*
Hendler, J. A., 1, 19, 23, 48, 55, 67, *286,
    288, 289, 291*
Hewitt, C., 47, 174, *285, 289*
Hillis, W. D., 33, 176, *289*
Hinton, G. E., 34, 191n, 206, 224, *288, 289,
    292, 295*
Hirst, G. J., 66, 67, 70, 144, 186, 188, 216,
    289, 293
Holbrook, J. K., 68, 69, 190n, *288*

J

Jones, R. D., 193, *290*
Juola, J. F., 185, *289*

K

King, D. R. W., 199, *289*
King, J., 45, *290*
Kogge, S., 171, *295*
Kolodner, J. L., 53, *289*
Koomen, J. A., 53, *285*

L

Laird, J. E., 189, *292*
Larkin, J. H., 192n, *289*
Leiman, J. M., 186, *293, 294*
Lewis, C. H., 199, *289*
Lipscomb, C., 193, *290*
Loftus, E. F., 183, 184–185, 185n, 190n, 196,
    197, *286, 288, 289*
Lorch, R. F., Jr., 190n, 193, *289, 290*
Lucas, M., 186, *290*

M

Manna, Z., 41, *290*
Martin, C. E., 70, *292*
Martin, N., 45, *290*
Massaro, D. W., 193, *290*
McClelland, J. L., 205n, 206, 208, 209, *290,
    292*
McDermott, D. V., 23, 47, 53, 149, 269, *286,
    290, 294*
McElvany, M., 171, *295*
McKoon, G., 193, *290, 292*
Meehan, J., 49, *290*
Meyer, D. E., 185, 190n, *290, 293*
Milheim, S., 211n, *292*
Moon, D., 68, *295*
Moore, R. C., 47, *290*
Myers, J. L., 193, *290*

N

Neisser, U., 192n, *290*
Nevins, A., 47, *291*

Newell, A., 39, 47, 59, 189, *287, 290, 291,* *292*
Nilsson, N. J., 29n, 39, 47, *288, 291*
Norvig, P., 70, 84, 112, 144, *291*

O

Onifer, W., 186, *291*
Orciuch, E., 189, *292*

P

Parker, J., 206, *291*
Pearl, J., 71, 189n, *291*
Phillips, B., 19, 67, *288, 291*
Pierson, R., 171, *295*
Pollack, J. B., 70, *291*
Posner, M. I., 192n, *291*
Post, R., 171, *295*

Q

Quillian, M. R., 32, 59–60, 137, 183, *287,* *291*

P

Ratcliff, R., 193, *290, 292*
Reggia, J., 211, 211n, *292*
Rieger, C., 49, *292*
Riesbeck, C. K., 70, *292*
Ringle, M. H., 181, *292*
Rips, L. J., 185, 185n, 193n, *292, 294*
Robinson, J. A., 47, *292*
Rosch, E., 185, 193, 193n, *292*
Rosenberg, C. R., 206, 222, *293*
Rosenbloom, P., 189, *292*
Rulifson, J. F., 47, *292*
Rumelhart, D. E., 205n, 206, 208, 209, *290,* *292*
Rychener, M. D., 47, *292*

S

Sacerdoti, E. D., 40, 44, *292, 293*
Sanborn, J., 55, *289*
Sanford, A. J., 193, *293*

Schank, R. C., 38n, 49, *392*
Schmidt, C., 50, *293*
Schneider, W., 192n, *293*
Scholz, R., 193, *290*
Schvaneveldt, R. W., 185, 190n, *290, 293*
Scott, C. A., 174, *293*
Seidenberg, M. S., 186, 196n, *293, 294*
Sejnowski, T. J., 34, 206, 222, 224, *288, 293*
Selman, B., 70, *293*
Sharkey, N. E., 209, *293*
Shastri, L., 213, 214, *293*
Shaw, J. C., 39, *291*
Shiffrin, R. M., 192n, *293*
Shoben, E. J., 185, 185n, 193n, *292, 294*
Simon, H. A., 39, *291, 293*
Simpson, R. L., 53, *289*
Small, C. L., 214n, *288*
Small, S., *293*
Smith, E. E., 185, 185n, 193n, *292, 294*
Smolensky, P., *294*
Snyder, C. R. R., 192n, *291*
Sobek, R. P., 48, *294*
Sridharan, N., 50, *293*
Stacy, E. W., 202n, *285*
Stallman, R. M., 58n, *294*
Steele, G. L., 58n, *294*
Stefik, M., 46, *290, 294*
Stuart, C., 47, *294*
Sussman, G. J., 41, 47, 89, *294*
Sutcliffe, R. F. E., 209, *293*
Swinney, D. A., 185, 186, 187, *291, 294*

T

Tanenhaus, M. K., 186, *293, 294*
Tate, A., 41, 45, *294*
Thareja, A., 171, *295*
Thorndyke, P. W., 199, *294*
Touretsky, D. S., 63, 191n, 224, *294, 295*
Tromp, J. W., 206, *287*

V

Vere, S. A., 46, *295*

W

Waldinger, R. J., 41, 47, *290, 292*
Waltz, D. J., 70, *291, 295*

Warren, D. H. D., 41, *295*
Warren, R. E., *295*
Weinreb, D., 68, *295*
Weiser, M., 171, *295*
Wilensky, R., 3n, 9n, 15, 49, 50, 52, 99, 279, 280, 281, *295*
Wilkins, A. J., 192, *295*

Wilkins, D. E., 47, *295*
Wilks, Y. A., 38n, *295*
Williams, R. J., 206, *292*
Winograd, T., 89, *294*
Wobcke, W. R., 209, *293*
Wong, D., 9, 279, *295*
Woods, D. R., 58n, *294*

Subject Index

Page numbers followed by n indicate footnotes.

A

Abductive unification, 121n, 122
Abstraction hierarchy, 40
Abstraction spaces, 46n
ABSTRIPS, 40–41
ACT*, 32, 71, 188–199
Activated nodes, 58
Activation, *see also* Spreading activation
  competitive, 211–212
Activation energy, 32
Activation markers, 70
Activation tags, 59
AFPLAN, 219–221
Algorithms, *see also specific system, e.g.,*
  NASL
  behaviors needed for, 5
  "local," 22
AND2 program, 43
Associationism, 182
Associative network, 8, 19, 57
ATLAST, 69–70
Attenuation, *see also* Zorch
  cognitive aspects of, 193–196
  of marking, 57, 128–133
Automatic spread of activation, 191–192

B

BACAS, 209–211
Backtracking, non-optimal solutions and, 10–14
Backward-chaining rule, 26–27
Bayesian statistics, spreading activation and, 71
BBN Butterfly, 174
Bidirectional breadth-first search, 67–68
Block's World task, 42
Boltzmann machine, 34, 224
Brown University, natural language work at, 64–67
Butterfly LISP, 174

C

Cancellation links, 62
Chaining rules, 26–27, 78–80
Child node, 58
Chunks, 35
CM-SCRAPS, 176–179
Coarse grained machines, 159
Cognitive issues, 31, 181–204

301

planning and, 201–204
spreading activation and, 182–201, *see also*
    Spreading activation, cognitive aspects of
Collins and Loftus model, 183–185
neurophysiology and, 190
Competitive activation, 211–212
Complex planning, 280–283
Concurrency, *see also* C-SCRAPS
reason for, 159–162
Connectionism, 33, 63–64, 205–227
    distributed representations and, 221–226
        distributed memory and, 224–225
        microfeatures of, 225–226
        weighted networks and, 222–223
    excitatory and inhibitory links in, 207–212
    learning and, 206–207
    massive parallelism and, 213–221
        connection machine planning system and,
        218–221
    neurophysiological plausibility and, 206
    themes in, 205–206, 226–227
Connection machine, 33, 176–179
    planning system for, 218–221
Conscious processing, 192
Context recognition, 64–65, 186, 283–284
Counterplanning, 50
C-SCRAPS, 22–23, 31, 159–180
    efficiency of, 167–171
    future versions of, 171–179
    implementation of, 162–167
    output of, 163
    parallel processes in, 72
    path evaluation in, 94n
    SCRAPS vs., output of, 250–263
    zorch and, 179–180
C$^+$-SCRAPS, 172

D

Date, in SCRAPS, 82
Date information, 134
Deduction, 19, 35
Deductive search, 19
Demons
    invocation of, 14–16, 99–102
    in SCRAPS path evaluation, 114–115
Design decisions, 124–128, *see also* Marker-
    passer design of
DEVISER, 46
    temporal reasoning in, 53
Direct-memory access parsing system, *see*
    DMAP-0

Disambiguation, 66, 186
    program for, 216–218
Distributed connectionism, 33, 221–226
    distributed memory and, 224–225
    microfeatures of, 225–226
    weighted networks and, 222–223
DMAP-0, 70, 126n
Dumb marker-passing, 126, 269

E

Energy, activation, 32
Evidential reasoning model, 214–216
Excitatory and inhibitory links, 207–212
Executor, 51
Explicit cancellation, 62

F

Fact retrieval paradigm, 199
Fahlman's NETL system, 60–64, *see also*
    NETL "Fail" flags, 116–117
Fine grained machines, 159
Flags, 58, 80
    cognitive aspects of, 201–204
    existence of, reason for, 106–107
    "fail," 116–117
    PERCEPTUAL, 83
        in SCRAPS path evaluation, 116
    use of, timing of, 107–109
Follow-on, 141–143
FORBIN, 53
Formula, in SCRAPS, 82
Forward-chaining rule, 26
FPS, 48
FRAIL, 23–24, 25, *see also* SCRAPS
    chaining in, 27n
    memory representation, 79
Frame problem, 91n
Frames, 35
    definition of, 35
    single-agent vs. multiple-agent, 29n
From-node, in SCRAPS, 82
Future C-SCRAPS, 174–176

G

"Garden-path" plans, 203–204
General Problem-Solver, *see* GPS
Goal-based planning, 48–52

Goal detector, 50–51
Goals, 37
Goal state, 37
  marker-passing starting at, 13
GPS, 34
  means-end analysis in, 39

H

HACKER, 41–43
Heuristics
  path evaluation
    demon rule, 114–115
    "fail" flag, 116–117
    intra-plan interaction, 117–118
    PERCEPTUAL flag, 116
    quick rejection, 112–113
  path ordering and, 144–145
"Human" planning, 49–50

I

Individual-nodes, 61
Inference finding, 68, 70
Inheritance hierarchy, NETL and, 63
Inhibitory and excitatory links, 207–212
Initial state, 37
Interactions within plans, 16–18, 102–105
  path evaluation and, 117–118
INTERPLAN, 41
Isa hierarchy, 23, 57–58

K

Knowledge representation system, 214–216
Knowledge structures, description of, 35

L

Learning
  connectionism and, 206–207
  planning as, 53
Least-commitment strategy, 44
Lexical access, 185–188
  mark decay and, 196–197
Lexical information network, 184
"Linearity" of plans, 40
Link(s), *see also* Isa hierarchy
  activation of, 198–199

excitatory and inhibitory, 207–212
  nodes and, 57, *see also* Associative network
  types of, 134–136
  weighted, cognitive aspects of, 192–193
Link unit, 60
LISP functions
  Butterfly, 174
  FRAIL and, 27n
  shortcoming of, 113n
"Local" algorithm, 22
Local connectionism, 33
Logic, temporal, planning as, 52–53
Logical alternatives, 88–91
Logical terminology, 35
Loops
  during marking, 136–137
  in paths, 143
Lunar robots, 54n

M

Mark(s)
  definition of, 32
  erasing, 143–144
  information on, 133–134
Mark decay, 196–197
Marker-passer
  added to problem-solver, 18–21
  cognitive aspects of, 200–201
  correctness of, 125–127
  design of, 124–158
    design issues in, 124–128
    follow-on and, 141–143
    link types and, 134–136
    loops and, 136–137
    loops in paths and, 143
    marker-passing issues in, 128–145
    multiple paths and, 138–141
    in SCRAPS, 145–158
    what is returned by, 124–125
Marker-passing
  connectionism and, 205–227, *see also* Connectionism
  as context mechanism, 283–284
  design of, path ordering and, 144–145
  dumb, 126, 269
  massively parallel, 156–158
  mechanism of, 8
  parallel vs. serial, 127–128
  problem-solving and, 18, 73–109, *see also* Problem-solving, marker-passing and
  smart, 126

spreading activation and, 57-72, *see also*
    Spreading activation
  systems for, design of, 21-22
  terminology of, 32
Marking
  attenuation of, 57, 128-133
  secondary, 273-275
Massive parallelism, 33, 156-158, 266, *see
    also* Parellel processing
  connectionism and, 213-221
    connection machine planning system and,
      218-221
    Rochester works on, 214-218
  C-SCRAPS and, 176-179
MCMOB, 171, 173
Means-end analysis, 39-41
Medium grained machines, 159
Memory
  distributed, 224-225
  FRAIL representation of, 79
  production, 198
  in SCRAPS, 74
    "active," 78-81
    network structure of, 74-78
  semantic, 59, 184-185
  spreading activation and, 183-185
Meta-planning, 46
MG-SCRAPS, 282-283
MOLGEN, 45-46
Multiple paths, 138-141

                  N

NASL, 23-24, 47-48
  basic planning algorithm for, 26
  choice mechanism for, 24, 26-29
  NOAH vs., 53-55
  SCRAPS and, 81
  SCRAPS vs., output of, 228-238
Natural language processing
  marker-passing and, 64-71
  program for, 216-218
  spreading activation and, 185-186
NEIGHBORS property, 155
NETL, 32, 60-64
  attenuation and, 129
Nets Of Action Hierarchies, *see* NOAH
NETtalk, 222-223
Network controller, 61
Neurophysiology, 190-191
  connectionism and, 206

NEXUS, 68
NISP, 149
NOAH, 44-45
  NASL vs., 47, 48, 53-55
  NOAH planner, 34
Node(s)
  links and, 57, *see also* Associative network
  preceding, pointer to, 133
  promiscuous, attenuation and, 130
Node unit, 60
Non-deductive search, 19
NONLIN, 45
Nonlinear planning, 41-47
Non-optimal solutions, backtracking and, 10-
    14
Noun grouping, 67, 68

                  O

Object-oriented programming, 68
One-way links, 134-135
Operators, 37
Opportunistic planning, 46n
Optimality criteria, 12
Order effects, 197-198
Origin, in SCRAPS, 82

                  P

PAM, 49-52
Parallel processing, *see also* Massive parallel-
    ism
  C-SCRAPS and, 72
  natural language, 70
  SCRAPS and
    future C-SCRAPS and, 174-176
    linked processors and, 171-173
    zorch and, 179-180
  serial processing vs., 127-128
Parent node, 58
Parsers, *see specific system*
Path(s)
  incorrect, 19
    debugging, 203-204
  loops in, 143
  multiple, 138-141
Path checker, 64
Path evaluation, 20-21, 110-123
  in C-SCRAPS, 94n
  formal explanation of, 118-121

SCRAPS use of, 122–123
in SCRAPS, 72, 84–85, 112, 268–269
demon rule heuristic, 114–115
"fail" flag heuristic in, 116–117
intra-plan interaction heuristic in, 117–118
PERCEPTUAL flag heuristic, 116
quick rejection heuristic, 112–113
weaknesses in, 273
Path information, 133–134
Path ordering, 144–145
Path strength, SCRAPS computation of, 148
PATI, 67–68
Pattern-directed invocation, 47
PERCEPTUAL flags, 83
cognitive aspects of, 202
in SCRAPS path evaluation, 116
Plan(s)
definition of, 37
interactions within, 16–18, 102–105
path evaluation and, 117–118
linearity of, 40
Plan interpreters, 47–48
Planning
cognitive aspects of, 201–204
complex, 280–283
definition of, 37
goal-based, 48–52
"human," 49–50
as learning, 53
nonlinear, 41–47
problem-solving and, 37–56, *see also*
Problem-solving
problem-solving vs., 10n, 34
SCRAPS and, 264–265
as search, 38–39
story comprehension and, 279
as temporal reasoning, 52–53
Plan projector, 51
Plan proposer, 51
Point of origin, 133
Polaroid Words, 66
Preconditions, 87–88
Prediction markers, 70
Prepositional phrase attachment, 67
Priming, 32, 58
automatic vs. effortful, 191–192
stimulus onset asynchrony and, 194–195
Priming paradigm, 185
Primitive task, 38
Problem-solver, marker-passer added to, 18–21

Problem-solving
definition of, 37
marker-passing and, 18, 73–109
demon invocation and, 99–102
examination of problems in, 86–87, 91
integration of, 86–109
interactions within plans and, 102–105
logical alternatives and, 88–91
non-optimal choice and, 95–99
preconditions for, 87–88
reason for flags and, 106–107
SCRAPS and, 74–85, *see also* SCRAPS
wrong choice and, 91–95
planning and, 37–56, *see also* Planning
planning vs., 10n, 34
previous work in, 38–48
means-end analysis, 39–41
nonlinear planning, 41–47
plan interpreters, 47–48
planning as search, 38–39
Production memory, 198
Production rules, in robot planning, 48
Production systems, 47
Promiscuous nodes, attenuation and, 130
Psychological issues, *see* Cognitive issues

Q

Quillian
semantic memory model of, 59
Teachable Language Comprehender of, 59–60

R

Reasoning, temporal, planning as, 52–53
Rejection, quick, in SCRAPS path evaluation, 112–113
Relevance, problem of, 91
Replanning, 279–280
Robot planning, *see also specific program*
lunar, 54n
production rules in, 48
Routing cycle, 178
Rule-based systems, development of, 47–48
RULE-IN rules, 28
RULE-OUT rules, 28, 85
Rules, *see* Demons; Heuristics; *specific type*

S

Schema, 35
SCRAPS, 22–23, 29–31, 55–56, 73–85
  "applied," 278
  attenuation in, 131–133
  complex planning and, 280–283
  concurrent implementation of, see C-
    SCRAPS
  connectionism vs., 211–212, 226–227
  Connection machine and, 176–179
  for a few communicating processors, 171–
    173
  flags in
    reason for, 106–107
    timing of use of, 107–109
  flow of control in, 20
  formal basis of path evaluation in, 122–123
  kludge in, 276–277
  limitations of, 277–278
  machines capable of running, 149n
  marker-passer in, 81–84, 145–158
    massively parallel processing and, 156–
      158
    pseudocode for algorithm for, 149–154
  massively parallel models relevant to, 213–
    221
  Rochester works on, 214–218
  memory in, 74
    "active," 78–81
    network structure of, 74–78
  NETtalk vs., 223
  output of, 228–263
    C-SCRAPS output vs., 250–263
    NASL output vs., 228–238
  path evaluation in, 84–85, 112, 268–270
    demon rules in, 114–115
    "fail" flags in, 116–117
    intra-plan interactions in, 117–118
    PERCEPTUAL flags in, 116
    quick rejection in, 112–113
    weaknesses in, 273
  planning and, 264–265
  problem-solver in, 81
  replanning and, 279–280
  spreading activation and, 71–72, 81–84, see
    also Spreading activation
  story comprehension and, 279
  "subconscious" process in, 284
  weaknesses of, 272–276
Scripts, 35

Search
  deductive, 19
  non-deductive, 19
  planning as, 38–39
Secondary marking, 273–275
Semantic enquiry desk, 66
Semantic memory model, 59, 184–185
Semantic priming, 32
Sense disambiguation, 66, 186
  program for, 216–218
Serial processing, parallel processing vs.,
    127–128
SIPE, 47
  compared with NASL and NOAH, 48
Smart marker-passing, 126
Solutions, non-optimal, backtracking and, 10–
    14
SPAN, 47
Spreading activation, 81–84
  cognitive aspects of, 182–201
    ACT* and, 188–189
    attenuation and, 193–196
    automatic vs. effortful priming and, 191–
      192
    lexical access and, 185–188
    link activation and, 198–199
    mark decay and, 196–197
    marker-passer and, 200–201
    memory model and, 183–185
    neurophysiology and, 190–191
    order effects and, 197–198
    weighted links and, 192–193
    zorch and, 199
  marker-passing and, 57–72
    definition of terms for, 32, 57–58
    natural language and, 64–71
    previous work in, 58–64
    SCRAPS related to, 71–72
  as memory model, 183–185
Stepwise refinement paradigm, 16–17
Stimulus onset asynchrony, priming and, 194–
    195
Story comprehension, planning and, 279
Story generation, 49
STRIPS, 29n
  means-end analysis in, 39–41
  NASL vs., 47
Subgoals, 37
Subtasks, 37
Symbolic approach, subsymbolic approach vs.,
    218

T

TALESPIN, 49
Tasks, 37
Teachable Language Comprehender, 59–60
Temporal reasoning, planning as, 52–53
Terminology
    for describing chunks, 35
    difficulties with, 32
    logical, 35
    for technique, 32–34
    for topic, 34
Theorem proving, 47
Time information, 134
TO-DO rules, 27–28
TWEAK, 47
Type-nodes, 61
Typicality relations, 192–193

U

Unification, 35, 121n
    abductive, 122
University of Rochester, connectionist models
    developed at, 214–218
UNIX^{TM} Consultant, 51–52

W

WARPLAN, 41
Weighted links, 135–136
    cognitive aspects of, 192–193
Weight information, 134
Wilensky's model, 49–52
WIMP, 66
Window, 46
Word recognition, 208
Word sense disambiguation, 66, 186
    program for, 216–218

Z

ZetaLisp, 68
ZMOB, 171–173
Zorch, 58
    attenuation and, 131–133, *see also* Attenuation
    cognitive aspects of, 199
    initial, 272
    parallelism and, 179–180
    in SCRAPS, 82, *see also* SCRAPS,
        marker-passer in

Milton Keynes UK
Ingram Content Group UK Ltd.
UKHW031135141024
449569UK00006B/165